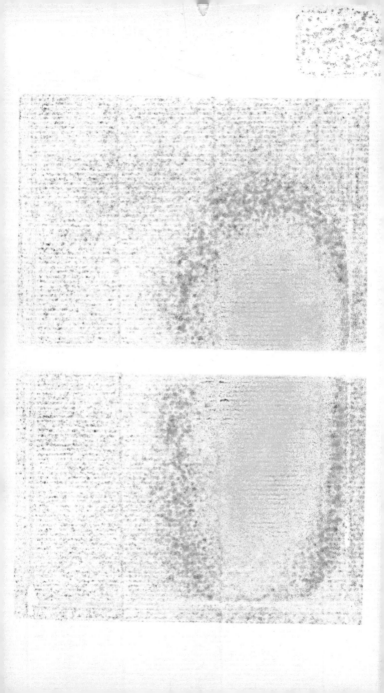

ENGLISH RECUSANT LITERATURE
1558—1640

Selected and Edited by
D. M. ROGERS

Volume 204

LUIS DE GRANADA
A Spiritual Doctrine
1599

LUIS DE GRANADA

A Spiritual Doctrine

1599

The Scolar Press

1974

ISBN o 85967 187 9

Published and printed in Great Britain by
The Scolar Press Limited, 59-61 East Parade,
Ilkley, Yorkshire and
39 Great Russell Street,
London WC1

1819627

A SPIRITVAL
DOCTRINE,
CONTEINING A RVLE

To liue vvel, vvith diuers Praiers and Meditations.

*ABRIDGED BY THE REVEREND FA-
ther* Levvis de Granada *of the holie order
of Preachers.*

AND DEVIDED INTO SIXE TREA-
tises, as is to be seene after the prefaces.

Nevvlie translated out of Spanish into English.

Psalm. 118. v. 35.
Deduc me in semita mandatorum tuorum.

Leade me (O Lord) in the path of thy commaundements.

Collegij *Anglis:*

Societ. *Jesu*

Bib: *Jun:*

AT LOVAN,
Imprinted by Laurence Kellam
1599.

ONORABLE Syr,
hauing latelie tranſ-
lated this little vo-
lume out of Spaniſh
into Engliſh, I began to thinke, to
vvhat perſon of our nation I might
dedicate the ſame, that not onelie
vvould gratefullie accept of ſo
ſmall a trauail, but alſo vvere able
to iudge, as vvel of the tranſla-
tion, as alſo of the fruite vvhich
maie be deriued to ſuch, as ſhall
liſt to reade it. At the length a-

† 2   mongſt

mongst all others , your honorable person seemed to me most fitte , for all the respects before mentioned . For if I regard your courtisie to all sortes of men , and your speciall good vvill and affection to those of mie coate in generall (to saie nothing of mie self in particular;) I maie vvith greate reason be esteemed verie vndiscreete , if I should think , that you vvould take this poore offer othervvise , then your Nobilitie and courtisie requireth . Also if I consider either your knovvledge in both languages English and Spanish , or youre experience , and vvounderful good affection to all sortes of spirituall, and Godlie Treatises, ioined vvith your Deuotion, Pietie,

Pietie and Zeale in the seruice of
God; I cannot but esteeme you to
be a sufficient Iudge as vvell of the
translation, as also of the profit,
that manie maie take by this little
vvoorke. Accept then, Honorable
good Syr, the same, as the first
frutes, & token of mie good vvill
tovvards you; accept it, Iaie, vntill
I haue put som other thing in order, vvhich maie further the spirituall auancement of deuoute persons, & be more vvorth your reading; and accept therevvithall mie
sincere affection, vvholie addicted
to praie for your long life, and
prosperitie, vvhich God grant
you, and preserue the same to his
greater honour and glorie, and
to your ovvne saluation and best

contentment. Chrift IESVS be
alvvaies in your fafegard. From
our college of the Societie
of IESVS in Louan this
19. of March 1599.
being the feaft of
S. Iofeph.

Yours moft humble affectionate.
Rich. Gibbons.

THE

THE TRANSLATOVR
to the gentle Reader.

I T hath seemed good to me, Gentle Reader, to let thee vnderstand in the beginning of this little booke, that som yeeres past, a vvorthie and vertuousGentleman of our nation, had begon to translate out of Spainish into English, the Memoriall, and other spirituall bookes, of that famous and Religious father *Levvis de Granada*, of S. Dominicks order. Of all vvhich, som haue ben put in print, som others, I knovv not vpon vvhat occasion, ar not yet com forth. But vvhatsoeuer the cause maie be, certeine it is that in the meane time, the same Religious father being verie desirous, that all sort of men should take the profit of such spirituall vvoorkes, as he vvith so greate paines had vttered to the vvoorld, for theire soules good, and auancement in the seruice of

† 4   God,

God, did, not long before his death, dravve
out an Abridgment of his forsaid bookes,
moued therunto for the reasons, vvhich he
him self hath set dovvne in his preface to
the Reader, as it goeth heere in the beginning of this little volume. VVhich vvoork,
vvhen I had read and perused the same,
liked me so much, that I resolued vvith
mie self to put it in Englifh, esteeming that
as all the other spirituall vvoorks of this deuout father, ar of greate comfort and consolation, to all the seruants of Almightie
God, so this vvould be of no lesse furthe-
rance in spirite, to such as vvould endeuour
to vse the same. Especiallie considering,
that all that is conteined in this little
booke, is matter apperteining rather to
practise of deuotion, and to kendle our affection in the loue of our svveete Sauiour,
then to frame greate discourses, and illuminate our vnderstanding; albeit this part
be also to be found heere, as much as it
maketh to the benifit of the other, and
standeth vvith the briefenes, vvhich the
Author novv pretended.

This being so, it remaineth Gentel
Reader, vvhoesoeuer, and of vvhatsoeuer
Religion thou be, that thou endeuour to
peruse this booke, to the end, for vvhich
                                                    it vvas

it vvas firſt vvriten, and is novv tranſlated into Engliſh, that is to thine ovvne good and ſaluation . VVhich thing thou ſhalt eaſilie perfourme, if thou procure, as neere as God ſhall aforde thee grace, to reade and vveigh that vvhich is heere conteined, vvith a repoſed and quiet ſpirite , vvith a meeke and humble ſpirite , vvith a ſpirite of patience and longanimitie, vvith a ſpirite altogether determined and reſolued, to ſeeke ſincerelie and purelie, not ſo much thine ovvne intereſt & contentment, as the honour and glorie of God, and to knovv his good vvill and pleaſure, and vvith all thy povver to put the ſame in execution. Neither muſt thou be ouercurious, or haſtie to paſſe on in reading the contents thereof, but rather endeuour to ſtaie thie ſelf ſom ſpace of time , in conſidering vvith much attention that , vvhich thou haſt read , and by this conſideration to ſtirre vp, and prouoke thy vvill and affection, to practiſe & excute that, vvhich thou ſhalt vnderſtand to be the beſt pleaſure of almightie God, and moſt profitable to thine ovvne ſaluation. This is that vvhich thou muſt doe, if thou pretend to take anie comfort or commoditie, by reading of ſpirituall and deuout bookes.

Novv

THE TRANSLATOVR

Novv then, deare Reader, hauing nothing els vvhereof to admonish thee, I
vvil end this mie preface, and remitte thee
to the Author him self of this little vvooke,
desiring thee, for mie small paines bestovved in the tranflation, to be mindfull
of me in thie praiers. Chrift
IESVS diect thee. At Lo-
uan the 25. of March,
1599.

*Thy hartie vvellvviller and feruant in Chrift
I ES V S. Rich. Gibbons.*

THE

THE AVTHOR TO
THE CHRISTIAN
READER.

T is a thing notorious , good Chriſtian reader , that the bread, vvhich vve dailie eate, is not ſo neceſſarie for the maintenance of our natural life, as is the doctrine of the vvoord of God, for the conſeruation of oure ſpiritual life. This doctrine teacheth vs tvvo principal things , to praie, and to vvoorke; vnto vvhich tvvo, be reduced al others vvhat-ſoeuer. Of theſe tvvo things infinite bookes haue ben vvriten. But for as much as this doctrine is ſo neceſſarie at euerie foote-ſteppe that vve make (by reaſon of the continual dangers, and temptations of our life) I haue determined to reſume heere in ſevv vvoords (gathered out of al mie bookes) that vvhich hath ſeemed to me moſt fit for this purpoſe; to the end thou maiſt eaſilie beare about vvith the in thie boſom, that vvhich ought to be alvvais vvriten in thie heart . And therfore I haue heere gathered and put together Six briefe treatiſes; one of Mental praier, taken ovvt of mie booke of Praier and Meditation, vvith al the fourteene meditations abbreuiated, vvhich vvere there ſet doune . And this treatiſe

Sixe treatiſes of this booke.

1

tife I haue put in the first place, because these meditations, besides that they giue vs abundant matter vvhereof to meditate, be also the best persuasions and mottues that can be found, to bring men to liue vvel and vertuouslie: So that yf they serue not in the beginning for the exercise of meditation, yet they vvil serue for persvvasion to induce men to the feare of God, and changement of life. But because al men doue not so much giue them selues to th'exercise of meditation, ether for their diuers affairs, or for other reasons vvhich they may haue, therfore that these also vvant not the succoar and help of praier, I haue added an other treatise of vocal praier, conteining manie praiers, vvhich serue to obteine such vertues, as be most necessarie for th'edification of our sovrles.

Trulie al holie scripture doth euerie vvhere declare vnto vs, the neede vvhich vve haue of these tvvo exercises, because they be the vveapons, vvhich vve haue most readie and at hand against our enimies, by vvhome vve be alvvais enuironed; & therfore vve must goe vvel armed vvith them, as long as our life lasteth. Heerehence it is that our Sa_uiour the night of his pasſion armed his disciples with praier, saying vnto them; vvatch ye and praie that ye enter not into tentation: and Dauid armed him self vvith meditation vvhen he said; vvere it not (o lord) that thy lavv is my meditation, I had then peraduenture prished

2

Matth. 26.
41.

Psal. 118.
29.

perished in my humilitie: *that is , I vvas then verie likelie to haue fallen vvhen tribulation came vppon me . Seeing therfore that these tvvo vveapons be so assured and prooued for our vvarfare, it seemed to me conuenient to put them in this brife manual, that by such meanes they might be alvvais at hand.*

Novv for so much as in the beginning vve diuided the vvhole summe of Christian doctrine into these tvvo things, praier, & vvoorke; hauing spoken alreadie of praier as vvel Mental as Vocal, it ensueth that vve treat hence forvvard of vvoork , that is of the instruction and order of our life , *hauing cheefelie regard of such as nevvlie begin to serue our Lord. And because of those sem there be, that begin this life remainning still in the vvoorld , som others entering into Religion ; for these last also I haue laid dovvne an other treatise,* in vvhich the thornes and brambles of our euil inclinations and passions be rooted out, and in their place ar set the plantes of vertues , *vvhich doe order and perfectionate our sovvles . And albeit these tvvo last treatises maie seeme to be different in the titles, neuertheles the documents conteined in them both (especiallie those vvhich concerne vertues) serue no lesse for the one treatise , then for the other : because such as desire to be saued, haue no other vvay for the same, but to goe* from vertue to vertue, vntil they see the God of Gods in Sion , *that is in*

3

4

Psal. 83.
8.

the

THE AVTHOR

the glorie vvhich is to com.

Besides this, to th'end there vvant nothing
for the dailie instruction of our life . I haue put
heere also tvvoe other little treatises, vvhereof the one is of Penance and Confession:
the other is of preparation for re-
ceiuing the blessed Sacrament
of the altare. And this may
suffice for the preface of
this little booke.

THE

A SPIRITVAL DOCTRINE DEVI-
ded into *fixe treatifes.*

The Firſt Treatiſe is, of *Mental Praier.*

The Second Treatiſe is, of *Vocal Praier.*

The Third Treatiſe is, *A Rule of good life for all ſorts of men.*

The Fourth Treatiſe is, *A Rule of good life for Religious men.*

The Fift Treatiſe is, of *The Sacrament of Penance.*

The Sixt Treatiſe is, of *receauing the bleſſed Sacrament, vvith a profeſſion of the Catholique faith, according to the holy Councel of Trent.*

THE FIRST
TREATISE OF MEN-
TAL PRAIER.

THE FIRST PART, VVHEREIN IS treated of Meditation.

OF THE FRVITE WHICH WEE
reape by Prayer an Meditation.

CHAP. I.

OR so much as this litle treatise speaketh of *Prayer* and *Meditation* , it shall bee good , in the beginning thereof, to laye dovvne in fewe vvordes the fruite which is reaped by his tholie exercise, to the ende that men may vvith a more francke and free heart giue themselues to the same.

It is a thing most euident, that one of the greatest impediments & lets, vvhich man hath to hinder him from his last felicity & blisse, is the euil inclination of his soule, & the difficultie & tediousnes vvhich he feeleth in doing good: in so much that, if this difficultie vvere not, it should be a most easie thing for him to runne the waie of vertues, and to obteine the end for vvhich hee

A   was

was created. And therfore the Apostle said.

I am delighted vvith the lawe of God according to the inwarde man: but I see another law in my members, repugning to the lawe of my minde, and captiuing me in the law of sinne. This is then the most generall reason that can be giuen of all our euill.

Rom, 7.22,

But now to quite our selus of this tediousnes & difficulty, & to make this affaire most easy, one of the things that most helpeth & furdereth is *deuotion.* For, as S. Thomas saith *deuotion* is nothing els, but a promptnesse and readines to work wel, which quiteth our soule of al this difficultie and teadiousnes, and maketh vs quick and nimble to all good. For deuotion is a spiritual refection, a refreshing and dew of heauen, a blast and breathing of the holy ghost, and a supernatural affectio, which so cóforteth, forceth, & trans formeth or changeth a mans hart, that it giueth him a new taste and desire of spiritual things, and a new disgust and hatred of things that be sensual. And this daily experience teacheth vs: for when a spiritual person cómeth from any deep & deuout praier, it is then that all his good purposes & desires be reneued: the be al his feruors and determinations to doe good: then he desireth to please and loue so good

and

and so sweete a lord, as God there shewed himself to be: and to endure new labours & paines, and that which is more, to spend his blood for him: & then finally is renued and flourisheth the freshnes of our soule.

And If thou ask me, by what means we come to obtaine this so mighty and noble affection of deuotion: to this answereth the same holie Doctor aforenamed saying, that it is attained by the meditation & contemplation of heauenly things, for that frō the deep meditation and consideration of them, riseth & springeth vp this affection and feeling in the wil, which we cal deuotion, and which inciteth and moueth vs to all good. And therefore is this holy & religious exercise so highly praised, & cōmended of all Sainčts, because it is a meane to obtaine deuotion, which, although it be but one vertue, maketh vs fit & moueth vs to all other vertues, & as it were a generall spurre for them all. And if thou desire to see how true this is, consider how plainly S. Bonauenture layeth it downe in these words following.

If thou wilt suffer with patience whatsoeuer aduersities and miseries of this life be a man of praier. l. meditation .vi- *If thou wilt obtaine force and strength to ouercome* ta Chri *the tentations of the enemie, be a man of praier.* If sti.

A 2   thou 27.

thou vvilt mortifie thine owne will, vvith her euill
appetites and passions, be a man of prayer. If thou
vvilt throughlie knowe the vilenes and subtilitie of
the diuile, and keepe thy selfe from his snares and de-
ceits, be a man of praiet. If thou wilt liue merelie
in the seruice of God and passe on the vvay of laboure
and affliction with sweetnes and contentement of
minde, be a man of prayer. If thou vvilt exercise thy
selfe in a spirituall kinde of life, and not make proui-
sion for the flesh in concupiscence, be a man of praier.
If thou wilt driue out of thy minde the importunate
flies of vaine cares and thoughts, be a man of praier.
If thou vvilt nourish thy soule vvith the fatnesse
and marrovv of deuotion, and haue it alvvaies ful of
good cogitations and holy desires, be a man of praier.
If thou vvilt fortifie thy heart, in the good pleasur
of God, vvith a stoute courage and stedfast purpose,
be a man of praier. Finally, if thou vvilt roote out all
vices of thy soule, and set vertues in their places, be
a man of praier, because in it is receaued the vnction
of the holic Ghost, vvhich teacheth our soule all
things that be needful. Moreouer if thou vvilt mount
vp to the height and top of contemplation, and enioye
the sweete embracings of the spouse, exercise thy
selfe in praier, because this is the vvay by vvhich the
soule climmeth vp to the contemplation and tast of
celestial things. Thou seest then of vvhat force and
vertue praier is. And for the greater proof of al that
hath bene said, setting aside the testimonie of holie
                                              scriptu-

*₃ Rom.
13, 14* (margin note)

ſcripture, let this ſuffiſe for the preſent, that we haue heard and ſeene, and ſee daily by experience manie ſimple and vnlearned perſons, who by the vertue of praier haue obtained al the forſaid things, and many greater alſo.   Hitherto be the vvordes of S. Bonauenture. VVhat treaſure then, I pray you, can be founde more riche, or vvhat marchants ſhoop better furniſhed with al ſort of goods, then this? But hearken what an other holie & religious Doctor Laurentius Iuſtinianus ſaith to this purpoſe, ſpeaking of the ſelfe ſame matter.

By reaſon of vnſpotted praier (ſaith he) the ſoule is clenſed from ſinne, the affection is comforted, Charitie is nouriſhed, the appetite of loue is increaſed, Faith is certified, Hope is ſtrengthened, the ſpirit reioyceth, the bowels tremble, the heart is pacified, ſiar is kindled, truth is diſcouered, tentatiō is put to flight, heauines is caſt off, the ſenſes ar renued, the ſtrength vvhich vvas vveakned, is repaired, feruor is ſtirred vp, luke vvarmnes is abandoned, the ruſtines of vices is conſumed, and in the ſame exerciſe the liuelie ſparcles of heauenly deſires doe ſhine brightlie, and the flame of godlie loue growveth vp more and more. For the vndeſiled praier of the ſoule is borne vppe vvith many prerogatiues of merites, and is adorned vvith the beautie of many ſpiritual priuileges, and vvith other principal vertues.   In ſo much that the heauens ſtande alwaies open to praier: ſo it diſco-

lib. de caſto conn. verbi & anima c. 22.

A 3   uered

uered and reueiled secrets: and the bearing of God is at all times attentiue to the same. This therfore may be sufficient for the preset to make vs in some manner to see the fruit of this holy exercise.

OF THE MATTER REQVISITE
to be vsed in meditation.

CHAP. II.

AVING hithertose ene of how great fruite *Prayer* and *Meditation* is, let vs now consider vvhat those thinges be of vvhich vve ought to meditate. To vvhich point I ansvvere, that for so much as this holye exercise is principally ordained to breede in our hearts the loue and feare of God, and the obseruation of his cōmaundements: therfore the matter, most conueniēt of this exercise, shalbe that vvhich most maketh this purpose. And althogh it be true that al things created, & all holy scripture incite and moue vs to this, neuertheles, speaking generally, the misteries of our faith vvhich be conteined in the *Simbole* named *Creede*, be most effectuall & profitable for this end: because in the same is created of the benefis of God: of the final iudgment, of the paines of hel of hel, and the glory of heauen, which be vehement motiues to ftir vp in our hearts the loue and feare of God: and in it alſo is comprehended the life and paſsion of our Sauiour Chriſt, in whch conſiſteth all our good. VVherfore with great reaſon it may be auouched that the moſt & proper matter of this exerciſe is the *Symbole*; although that alſo that may be good for ech one in particuler, vvhich ſhall mooue his heart to the loue and feare of God.

Novv according to this, for th'inſtructió of thoſe that be nouices & beginners in this vvay, to vvhome it is expedient to giue meat as it vvere chevved & digeſted before I vvil ſet dovvn here briefely tvvo ſorts of meditatiós for al the daies of the vveek, one for night, and the other for morning, dravven, for the moſt part, out of the myſteries of our faith: to the end that as vvee giue daily to our bodie tvvo refections, ſo likevviſe vvee giue our ſoule, vvhoſe foode is the meditation and conſideration of heauenlie things. Of theſe meditations ſome appertaine to the myſteries of the ſacred paſsion & reſurrection of Chriſt, ſom others to the other miſteries of vvhich vve haue ſpoken heretofore. And if peraduenture any bodie ſhould not haue ſo much

time

tyme as to recolle&t himself twise a day, at
the leaſt he may meditate one part of theſe
myſteries in one weeke, and th'other in an
other, or els entertaine himſelf in thoſe on
of the paſſion and life of Chriſt, which be
the moſt principall; albeit the others muſt
not be left, eſpeciallie in the beginning of
any mans conuerſiõ, becauſe they be moſt
conueniẽt for that time, in which the feare
of God, togeather with ſorow and dete-
ſtatiõ of our ſinnes, is principally required.

HERE FOLLOVV THE
FIRST SEVEN MEDITA-
tions for the daies of the weake.

Mondaie night. Of the knovvledg of thy ſinnes
and thy ſelf.

T HIS day thou maiſt attend to the
knowledge of thy ſinnes, and to the
knowledg of thy ſelf, that in the one thou
ſee how many euils thou haſt, and in the
other thou vnderſtand that thou haſt no
good which cõmeth not frõ God, Which
is the way to obtaine Humility mother of
all vertues.

For this thou muſt firſt thinke vpon the
numbre of the ſinns of thy life paſt, ſpecial-
ly vppon thoſe offences which thou did-
                                          eſt

deſt commit in the time when thou hadſt
leaſt knowledge of God. For if thou canſt
well vew them, thou ſhalt find that they
haue exceeded in nūber the verie haires of
thy head, and that thou didſt liue at that
thine as a heathen that knoweth not what
God is.

After this runne ouer breefly the ten com
mandements, and the ſeuen deadly ſinnes,
and thou ſhalt ſee that there is no one of
them al, in which thou haſt not oftentimes
offended in worke, word, or thought.

Secondly runne ouer all the benefits of
God, and all the times of thy former life,
and conſider wherein thou haſt imploied
them, for ſo much as thou muſt geue accompt of them all to God. Wherfore tell
me now, wherein haſt thou ſpēt thy childhood? wherein thy infancy? wherein thy
youth? and finallie in what al the daies of
thy life? wherein haſt thou occupied thy
bodily ſenſes, and the powers of thy ſoule,
which almighty God gaue thee to the end
thou ſhouldeſt know & ſerue him? where
in haſt thou imploied thine eyes, but in
beholding vanities? wherein thine eares,
but in hearing lies? wherein thin toūg, but
in a thouſand manners of ſwearing & mur
muration? wherein thy taſt, ſmelling and
tou-

touching, but in delites & senfual pleafures

VVhat profit haft thou taken by the holie Sacraments, which God ordeined for thy remidie? what thankes haft thou giuen him for his benefites? How haft thou anfwered to his infpirations? wherein haft thou fpent thy health, and the ftrength & habilities of nature, and the goods which are named of fortune, & the means & opportunities to liue well? what care haft thou had of thy neighbours, which God hath commanded vnto thee, and of thofe works of mercy, which he appointed thee to vfe towards them? Think thē, what anfwere wilt thou make at the daye of accompt, when God fhal fay vnto thee, Giue me an accompt of thy ftewardfhip, & of al my goods committed to thy charge, for the time is now expired, and thou fhalt haue no more to doe with them.

O dry & withered tree, ready for euerlafting torments! what wilt thou anfwere at that day, whē fhal they aske thee an accompt of all the time of thy life, and of all the minutes and moments of the fame?

Thirdly thinke vpon the finnes which thou haft committed, and doeft euery daie commit fince the time thou haft had more light to know God, and thou fhalt finde
that

that yet ſtill the ould Adam liueth in thee with many of his ould rootes & cuſtoms. Conſider then how vnreuerent thou haſt ben, and yet art towards God, how vnthankful for his benifits how rebellious & ſtifnecked to his inſpirations, how ſlowthful in things apparteining to his ſeruice: which thon neuer doeſt with ſuch readines and diligence, nor with ſuch pure intention as thou oughteſt, but for ſom other reſpects and commodities of the world.

Conſider alſo how ſeuere & hard thou art with thy neighbour, and how pitifull and fauourable towards thy ſelfe, what a frind of thine own will, of thy fleſh, of thy eſtimation, & of al other thy commodities. Behould how thou art alwaies prowde, ambitious, angry, raſh, vain glorious, enuious, malitious, delicate, inconſtant, lighſenſual, a frind of thy paſtimes, of pleaſant companies, of laughing, ieſting, & babling.

Conſider likewiſe how changeable thou art in thy good purpoſes, how vnaduiſed in thy wordes, how head-long in thy deedes, how cowardous & fain thearted in what ſoeuer matters of weight and importance,

Fourthly when thou haſt conſidered 4 in this order the multitude of thy ſinnes,

behould

hould forthvvith their grieuoufnes, that
thou maift fo perceiue hovv thy miferies
be increafed on euery fide : to vvhich purpofe thou muft view vvel thefe *three cir-
circumftances* in the finnes of thy life paft, to
vvit, *againft vvhom* thou haft finned , for
vvhat caufe thou haft finned, and in what
manner thou haft finned.   If thou confider *againft vvhome* thou haft finned, thou
fhalt finde that thou haft finned *againft
God*, whofe goodnes & maieftie is infinite,
whofe benefits & mercies towards man-
kinde doe exceede euen the fandes of the
fea, in whom be all titles of excellencie &
honour that can be imagined, & to whom
all dutie and homage is due euen in the
higheft degree of bonden dutie.   If thou
confider *the caufe for vvhich* thou haft finned, it vvas but for a point of eftimatió, for
a beaftly delight, for a trifle of cómoditie,
and oftentimes without any commoditie
at al, only for cuftom & contempt of God.
Et now , *after vvhat manner* haft thou finned? Surely with fuch facilitie, vvith fuch
boldnes, fo vvithout fcruple & remorfe of
confcience, fo vvithout feare, yea for the
moft part vvith fuch eafines and contentment, as if thou haddeft finned againft a
God of ftraw, that neither knewe nor faw
                                    vvhat

what paffeth in the world. Is this then the honour due to fo high a maieftie? Is this the thankf-giuing for fo manie benefits? Is this the recompéce worthie to be made for his pretious blood fhed vpon the Croffe ? and for thofe ftripes and buffets which he fuffred for thy fake? O miferable & wretched creature that thou art miferable! for that which thou haft loft, more miferable,for that which thou haft committed,and moft miferable of all, if yet thou fee not thine owne perdition.

After all this,it is a thing of great profit & importance to fix the eies of thy confideration in thinking vpon thine ovvne bafenes, that is,how of thy felfe thou haft nothing elfe, but nothing and finne, and that whatfoeuer is befids that is of God,it being a thing moft euident, that as well all the goods of *Nature*,as alfo thofe of *Grace*,which be the greateft, be al & wholy his & from him. For his is the gate of *Predeftination*, which is the fountain of al other graces,his is the grace of *Vocation*, his the grace *Concomitant*,which afsifteth thee in dooing all good, his the grace of *Perfeuerance*, and finallie,his the grace of *Euerlafting life*. This being fo, vvhat haft thou of thy felf, wherof to glory and vaunt , but nothing and finne?

sinne? Repose then a little in the consideration of this thy nothing esteming this on
ly to be thyne owne riches, and all the rest
that thou hast, to be of the law of God: to
the end thou maist see cleerely, and as it
were feele with thy hands what thou
art, and what God is, how poore thou art,
and how rich he is: Consequently how
little thou oughtest to trust & esteeme thy
self, and how much to trust in God, to loue
him, and to glory in him.

when thou hast vvel considered al these
things aforesayd, think then of thy selfe as
basely as thou possibly canst. Thinke that
thou art a place vvhere reedes grovv,
VVhich be chaunged with euery vvinde,
without weight, without force, without
firmnes, without stay, & without any manner of being. Think that thou art a lazarus
lying fower daies dead, that thou art a
stinking and abomible carcas, so full of
wormes and of so vyle a stentch, that so
many as passe by thee, doe stoppe theire
noses, and shut their eys that they may not
see thee. Think that in this sort thou doest
stinck in the sight of God and of his Angels
and esteeme thy self vnworthy to lift vp
thy eyes towards heauen, vnworthy that
the earth should beare thee, vnworthy that
any

any creatures fhould ferue thee, vnworthy of the bread thou eateſt, and vnworthie of the light and ayer that thou receaueſt.

Caſt thy ſelfe downe proſtrate with that publicke woman ſinner at our Sauiours feete, aud couering thy face for very ſhame and confuſion, with the like ſhame that a womā would appeare befor her husband, when ſhe hath committed treaſon and ad-ulterie againſt him, and with great ſorrow & repentance of hart deſire him to pardon thy ſinnes and offences, and that of his in- finite pitie and mercie it wil pleaſe him to receaue thee againe into his houſe.

Luk. 7.3

Teuſday night. *Of the miſerie of mans life.*

THIS day thou haſt to meditate vp-on the miſeries of mans life, that by them thou maieſt ſee how vaine the glory of this worlde is, and howe litle to be ac-coumpted of, ſeeing it is built vpon ſo weak a foundation as this miſerable life of ours is. And albeit the diſtreſſes and miſe-ries of this life be almoſt innumerable, yet maiſt thou, for the preſent, conſider chiefly theſe ſeuen.

Firſt conſider how ſhort this life is, ſeeing the longeſt terme therof, paſſeth not three-
ſcore

1

score and ten, or fowerscore yeares: for all
the rest, if it be any thing prolonged, as the
Prophet saith, is but labour & sorrow. And
If thou take out of this the time of thy infancy, which is rather a life of beastes then
of men, and that which is spent in sleeping
when we doe vse neither sense nor reason
which maketh vs men, thou shalt find it to
be a great deale shorter, then it seemeth vnto thee. Besides al this, If thou compare the
present life with th'eternity of the life to
com, it wil scarsly seem vnto thee so much
as a minute, whereby thou shalt easily perceaue how far out of the right way those
persons be, who to enioy the little blast of
so short a life, do put themselues in hazard
to loose the quiet rest of the life, that shall
endure for euer.

2   Secondly consider how vncertain this life
is, which is an other misery besids the former, for it is not only of it self very short,
but eue that smale cotinuace of life, which
it hath, is not assured but doutful. For how
many arriue to those threescore & ten, or
fourscore yeares which wee spake of? In
how many is the webbe cut off, euen whe
it is scarcely begon to be wouen? How many flitter out of this worlde, euen in the
flovver (as they terme it) of their age, and
in

Psal.
89

in the very bloſſom of theyr youth? *Ye* *Mat. 13.* *knovv not* (ſaith our Sauiour) *vvhen the lord of* *3 5.* *the houſe commeth, at euen, or at midnight, or at* *the cock crovving, or in the morning.*

And the better to vnderſtand this, and to haue ſom feeling of the matter, as in deede it paſſeth, it ſhal be a good help vnto thee to cal to mind the death of manie perſons vvhich thou haſt knovven in this vvorld, eſpeciallie of thy frinds and acquaintance, and of ſome vvorſhipful & famous perſons, vvhom death hath aſſaulted in diuers ages, and vtterlie be-guiled of al theyr fond deſignments & vaine hopes.

Thirdlie conſider hovv fraile and brickle   3
this life is, and thou ſhalt find, that there is no veſſel of glaſſe ſo fraile as it is, in ſo much that the ayer, the ſonne, a cuppe of cold vvater, yea the verie breath of a ſick man, is ſuffici-ent to bereue vs of our life, as it appeareth by dailie experience of manie perſons, vvhom the leaſt occaſion, of the afore reherſed, hath ben able to ouerthrovv and beate to the grovvnd, euen in the moſt floriſhing time of their age.

Fovverthlie conſider hovv mutable this   4
life is, and hovv it neuer continueth in one ſtay, for vvhich purpoſe thou muſt conſider the great alterations of our bodies, vvhich
          B   neuer

neuer remaine in one ftate of health and difpofition ; and much more the mutations and
changements of our mindes , vvhich be alvvais altered, as the fea, vvith diuers vvinds
and vvaues of pafsions, appetites, and cares,
vvhich trouble & difquiet vs euerie hovver;
and finallie the varieties , vvhich they terme
of *fortune* , vvhich neuer fuffereth the affairs
of mans life to perfeuer in the felf fame ftate,
and in the fame profperitie and contentment,
but alvvais turneth her vvheele, and roleth
vp and dovvne from one place to an other.
And aboue al this confider hovv continual
the mouing of our life is , feeing it neuer ref-
teth day nor night, but goeth fhortening
from time to time . Novv according to this
reckning vvhat is our life, but a candle that
ftill confurreth and the more it burneth and
giueth light, the more it vvafteth avvay?
vvhat is our life but a floure that openeth in
the morning, that at noonetide fadeth avvay
and at euening is cleene dried vp?

In refpect of this continual mutation and
changement, God faid by the Prophet Ifaie.
Ifaie 40.
6. *Al flefh is hay , and al the glorie thereof is as the
flovver of the feeld.* Vppon vvhich vvoords S.
Hierom faith . *Trulie vvhofoeuer vvil confider the
frailtie of our fleafh, and hovv in al minutes and moments of times vve grovv and vvax avvay and neuer
                                                    abyde*

abyde in one state, and hovv euen this, in vvhich vvee speake, copy and vvrite, is so much past of our life; he vvil nothing dout to call our flesh hay, and al the glorie of the same as the flovver of hay, or as the medovves of the feelds. He that vvas an infant, becommeth a child; he that vvas a child, vvaxeth suddenlie a young man; and by vncertaine spaces of time is chaunged to be old and aged, and doth before maruaile to see him self aged, then he vvondereth that he is not young. The beavvtiful vvoman vvhich did dravv after her so manie companies of foolish young men, shevveth her vvrinckled forhead, and she that before vvas so greatlie loued, is aftervvards vtterlie contemned.

Fiftlie consider hovv deceitfull our life is, (vvhich peraduenture is the vvoorst propertie it hath, for so much as it deceaueth so manie, and yet hath so manie blindlouers of it,) becaufe being in deede verie laide and filthie, it seemeth vnto vs beautiful; being bitter, it seemeth svveete; being but short, to euerie one his ovvne life seemeth long; and being so miserable, it seemeth so amiable that there is no trauel nor daunger, to vvhich men doos not expose them selues for the same, although it be vvith peril and hazard of their life euerlasting, dooing things vvhereby they com to lose it.   5

Sixtlie consider hovv besides this that our   6

B 2   life

life is so short, as hath ben said, yet that litle
time vve haue to liue is so subiect to so manie
miseries both of the soule and bodie, that all
it laied together is nothing els but a vale of
teares, and a maine sea of infinite miseries.
Sainct Hierom vvriteth, that Xerxes that
most mightie king, vvho threvv dovvne
mountaines & dried vp the seas, as on a time
he vvent vp to the toppe of a high hill, to take
a vevve of his huge armie, vvhich he had gathered together of infinite people, after he
had vvel seene them, it is said that he vvept.
And being demanded the cause vvherefore
he vvept? he ansvvered and said; I vveepe because vvithin these hundred yeares, there shal
not one of al this huge armie, vvhich I see
here present before me, be left aliue.

O that vvee might, saith S. Hierom. *ascend vp
to the toppe of som high place, that vve might see frō
thence al the vvhole earth vnderneath our feete.
From thence shouldest thou see the ruines and miseries of the vvhole vvorld, and nations destroied by
nations, and kingdoms by kingdoms. Thou shouldest see hovv som vvere tormented, som murdered,
som drovvned in the sea, som others lead avvaie cap-
tiues. In one place thou shouldest see mariages and
mirth, in an other dolefull mourning and lamentatiō,
heere som borne, there som others die, som flovving in
riches, and others begging from dore to dore. To be*
                                          short

tom. 1.
epistol. 3.
cap. 11.

short thou shouldest see not onlie the huge armie of Xerxes, but also al those in the vvorld that be novv aliue, vvithin these fevv daies to end their liues.

Runne ouer al the diseases and paines of a mans bodie; and al the afflictions and cares of the mind: and al the perils and daungers vvhich be incident as vvel to al eftates, as to al ages of men, and thou shalt see yet more euidentlie hovv manifold the miferies of this life be : for bv feeing hovv little a thing al that is, vvhich the vvorld can aford thee, thou shalt com more eafilie to defpife & contemne vvhatfoeuer the fame hath in it.

Finallie after al thefe miferies, there folovveth the laft miferie that is death, vvhich is as vvel to the bodie as to the fovvle, of al terrible things the verie laft, and moft terrible. For the bodie fhall in a moment be depriued, and fpoiled of vvhat foeuer it hath: and of the fovvle there fhal then be made a refolute determination, vvhat fhal becom of it for euer and euer.

Al this vvil make thee vnderstand hovv breefe & miferable the glorie of the vvorld is, for as much as the life of vvorldlings, vppon vvhich it is founded, is fuch as vve haue heere laid dovvne: and confequentlie hovv the fame deferueth to be abhorred, defpifed, contemned.

VVenfdaie·night. Of the houre of death.

THIS daie thou muſt meditate vppon the hovver of death , vvhich is one of the moſt profitable conſiderations that may be, as vvel for the obteining of true vviſdom, and eſchevving of ſinne, as alſo for begining to prepare thy ſelf for the hovver of accoumpt.

1 Conſider then firſt of al hovv vncertaine that hovver is in vvhich death vvil aſſault thee, becauſe thou knovveſt not nether in vvhat time, nor in vvhat place, nor in vvhat diſpoſition it vvil com vppon thee. Onlie thou knovveſt for certaine that die thou muſt, al the reſt is vncertaine, ſauing that ordinarilie this houre is vvont to ſteale vppon vs, at ſuch time as a man is moſt careles, and thinketh leſt of it.

2 Secondlie conſider the ſeparation vvhich ſhalbe at that time, not onlie betvvixt vs & al ſuch things as vve loue in this vvorld, but alſo betvvene the ſovvle and the bodie ſuch auncient and louing companions. If the baniſhement from our natiue countrie, and frō the natural ayer in vvhich a man hath ben bredde and brought vp , ſeeme a thing ſo grieuous, although the baniſhed man might carie avvaie vvith him vvhat ſoeuer he loueth

vveth;hovv much mo.e grie ous then fhal
that vniuerfal banifhment be from al things
that vve haue, from our hovvfes, from our
goods, from our frinds, frō our father, from
our mother, from our children, f om this
lightand common ayer, and finallie from al
things of this vvorld. If an oxe make fo
great a bellovving vvhen he is feparated
from an other oxe vvith vvhom he did
dravve the plovve; vvhat a bellovving vvil
thie heart then make, vvhen thou fhalt be
feparated from al thofe, in vvhofe companie
thou haft caried the yoke and burthens of
this life?

Confider alfo the paine vvhich a man
fhall then receiue, vvhen he fhal fee reprefented before him in vvhat cafe his bodie &
fovvle fhalbe after his death: for as tovvching the bodie, he knovveth alredie that
better prouifion can not be made for it, then
a pitte of feuen foote long in the companie
of other dead bodies. But as concerning the
fovvle, he knovveth not certainlie, vvhat
fhal becom of it, nor vvhat fort fhal befall it.
This is one of the greateft angvv fhes and
griefes that men ar then trovvbled vvith, to
vvit, that there is to enfue glorie and paine
eue.lafting, & that they be then fo neere to
th'one and th'other, & yet knovv not vvhi-

3

ther of these tvvo lottes, being so far different
as they ar, shall fall vnto theyr share.

After this angvvish there folovveth an
other no lesse then this, to vvit the accompt
vvhich must be giuen there , and vvhich is
such that it maketh euen the most stovvtest
to tremble ahd quake. It is vvriten of holie
Arsenius that being at the point of death he
began to be afraied. And as som of his disciples said to him, vvhat, father, ar you novv
afraied ? he ansvvered. Mie sonnes this feare
is not nevv to me, because I haue alvvaies
liued vvith the same. Moreouer at that time
al the sinnes of a más life past, ar represented
vnto him like a squadron of enemies that
com to assault him; and those vvhich be the
greatest, and vvherein he tooke greatest delight, ar then represented more liuelie , & ar
cause of greater feare . O hovv bitter shal
the remembrance of delights and pleasures
past be at that time , vvhich in other times
seemed so svveete? Trulie the vviseman had
good reason to saie. *Regarde not the vvine vvhen
it is redd, and vvhen it shevveth his colour in the
glasse; for although at the time of drinking it seeme
delectable , yet at the end it vvil bite like a serpent,
and poison like a cocatrice.* These be the dregges
of that poisoned cuppe of the enimie. These
be the leauings of the cuppe of Babylon so
gylted

Prou. 23.

gylted vvithout. At that time a miſerable man, ſeeing him ſelf enuironed vvith ſo manie accuſers, beginneth to feare the threed of this iudgement, and to ſaie vvith him ſelf. O miſerable vvretch that I am vvho haue liued ſo deceaued, and haue vvalked ſuch vvaies? vvhat ſhal becom novv of me in this iudgement? If S. Paul ſaie that *VVhat things* *a man doth ſovv, thoſe alſo ſhal he reape.* I that haue ſovven no other thing but vvorks of fleſh, vvhat hope I to reape thereof but corruption? yf S. Iohn ſaie that no polluted thing ſhall enter into that ſoueraigne Citie vvhich is al of pure gold, vvhat hope maie I haue vvho haue liued ſo abominablie and ſo filthilie?

Galat.6.8

Apoc.21.

After this there folovv the Sacraments of Confeſsion, of the Altar, and of Extreme vnction, vvhich is the laſt ſuccour that the Catholique Church can help vs vvithal in that trovvbleſom time: & therefore as vvel heerein as in other things, thou muſt conſider the griefes and angvviſhes of mind, vvhich a man ſhall then ſuffer for his vvicked life paſt; and hovv gladlie he vvil vviſh that he had taken an other vvaie: and vvhat kind of life he vvould then lead, yf he might haue time to dooe the ſame; and hovv he then vvil enforce him ſelf to call vppon almighte God,

5

God, vvhen the paines and increasing of his sicknes vvil scarcelie permitte him to dooeit.

6   Consider also those last accidents & pangs of sicknes', vvhich be as it vvere messangers of death, hovv terrible and fearful they be: the breast riseth and panteth; the voice vvaxeth hoarce; the feete begin to die; the knees vvax cold & stiffe; the nostrels runne out; the eys sink into the head: the countenance seemeth dead: the toung faultereth & is not able to doe his office: & finallie by the hast vvhich the sovvle maketh to depart out of the bodie, all the senses being troubled doe lose theire force and vertue.

7   But aboue al, the sovvle is shee that then suffreth greatest troubles: for at that time shee is in a great conflict and agonie, partlie for her departure, and partlie for feare of the accoumpt vvhich she must giue; because she is naturallie loth to depart from the bodie, and liketh vvel her abode therein, and feareth her reckoning.

Novv vvhen the sovvle is departed from the bodie, there remaine yet tvvo vvais to goe: th'oneis to accompaine the bodie vnto the sepulchre; th'other is to folovv the sovvle vntil her cause be determined: and thou must vievv vvhat shall befall to ech of these parts.

Con-

Confider then in vvhat fort the bodie re-maineth after his fovvle hath forfaken it, &
vvhat a vvorthie garment that is vvhich they
prouide to burie it in, and vvhat haft they
make to get him ridde ovvt of the hovvfe.
Confider his funeralls vvith al that paffeth
in the fame, the ringing of bells; the praying
for him; the doleful feruice and finging of the
Church; the accompanying, and forovv, &
vveeping of frinds; and finallie al th'other
particulers that ar then vvoont to happen,
vntill the bodie be left in the graue, vvhere it
fhall lie buried in that earth of perpetual ob-liuion and forgetfulnes.

VVhen thou haft left the bodie in the grave   9
folovv forthvvith the fovvle, and behould
vvhat vvay fhe taketh through that nevv
region, and vvhat fhal becom of her, and
vvhat iudgement fhe fhall haue . Imagin
that thou art novv prefent at this iudgemét,
and that al the court of heauen expecteth
the end of this fentence, vvhere the fovvle
fhal be charged and difcharged of al that
fhe hath receaued euen to the valevv of a
pinnes point . There fhalbe taken accoupt
of the life, of the goods, of the familie and
hovvfhold , of the infpirations of God, of
the means and opportunities vve had to lead
a good life , and aboue al of the accoumpt
vve

vve haue made of the moſt pretious bloud
of our Sauiour, and of the vſe of his ſacra-
ments. And there ſhal euerie one be iudged
according to the accoumpt he ſhall make of
that, vvhich he hath receaued.

Thurſdaie night . Of the date of iudgment.

THIS daie thou ſhalt meditate vppon
the daie of the general iudgement, that
by meanes of this conſideration, thoſe tvvo
principall affeċtions maie be ſtirred vp in
thy ſoule, vvhich euerie faith full Chriſtian
ought to haue, to vvit the feare of God, and
abhorring of ſinne.

I   Conſider firſt vvhat a terrible daie that
ſhalbe, in vvhich the cauſes of al the childrē
of Adam ſhalbe examined, the proceſſes of
al our liues concluded, and a definitiue ſentence giuen vvhat ſhal be of vs for euermore.
That daie ſhall compriſe in it ſelf al the daies
of al ages, as vvel preſent and paſt, as to com;
becauſe in it the vvorld ſhall giue accoumpt
of al thoſe times, and in it ſhall almightie
God povver out his anger and indignation,
vvhich he hath gathered & laid vp in al ages.
Hovv violentlie ſhal the maine floud of
Gods indignation breake out at that daie,
conteining in it ſo maine flouds of anger
and

and vvrath, as there haue ben sinnes committed since the creation of the vvorld.

Secondlie cõsider the fearful signes vvhich shal goe before that daie: for as our Sauiour saith, before the comming of this daie, there shalbe signes in the sunne, in the moone, and in the starres, and finallie in all the creatures of heauen and earth, for they all shal haue as it vvere a feeling of their end, before they end in deede; and shal tremble and beginne to fal, before they fal in deede. But men (saith he) shal goe dried vp and vvithered for feare of death, hearing the terrible rorings of the sea, and seeing the great vvaues and tempestes vvhich shal rise in it, and foreseeing by this the great calamities and miseries vvhich such feareful signes dooe threaten to the vvorld. And so shal they goe astonied and amazed, their faces pale and disfigured, them selues dead before death, and condemned before sentence be giuen; measuring the perils imminent, by their ovvne present feares, & euerie one so occupied vvith his ovvne affairs, that none shal think of others, no not the father of his sonne. None shal then haue to doe vvith anie, or for anie, becaufe none shalbe sufficient for him selfalone.

Thirdlie consider that vniuersal floud of fier that shal com before the iudge, and that

dread-

dreadful fovvnd of the trompet vvhich the
Archangel fhal blovv to fommon and call
al the generations of the vvorld to affemble
together in one place, and to be prefent at
there iudgement, and aboue all that dreadful maieftie vvith ,vvhich the iudge fhall
com.

4   After this confider the ftreight accoumpt
vvhich fhal there be required of euerie mā.

Iob 9.   *Trulie* (faith Iob) *I knovv it is fo, and that no man
can be iuftified, yf he be compared vvith God. If he
vvil conted vvith him* (in iudgement) *of a thovvfand things* (that he fhall charge him vvithal)
he fhal not be able to anfvvere vnto one. VVhat
then fhal euerie vvicked perfon think at
that time vvhen God fhal enter vvith him
into this examination, & fhal there vvithin
his ovvne confcience faie thus vnto him.
Com hither thou vvicked felovv ,̧ vvhat
haft thou feene in me that thou fhouldeft
thus defpife me, and goe to mine enimies
fide ? I haue created thee to my image and
likenes: I haue giuē thee the light of faith &
made thee a Chriftiā, & redeemed thee vvith
mine ovvne propre bloud , for thee haue I
fafted, traueilled from place to place, vvat-
ched, laboured & fvveat droppes of bloud,
for thee haue I fuffred perfecutions, fcour-
gings, blafphemies, reproches, buffetings,
                         difho-

dishonours, torments, and the Crosse. VVitnes be this Crosse and nailes vvhich appeare heere. VVitnes be these vvounds of my hāds & feete vvhich remaine in mie bodie. VVitnes be heauen & earth before vvhom I suffered. Novv vvhat haft thou donne vvith this thy foule vvhich I vvith my bloud purchased to be mine ? In vvhose feruice haft thou emploied that vvhich I bought so deerelie? O fooliſh and adulterous generation ! VVhie vvouldeft thou rather ferue this thy enimie vvith paine, then me thy Creator & Redeemer vvith ioy? I called you oftentimes, & ye vvould not anfvvere me ; I knocked at your gates, and ye vvould not avvake ; I ftretched out my hands on the croſſe, & ye vvould not behold them. Ye haue defpifed my counfels vvith al my promifes & threatnings: vvherfore fpeake novv o ye Angels, iudge ye other iudges betvvixt me and my viniard, vvhat could I haue donne more for it then I haue donne?

Novv vvhat anfvvere can the vvicked make heere ? fuch as fcoffe at holie things ? fuch as mocke vertue? fuch as contemne fimplicitie ? fuch as haue made more accoumpt of the lavves of the vvorld then of the lavves of God? fuch as haue bene deaffe at al his callings, vnfenfible to all his infpirations,

rebel-

rebellious againſt his commandements, ob-
durate and vnthankful for al his chaſtiſe-
ments & benefits? vvhat vvil thoſe anſvvere
vvho haue liued,as if they had beleeued that
there vvere no God; and ſuch as haue made
accoumpt of no lavve, but onlie of their
ovvne intereſt and commoditie? *VVat vvil ye*

Iſai. 30.
27.

dooe(ſaith the Prophet Iſaie) *in the daie of viſita-
tion and calamitie vvhich commeth from a farre*?
Vnto vvhome vvil ye flie for ſuccour and
help,and vvhere vvil you leaue your glorie;
that ye be not caried avvaie priſoners,and fal
vvith thoſe that ar dead?

§ Fiftlie conſider after al this that terrible
ſentence vvhich the iudge ſhal thunder out
againſt the vvicked;and that dreadful ſaying
vvhich ſhal make the ears of al that ſhal

Iſai. 10.
3.

heare it to glovve and tingle. *His lippes* (ſaith
the Prophet Iſaie) *ar ful of indignation , and his
toung like a conſuming fiar* . VVhat fiar ſhal
byrne ſo hoat as theſe vvords; *Depart from me*

Math. 25.
41.

*ye vvicked and curſed into euerlaſting fiar, vvhich is
prepared for the diuel and his Angels*; In vvhich
vvords and eche of them thou haſt much to
feele & think of,as of that doleſul departing;
of that malediction and curſe;of that fiar; of
that companie of diuels and vvicked ſpirites;
and that vvhich is aboue al,of that eternitie
vvhich ſhal neuer end.

Fridaie

Fridaie night of the paines of hell.

THIS daie thou shalt meditate vppon the paines of hell, that vvith this consideration also, thy sovvle maie be the more confirmed in the feare of God, & abhorring of sinne.

These paines, saith Sainct Bonauenture, ar to be conceiued vnder som such corporal formes and similitudes, as the Sainchs haue taught vs. VVherfore it shalbe a thing verie conuenient to imagin the place of hell (as the same doctor saith) to be as it vyere an obscure and dark lake vnder the earth; or as a most deepe pitte full of fier; or as a horrible and dark Cittie vvholie burning vvith fierce flames of fier : in vvhich none other noise vvere to be heard, but the hovvlings and lamentations of hellish tormentors, & tormented persons, vvith continual vveeping and gnashing of teeth.

Bonauent. in fasciculario c. 3.

Novv in this vnfortunate place the damned suffer tvvo principal sorts of paines, th'one called by the Diuines *pænam sensus*, a sensible paine; th'other *pænam damni*, a paine of losse. As tovvching the first paine, to vv.t of the sense, consider that then, there shalbe no sense at all, neither vvithin, nor vvithout the sovvle, vvhich shal not suffer h's propre

C   torment.

1

2

torment . For like as the vvicked offended
God vvith al theire membres and senses, and
made armour of them al to serue sinne, euen
so vvil he ordain that ech one of them shalbe
there tormented vvith his peculiar torment
and paie according to his desert. There shall
the vvanton and lecherous eyes be tormented vvith the vglie sight of diuels. There
shall the eares vvhich vvere accustomed
to heare lies and filthie talke, heare perpetual
blasphemies and lamentations. There the
nostrels, vvhich so much loued perfumes &
sensual smels, shalbe filled vvith intolerable
stench. There the taste, vvhich vvas cherished
vvith so diuers kinds of meats and delicacies,
shalbe tormented vvith rauenous hunger &
thirst. There the toung, so much giuen to
murmuring and blaspheming, shalbe extreme bitter vvith gall of serpents. There the
touching, so great a frind of delicate and soft
things, shal svvimme as it vvere in the cold
yse of the riuer Cocytus, and betvvixt the
extreme heates and flames of fiar. There the
imagination shal suffer vvith the apprehen-
sion of greefes present; the memorie by calling to mind the pleasures past ; the vnderstanding vvith the representation of euils
that ar to com; & the vvil vvith the extreme
anger and furie vvhich the vvicked haue

in

in that place againſt God . Finallie there
ſhalbe heaped together al the miſeries and
torments that poſsiblie can be imagined.
For as S. Gregorie ſaith, there ſhalbe cold in- *Gregor.*
tollerable: fiar vnquenchable, the vvorme of
cõſcience immortall, ſtenche inſupportable;
darknes palpable: vvhippes of tormentours:
viſion of diuels: confuſion of ſinnes: and deſ-
peration of al goodnes. Novv tel me , yf it
ſeeme a thing intollerable to ſuffer the leſt of
al theſe paines that vve indure in this vvorld
though it vvere but for a ſmall time , vvhat
ſhall it be to ſuffer there at one time al this
multitude of torments, in al the members &
ſenſes both invvard and ovvtvvard? & that
not for the ſpace of one night alone, nor of
a thouſand nightes, but for the ſpace of an infinite eternitie. VVhat vnderſtanding, vvhat
vvordes , vvhat iudgement is there in the
vvoorld, that is able to conceiue and expreſſe
this matter as it is in deede?

And yet this is not the greateſt paine that *3*
is there to be ſuffered : for an other there is
farre greater vvithout anie compariſon ,
that is, that vvhich the Diuines terme *pænam
damni,* the paine of damnatiõ or loſſe: vvhich
is to be depriued for euer of the ſight of God,
and of his glorious companie . For ſo much
greater is anie paine, by hovv much it depri-

ueth vs of agreater good:and becauſe God is
the greateſt good of al goods, ſo to vvant
him ſhall be the greateſt euill of all euils,
vvhich in deede is this.

4   Theſe ar the paines that generallie appertaine to al the damned: but beſides theſe ge-
ne all paines, there be other particuler paines
vvhich euerie one ſhal ſuffer according to
the qualitie of his ſinne. For there ſhal be
one kind of paine for the provvde man, an
other for the enuions: one for the couetous,
an other for the leacherous, and ſo in like
manner for all other ſinnes. There ſhal the
paine be eſteemed avvnſvverable to the
pleaſures before receiued: and the confuſion
anſvverable to the preſumption and pride:
& the nakednes anſvverable to the ſuperflui-
tie and abundance:and the hunger and thirſt
avvnſerable to the delicatenes and fullnes
paſt.

5   Vnto all theſe paines there is added an
eternitie, or euerlaſtingnes of ſuffering them,
vvhich is as it vvere the ſeale and key of
them all: for al the reſt aforeſaide vvere yet
ſomvvhat tollerable, if it might be ended:
for ſo much as nothing is great that hath an
end. But paines that haue no end, no eaſe, no
mitigation, nor declination, no nor hope
that euer ether the paines, or he that giueth
                                                      them,

them, nor he that fuffereth them fhall finifh
and haue an end, but to be as it vvere a per-
petuall banifhment, and an infamie neuer to
be remitted; this is a matter able to make anie
man befides him felf, that fhould confider
it deepelie and vvith due attention.

This is then the greateft paine that of all
others is to be fuffered in that vnfortunate
place: for yf thefe paines vvere to be endured but for fom certaine tyme, although it
vvere a thovvfand or a hundred thovvfand
years, or, as a certaine doctor faieth, yf there
vvere anie hope that they fhould end in fo
much time, as al the maine occeá fea fho:ld
be confumed drop by drop, taking out of it
euerie thoufand yeare but one drop onlie,
yet this vvoold be fom kind of comfort and
confolation. But it paffeth not foe in this
cafe, for the paines fhal be correfpondent to
the eternitie of almightie God, and the continuing of this miferie, to the perpetuitie of
his diuine glorie. So long as God fhal liue,
fo long fhall they die, & vvhen God fhal be
no more that vvhich he is novv, then fhall
they alfo ceafe to be that vvhich they ar.
Novv in this duratió, in this eternitie, I vvifh
thee good brother, to fettel & reft for fom
time thy confideration, & as a cleene beaft
to ruminate this paffage novv vvith thie
C 3 felf,

self, for as much as the eternal, & euerlasting truth crieth, and auovvcheth saying. *Heauen and earth shall passe, but my vvordss shall not passe.*

Matthæ.
24. 35.

Saturdaie night . Of the glorie of beauen.

THIS daie thou shalt meditate of the glorie of those that be blessed and happie in heauen, thereby to moue thy heart to the contempt of the vvorld, and to an earnest desire to be in the companie of celestiall citizens.

To th'end therfore that thou maist in som sort vnderstand somyvhat of this felicitie, thou hast to consider, a mong other things, these fiue that ar in it. The excellencie of the place; the ioy of the companie; the vision of God; the glorie of the bodies; & finallie the sacietie, and perfect store of al good things vvhich is there.

First then consider th'excellencie of the place, and especiallie the greatenes thereof, vvhich is vvonderfull. For vvhen a man readeth in certaine graue authors, that e erie starre in heauen is greater then the vvhole earth, & moreouer that there be som starres of such exceeding greatenes, that they be ninetie times bigger then al the vvhole earth; and vvith this lifteth vp his eyes to heauen, heaven, and seeeth in the same such a number of starres, and so manie voide spaces, vvhere manie more starres might be set, vvhen he seeeth this, I saie, hovv can he but vvoonder? hovv can he but be astonied & as it vvere besides him self, considering the passing greatnes of that place, and much more of that Souerain lord that created the same?

Novv as for the beavvtie of that place, it is a thing that cannot be expressed vvith vvords; for yf God hath created so vvonderful and so bevvtiful things in this vale of teares, vvhat hath he created (trovv ye) in that place, vvhich is the seate of his glorie, the throne of his statelines, the pallace of his maiestie, the hovvse of his elect, and the paradise of all delightes?

After the excellencie of the place consider the vvorthines of the dvvellers in it, vvhose number, holines, riches, & bevvtie doe far exceede vvhat soeuer can be imagined. S. Iohn saith that the multitude of the elect ar so great, that no man is able to count them. S. Dionisius saith, that the Angels ar so manie, that they exceede vvithout comparison al corporal and material creatures vppon the earth. S. Thomas agreeing vvith this opinion, saith, that like as the heauens in great-

2.

Apocal.
7. 9.

Cælest.
Hierar.
c. 14.

1. p. q. 50.
ar. 3

C 4   nes

nes exceede the earth vvithout anie proportion: so doth the multitude of those glorious
spirites exceede the nombre of all corporall
things that ar in this vvoorld vvith like ad-
vantage and proportion. Novv vvhat thing
can be imagined more vvoonderfull then
this? Certainlie this is such a thing, that if it
vvere vvel considered, it vvere sufficient to
make al men astonied. And yf eche one of
those blessed spirites (yea though it be the
verie least among them) be more beautiful
to behold, then al this visible vvoorld, vvhat
a sight shall it be, to behold such a number
of beautiful spirites, & to see the perfections
and offices of euerieone of them? There the
Angels be sent in ambassages; The Archangels ministre and serue ; the Principalities
triumph; The Povvers reioice; The Domi-
nations gouerne; The Vertues shine ; The
Thrones glister; The Cherubines giue light.
The Seraphines burne in loue; and al sing
lavvdes and praises to God. Novv yf the
companie and mutual conuersation of good
and vertuons persons, be a thing so svveete
and so amiable as vvee dailie proue; vvhat a
thing shall it be to conuerse there vvith so
manie blessed Sainčts, to talk vvith the Apostles, to deale vvith the Prophets, to communicate vvith the Martyrs, and to háue a perpetual

petual familiaritie vvith al the elect?

More yf it fhal be fo great a glorie to en- **3**
ioy the companie of the good; vvhat fhal it
be to enioy the companie and prefence of
him, vvhome the morning ftars dooe praife,
at vvhofe excellent beautie the fonne and
moone dooe vvonder, before vvhofe maieftie the Angels and al thofe bleffed fpirites
dooe bovve theire knees? vvhat fhal it be
to behold that vniuerfal and fupreme good,
in yvhome al good things ar conteined? that
greater vvoorld, in vvhich ar included al
vvoorlds? and to fee him, vvho being one, is
al things; and being moft fimple in him felf,
and vvithout al kind of mixture, doth yet
comprehend in him felf the perfections of al
things? If to heare &fee king Salomō, vvere
thought fo great a matter, that the Queene
of Saba faid of him . *Bleffed ar the men , and* 2. *Regu.*
bleffed ar thefe thy feruants, that ftand in thy pre- 10. 8.
fence and heare thy vvifdom: VVhat fhal it be
to behold that moft high Salomō? that eternal vvfdom? that infinite greatnes? that ine-
ftimable bevvtie ? that exceeding goodnes,
and to enioie the fame for euer and euer?
This is the effential glorie of the Saincts:
this is the laft end and harborough of our
defires.

Afther this contemplate the glorie of the **4**
bodies,

bodies, vvhich fhalbe endued vvith thofe fovver finguler qualities and dovvries, to vvit vvith *Subtilitie*, *Svviftnes*, *Impaßibilitie* and *Cleerenes* : vvhich *Cleerenes* fhalbe fo great, that ech one of the Sainꝭts bodies fhal fhine like the funne in the kingdom of their father. Novv if the funne vvhich ftandeth in the middeft of the heauens being but one, be yet fufficient to giue light and comfort to al this vvorld, vvhat a light fhal fo many funnes and lamps make, as fhal fhine togetherin that place?

¶   But vvhat fhal I fay novv of al the other goods vvhich are there ? There fhal be Health, vvithout infirmitie; Libertie, vvithout bondage; Bevvtie vvithout deformitie; Immortalitie, vvithout corruption ; Abundance, vvithout neceffitie ; Quietnes, vvithout vexatiō; Securitie, vvithout feare; Knouledge, vvithout error; Fulnes, vvithout lothfomnes; Ioy, vvithout heauines; and Honour *August.*   vvithout contradiction. There (as S. Auguftine faith) fhal be true glorie : for none fhal be praifed by error or flatterie . There fhal be true honor: for it fhal nether be denied o fuch as deferue it, nor giuen to fuch as merite it not. There fhalbe true peace: for no man fhalbe molefted either by him felf, or by others . The revvard of true vertue, fhalbe
                                                    euen

euen he that gaue the vertue, & hath promifed him felf for a revvard of the fame; vvhom
vve fhâl fee vvithout ceafing, loue vvithout lothfomnes, and praife vvithout vvearines. There the place is large, beutiful,
bright, and fecure; the companie verie good,
and pleafant ; the time alvvaies after one
manner; not diuided into euening and morning, but continued vvith one fimple eternitie. There fhalbe a pepetual fpring-time,
vvhich fhal florifh for euermore vvith the
frefhnes and fvveete breathing of the holie
Ghoft. There al fhal reioice, al fing, and giue
continuall praife to that high giuer of al
things, through vvhofe bountiful goodnes
they liue and raigne for euer. O heauenlie cittie! fecure dvvelling place! countrie
vvhere al pleafant things ar to be found!
people vvithout grudging and murmuring!
quiet neighbours! and men vvithout anie
yvant or necefsitie. O that the ftrife and
contention of this prefent ftate vvere ended!
O that the daies of my banifhment vvere
once finiffhed! vvhen fhal this daie com?
vvhen fhal I com, and appeare before the
face of my fvveete lord and Sauiour?

Sundaie

Sundaie night, of the benifits of almughtie God.

THIS daie thou shalt meditate vppon the benifits of God , therebie to giue him thanks for them , and to enkendle in thy selfa more feruent loue of him vvho hath ben so bountiful tovvards thee . And although these benifits be innumerable , yet maist thou at the least consider these fiue most principal: to vvit, the benifits of *Creatiõ, Conseruation, Redemption, Vocation, and other particuler and Secrete benifits.*

I   And first of al , touching the benifit of *Creation* , consider vvith great attention vvhat thou vvast before thou vvere created, and vvhat God did for thee, and bestovved vppon thee , before thou diddest merite or deserue anie thing ; to vvit he gaue thee thy bodie vvith al thy membres and senses : and thy sovvle of so great excellencie, endued vvith those three noble povvers , vvhich be *Vnderstanding, Memorie, and VVill.* And consider vvel , that to giue thee this sovvle , vvas to giue thee al things, for so much as there is no perfection in anie creature , vvhich a man hath not in him in his manner. VVhereby it appeareth that to giue vs this thing alone, vvas to giue vs at once al things together.

As

As conce:ning the benifit of *Conſeruation*,   2
conſider hovv al thy vvhole being dependeth of Gods prouidence; hovv thou couldeſt not liue one momēt, nor make ſo much
as one ſteppe, vvere it not by means of him;
hovv he hath created al things in this vvorld
for thy vſe and ſeruice, the ſea, the earth, the
birds, the fiſhes, the liuing beaſts, the plants,
and finallie, the Angels of heauen. Conſider
moreouer the health vvhich he giueth thee,
the ſtrength, life, ſuſtenance, vvith al other
temporal helps and ſuccours. And aboue al
this vvaigh vvel the miſeries and calamities, into vvhich thou ſeeeſt other men fall
euerie daie; and thou thy ſelf mighteſt alſo
haue fallen into the ſame, yf God of his great
mercie had not preſerued thee.

Touching the benifit of *Redemption*, thou   3
maiſt cōſider therein tvvo things. Firſt hovv
manie & great the benifits haue ben, vvhich
ovvr Sauiour hath giuen vs by means of the
benifit of Redemption: and ſecondlie hovv
manie and hovv great the miſeries vvere,
vvhith he ſuffred in his moſt holie body and
ſovvle, to purchaſe vs theſe benifits. But to
the end thou vnderſtand better, and feele in
thy ſelf hovv much thou ovveſt vnto this
thy lord, for that vvhich he hath endured for
thy ſake; thou maiſt conſider theſe fovver
prin-

principall circumstances in the misterie of
his sacred Passion; to vvit, vvhoe is he that
suffreth; vvhat he suffreth; of vvhome; and
to vvhat end he suffreth . VVhoe is he then
that suffreth ? God. VVhat suffreth he? The
greatest torments and dishonour, that euer
vvere suffred. Of vvhome doth he suffer? Of
hellish and abominable creatures , vvho in
theire vvoorks ar like euen to the diuels
them selues . To vvhat end doth he suffer?
not for anie comoditie of him self, or anie
merite of our part, but onlie for the bovvels
of his infinite charitie and mercie.

4　　As concerning the benifit of *Vocation,*
consider first of al, vvhat a great mercie it
vvas of God to make thee a Christian, and
to call thee to the Catholique faith by the
means of holie Baptisme; and to make thee
also partaker of the other Sacraments. And
yf after this calling , vvhen thou hast by
deadlie sinne lost thine innocencie, our lord
hath raised thee vp from sinne , and receaued thee againe into his grace , and set thee
in the state of saluation ; hovv canst thou be
able to praise him for this so singular a benifit ? vvhat a great mercie vvas it to expect
thee so long time ? to suffer thee to commit
so manie sinnes? and to send thee so manie
godlie inspirations? and not to shorten the
daies

daies of thy life, as he hath donne to diuers
others that vvere in the same state? and last
of al to call thee vvith so mightie a vocatiõ,
that thou mightest rise vp againe from death
to life, and open thine eys to the eternal
light? vvhat mercie vvasit also, after thou
vvast conuerted, to giue the grace not to returne vnto deadlie sinne againe, but to vanquish thine enimie, and to perseuer in
good life?

These ar the publique and knovven benifits; but there be other secrete benifits,
vvhich no man knovveth, but he onlie that
hath receaued them: and againe there be
som so secrete, that euen he him self vvho
hath receaued them, knovveth them not; but
he onlie that gaue them. Hovv manie times
hast thou deserued in this vvorld either
through thy pride, negligence, or vnthankfulnes, that God should vtterlie forsake thee
as he hath donne to manie 'others for som
one of these causes, and yet hath not he
dealt thus vvith thee? Hovv manie euills &
occasions of euills hath our lord preuented
vvith his prouidence, ouerthrovving 'the
snares of thine enimie, and stopping his passage, and not permitting him to execute his
vvilie practyses and designements vppon
thee? Hovv ofentimes hath he donne for
                                        euerie

Luc. 22.
31.

euerie one of vs that vvhich he said to S.
Peeter. *Behold Satan hath required to haue youv*
for to sift as vvheate : but I haue prayed for thee that
thy faith faile not. Novv vvho knovveth these
secretes but onlie God? The positiue benifits be such as a man may somtimes vnderstand and knovv them : but priuatiue benifits vvhich consist not in dooing vs good,
but in deliuering vs from euils, vvho is able
to vnderstand? VVherefore as vvel for these,
as for the others, it is reason vvee should
alvvais be thankful to our lord, and vnderstand hovv farre in arrerages vvee be
in our reckoning vvith him, and hovv
much more vve be indetted vnto him, then
vvee ar able to paie, seeing vvee ar yet not
able to vnderstand them.

6   But that thou in som sort knovv better
the greatnes of these benifits vvhich God
hath bestovved vppon thee, it maketh much
to the purpose that thou consider eche one
of these benifits vvith the circumstances
annexed vnto them vvhich be : vvhoe he is
that giueth the benifit; vvho he is that receaueth the same; vvherefore it is giuen; and
in vvhat sort.

As touching the first circumstance thinke
vvel vvith thy self, howv great he is that bestovveth these benifits vppon thee, seeing he
is

is God; confider the greatenes of his omnipotencie, vvhich is declared vnto vs fuf-
ficientlie by the vvoork-manſhip of this
vvoorld, vvith the vvhole vniuerſitie of
creatures conteined therein . Confider alſo
the greatenes of his vvifdom, vvhich is knovven by the ordre, agreement, and maruailous prouidence vvhich vvee fee in al things.
For yf thou meditate vvel vppon this circumſtance, thou ſhalt com to vnderſtand,
that not oulie the afore-ſaid benifits, but
alſo the leaſt thing that maie be, as for exam-
p̃le an apple, or nut, ſent thee by this ſo great
and vvorthie a king, ought to bee highlie
eſteemed of thee, for the vvorthines of him
that giueth it.

The greatenes alſo of theſe benifits is no
les to be eſteemed in reſpect of the ſecond
circumſtance, that is of the baſenes of him
that receaueth them, then in reſpect of the
excellencie of him that giueth them. And
therefore the Prophet Dauid ſaid. O lord
vvhat is man that thou art mindful of him, or the. Pſal. 8. 5.
ſonne of man that thou viſiteſt him? for yf al the
vvhole vvoorld be ſcarce as much as an
emmot or ant in compariſon of the maieſtie
of almightie God; vvhat then may man be
in reſpect of him, vvhoe is but ſo ſmall a portion of the vvhole vvoorld? And therefore
D   hovv

hovv can it be but great mercie and maruail, that so high and Soueraine a Lord should haue so particular and speciall care to dooe so much good to so little an emmot?

But novv vvhat vvilt thou saie, yf thou consider the cause of these benifits, that is, vvherefore they be giuen thee? It is euident that no man doth good to an other, nor maketh as much as one steppe for him, vvithout som hope or pretense of interest . Onlie this our lord bestovveth al these benifits vpon vs, vvithout anie pretense or hope, that vvee of our part maie dooe anie thing redounding to his commoditie and profit . In so much that vvhatsoeuer he doth for vs, he doth it of pure fauour and grace, moued thereunto by his onlie goodnes and loue . And yf thou think othervvise, tell me, I praie thee, yf thou be predestinated, vvherefore els did he predestinate thee ? vvherefore aftervvards create thee? redeeme thee? make thee a Christian? & call thee to serue him? vvhat might there be heere, that might moue him to bestovv such exceeding great benifits vppon thee, other then his onlie goodnes, and loue tovvards thee?

Neither is it a thing of les importance for this purpose, to consider the means and the manner, vvith vvhich he doth vs so much good,

good, that is the hart and vvill vvith vvhich
he doth it: for that all the good the vvhich
he hath donne vnto vs in time, he determined from al eternitie to dooe it. And so from
al eternitie he hath loued vs vvith perpetual
charitie; and for this charitie and loue tovvards vs he determined to dooe vs al this
good, and to haue an especial care of our saluation: to vvhich he still attendeth vvith
such prouidence and ouersight, as yf void of
al other affairs, he had nothing els vvhereto
to attend, but to the saluation of eche one in
particular. Heere then hath euerie deuovvt
sovvle vvhere vppon to ruminate and consider as a cleane beast, night and daie, and
vvhere she shall find most abundant and
svveete pasture for all her life.

OF THE TIME AND FRVITE OF
the foresaid meditations.

CHAP. III.

HESE be the seuen first
meditations, good Chri-
stian reader, vppon vvhich
thou maist discourse aud
occupie thy thought al the
daies of the vveeke ; not
that thou maistnot think also as vvel of som
other things, and in other daies besides these;

for,

for, as hath ben said in the beginning, vvhat soeuer thing induceth our hart to the loue and feare of God, and to the obseruation of his commaundments, is fit matter for meditation. Neuer-theles the aforesaid passages & considerations haue ben heere set dovvne for tvvo causes: the first vvhereof is, because they be the principal mysteries of our faith, and such as of them selues, moue vs more to that vvhich vve said, to vvit to the loue & feare of God. The second is, that young beginners, vvhoe haue neede of milke, maie find heere chevved & digested those things, of vvhich they ar to meditate, to th'end they goe not, as pylgrims in a straunge countrie, vvandring vp and dovvne through vn-knovven places, and taking som things, and leauing others, vvithout hauing anie stabilitie or stedfastnes in anie.

It is also to be noted that the meditations of this vveeke ar most fit, as hath ben said, for the beginning of a mans conuersion, that is vvhen a man nevvlie turneth him self to God; for that then it behoueth to begin vvith those things, vvhich maie moue vs to sorovv & detestation of sinne, to the feare of God and contempt of the vvoorld, vvhich be the first entries of this vvaie, and therefore those that begin must perseuer for som space

of

of time in the confideration of thefe things,
that they maie by thé, be better founded in
the vertues and affects before mentioned.

OF THE OTHER SEVEN MEDI-
TATIONS OF THE SACRED
Pafsion, and of the manner vvhich vve
muft obferue in them.

AFTER the meditations , vvhich
before vve haue laid dovvne, there
follovv other feuen meditations of the holie
Pafsion, Refurrection, & Afcenfion of Iefus
Chrift, to vvhich alfo maie be annexed and
ioyned the other principal paffages of his
moft bleffed life.

But heere vvee muft vnderftand, that there
be fixe things to be cheefelie confidered in
the Pafsion of our Sauiour Chrift; to vvit.
The greatenes of his paines : that vve maie
take compafsion of them. The grieuoufnes
of our finnes; vvhich vvas caufe of his paines, that vve may abhor them. The excellencie of the benifit : that vve maie bee
thankful for it. The magnificencie of the
goodnes , and charitie of almightie God
vvhich is heere difcouered : that vve maie
hartilie loue the fame. The conueniencie of
this myfterie : that vve may admire it. And
the multitude of the vertues of our Sauiour

D 3   Chrift

Chrift vvhich dooe fhine heere fo brightlie
that vve maie be prouoked thereby to imitate them.

Novv according to this, vvhen vve goe to
meditate the Paſſion, vve muft endeuour to
incline our hart ſom times to haue compaſ-
ſion of the paines of our Sauiour Chriſt, for
that they vvere the greateſt that euer vvere
ſuffred in this vvorld, as vvel for the tendernes of his complexion, as for the greatenes of
his charitie, and alſo for that he ſuffred vvithout anie manner of conſolation, as in an
other place is declared.

Som other times vve muft procure to dravv
out of this holie paſſion motiues of ſorovv
for our ſinnes, conſidering that they vvere
the very cauſe, vvhy our Sauiour ſuffred ſuch
& ſo grieuous paines, as in deede he ſuffred.

Som other times vve muft take from hence
motiues of loue and thankſgiuing; conſidering the greatenes of the loue, vvhich our
Sauiour by this meane diſcouered vnto vs; &
the greatenes of the benifit vvhich he beſtovved vppon vs, redeeming vs ſo liberallie
vvith ſo great coſt of his, and ſo great commoditie of ours.

At other times vve muft lift vp our eyes to
conſider the conueniencie of the manner
of this miſterie vvhich almightie God did
chooſe

choose to heale and cure our miserie; that is to satisfie for our debts; to succour our necessities; to merite for vs his grace; to beate dovvne our pride; & to induce vs to the contempt of the vvorld; to the loue of the Crosse; of Pouertie; of Asperitie; of Iniuries; and of all other vertuous and laudable labours.

Som other times vve must fix our eys in the examples of the vertues, vvhich shine in the most holie life and death of our Sauiour: in his Meekenes, Patience, Obedience, Mercie, Pouertie, Charitie, Humilitie, Benignitie, Modestie, & in al the other vertues, vvhich in al his vvoorks and vvoords shine more brightlie, then the starres in heauen; to the intent vve maie imitate somvvhat of that vvhich vve see in him, and that vve receaue not in vaine the spirite and grace, vvhich he hath giuen vs for this end, but that vve endeuour to goe to him by him. This is the highest and most profitable manner of meditating the passion of our Sauiour Christ, vvhich is by vvay of imitation, for that by imitation vve com to be transformed, and so to saie vvith the Apostle, *I liue, novv not I, but Christ liueth in me.* Galat. 2, 20.

Beside that vvhich vve haue hitherto said, it is verie expedient in the misteries of the

D 4   holie

holie paſſio to haue Chriſt as it vvere preſent before our eyes, and to make account that vve ſee him before vs vvhen he ſuffereth, and to haue an eye not onlie to the hiſtorie of the ſacred paſſion, but alſo to al the circumſtances of the ſame, & eſpeciallie to theſe fovver as vve haue touched before : that is, vvhoe ſuffereth; for vvhome he ſuffereth; hovv he ſuffereth; and for vvhat cauſe. VVhoe ſuffereth? Almightie God, vvhoe is infinite, immenſe &c. For vvhome ſuffreth he? for the moſt vngrateful and vnmindful creature in the vvorld. Hovv ſuffreth he? vvith exceeding great humilitie, charitie, benignitie, meekenes, mercie, patience, modeſtie &c. For vvhat cauſe ſuffreth he? not for anie, commoditie of his ovvne, nor anie merite of ours, but onlie for the bovvels of his infinite pittie and mercie.

Moreouer vve muſt not be content, to conſider that onlie vvhich our bleſſed Saniour ſuffred outvvardlie in his bodie, but much more that vvhich he endured invvardlie, becauſe vve haue much more vvhereof to contemplate in the ſovvle of Chriſt, then in the bodie of Chriſt; and this as vvel in the feeling and compaſsion of his paines, as alſo in other affections & conſiderations vvhich vvere in him.

Novv

Novv this litle preambule or preface being thus presupposed, let vs begin to separate & put in ordre the misteries of this most sacred and holie passion.

HEERE FOLOVV THE
OTHER SEVEN MEDI-
rations of the holie Passion.

Mondaie morning. Of our Sauiours entring into Ie-rusalem; vvasßhing his Apostles feete; and insti-tution of the most blessed Sacrament.

THIS daie vvhen thou hast made the signe of the crosse, vvith such prepara-tion as aftervvard shalbe declared, thou hast to meditate vppon the entring of our Sa-uiour into Ierusalem vvith boughs ; vppon the vvasshing his Apostles feete; and vppon the Institution of the most blessed Sacra-ment of the altar.

Of our Sauiours entring into Ierusalem.

VVHEN the lamb vvithout spot had finished his sermons & prea-ching of the ghospel , and that the time of that great sacrifice of the Passion vvas novv neere at hand, it pleased him to com to this place , vvhere he vvas to make an end of the Redemption of mankind. And that it might

be

I

be knovven vvith hovv greate charitie &
ioy of mind he vvent to drink this chalice
for vs, he vvould be receaued this daie vvith
great triumph, the people going foorth to
meete him vvith great acclamations and
praifes, vvith boughs of oliue trees and palmes in theire hands, & manie fpreding their
garments in the vvaie vnderneath him, and

Matt. 21.
9.

crying vvith one voice, and faying. *Bleſſed is
be that commeth in the name of our Lord. Hoſanna
in the higheſt.* Ioyne then alſo, my deare brother, thie cries vvith their cries, and thy praiſes vvith their praiſes, & giue thanks to our
Lord for this ſo great a beniſit, vvhich he
novv beſtovveth vppon thee, & for the loue
vvith vvhich he beſtovveth it. For albeit
thou ovve him much for that vvhich he ſuffred for thee, yet thou oueſt him much more
for the loue vvith vvhich he ſuffred it. And al
though the toi ments of his paſſion vvere exceeding greate, yet greater vvas the loue of
his hart; and ſo he loued much more then he
ſuffred; and vvould alſo haue ſuffred much
more, yſit had ben neceſſarie for vs.

2   Goe forth aftervvard into the vvaie, there
to receaue this nevv triumpher; and receaue
him vvith acclamatiõ of praiſes, vvith oliue
bovvghs, and vvith palmes in thy hands,
ſpreading likevviſe thy proper garments
vppon

vppon the grovvnd to celebrate this feast
of his entring. The acclamations of praises,
be praier and thankſgiuing . The oliue
bovvghs, be vvoorks of mercie; and the palmes be mortification and victorie ouer our
paſsions : and the ſpreading of garments in
the vvaie, is the chaſtiſing and hard vſing of
the bodie. Perſeuer then in praier, thereby
to glorifie almightie God : vſe mercie alſo,
thereby to ſuccour thy neighbours neceſsities; and vvith this mortfie thy paſsions, and
chaſtiſe thy fleſh, and in ſuch manner thou
ſhalt receaue in thy ſelf the ſonne of God.

Thou haſt alſo heere a great argument &
motiue to deſpiſe the gloꝛie of the vvorld,
after vvhich men runne ſo deſperatelie, and
for vvhoſe ſake they commit ſuch great ex-
ceſſes. But vvilt thou ſee vvhat account there
ought to be made of this glorie? Caſt thine
eys vppon this honour, vvhich the vvoorld
heere giueth to this thy lord, and thou ſhalt
perceaue that the ſelf ſame vvoorld, vvhich
to daie receaued him vvith ſo great honour,
fiue daies after eſteemed him to be vvoorſe
then Barabbas, demaunded vvith great inſtancie his death, and cried out againſt him
ſaying ; Crucifie him; Crucifie him . So that
the vvoorld, vvhich this daie proclaimed him
for the ſonne of Dauid, that is for the moſt
holie

3

holie of holies, to morovv esteemeth him to
be the vvoorst of all men, and more vnvvorthie to liue then Barabbas. Novv vvhat
example can be more euident, thereby to
see vvhat the glorie of the vvoorld is, and
vvhat account ought to be made of the iudgments of men? vvhat thing can there be
more light, more vvilfull, more blind, more
disloyall, and more inconstant in his opi-
nions, then the iudgment of this vvoorld?
To day he affirmeth, to morovv he denieth:
to daie he praiseth, to morovv he blasphe-
meth: to daie vvith much inconstancie and
lightnes he setteth you aboue the skyes, to
morovv vvith more lightnes he throvveth
you dovvne to the verie depth: to day he
saith that you ar the sonne of God; and to
morovv he saith that you ar vvoorse then
Barabbas. Such is the iudgment of this beast
of manie heads, and of this deceitful monster,
vvhich keepeth no faith, lealtie, or truth to
anie bodie, nether measureth vertue or valour but by his ovvne interest. None is good,
but he that is prodigal vvith him, yea although he be a panime and infidel; and none
is euil, but he that vseth him as he deserueth,
yea albeit he vvoork miracles; and this because he hath no other vveight vvherby to
vveigh vertue, but his ovvne interest and
com-

commoditie.

Novv vvhat ıhall I faieof his lies & de-
ceits?vvith vvhome hath he euer faithfullie
kept his vvoord? To vı home hath he giuen
that vvhich he promifed ? vvith vvhome
hath he had perpetual frindſhip ? To
vvhome hath he affured for long time that,
vvhich he gaue him ? To, vvhome hath he
euer fold vvinevvhich he gaue not througlie
vvatered ? He hath onlie this of faithful,
that he is faithful to none. This is thatfalſe
Iudas vvhich kiſsing his frinds, deliuereth
them to death : This is that traitour Ioab, 2. *Regu.*
vvhich imbracing him vvhome he faluted 3. 27.
as a frind, fecreatlie thruſthis dagger thorough his bodie. He crieth vvine, and felleth
vinagre; he promifeth peace, and fecreatlie
denounceth vvarre. He is euil to be kept;
vvoorſe to be gotten; daungerons to be holden; aud verie hard to be left and forfaken.
O peruerſe vvoorld ! falſe promifer, affured
deceiuer, fained frind, true enimie, common
liar, fecreat traitour, ſvveete in the beginning, bitter in the end, faire faced, cruel han-
ded, fcarſe in gifts, prodigal in grifes, in
ovvtvvard fhevy fomthing, invvardlie void
and nothing, in appearence florifhing, but
vnder thy flovvres ful of thornes.

of

Of the vvaſhing of feete.

TOuching this myſterie contemplate, o my ſovvle, in this ſupper thy ſvveete and myld Ieſus. Behold this vvonderful example of ineſtimable humilitie, vvhich he heere ſhevveth vnto thee, riſing from the table, and vvaſſhing his diſciples feete. O good Ieſus, vvhat is this that thou doſt? O ſvveete Ieſus, vvherfore doth thy maieſtie ſo abaſe it ſelf? vvhat vvouldeſt thou haue thought, o my ſovvle, yf thou haddeſt there ſeene God him ſelf kneeling before the feete of men, yea euen before the feete of Iudas? O cruel Iudas, vvhy doth not this ſo great humilitie mollifie thy heart? vvhy doth not this ſo vvonderful meekenes cauſe euen thy very bovvels to burſt and riue in ſunder? Is it poſsible that thou haſt conſpired to betray this moſt milde and gentel lamb? Is it poſsible that thou haſt no remorſe and compunction in beholding this example? O beutiful hands, hovv could ye touch ſtich lothſom and abominable feete? O moſt pure and cleane hands, vvhy diſdaine yee not to vvaſh thoſe feete ſo mired & durted in fovvle vvaies, vvhiles they ſought to ſhead your blovvd? O ye bleſſed Apoſtles,
                                        hovv

hovv tremble ye not feeing this fo great
humilitie? Peter vvhat doft thou? vvilt thou
confent that the lord of maieftie fhall vvafh
thy feete?

Sainct Peter vvhen he favv our Sauiour
kneeling before him, being greatlie amazed
&vvoondering at the matter, began to faie.
VVhat? vvilt thou o Lord vvafh my feete?
Art not thou the fonne of the liuing God?
Art not thou the Creator of the vvorld? the
bevvtie of heauen? the paradife of Angels?
the remedie of men? the brightnes of the
glorie of the father? the fovvntaine of the
vvifdome of God, vvhich dvvelleft in the
higheft? vvilt thou then vvafh my feete?
vvilt thou being a lord of fuch maieftie and
glorie take fo vile & bafe office vppon thee?

Confider alfo hovv after our Sauiour had
vvafhed theire feete, he vviped them and
made them cleane vvith that facred tovvel
vvhere vvith he vvas girded: and lift vp the
eys of thy fovvle fomvvhat higher, & thou
fhalt fee there reprefented the myfterie of
our Redemption. Confider hovv that faire
tovvell gathered and receaued into it felf, al
the filth and vncleanenes of thofe feete fo
mirie and fovvie; and fo the feete remained
cleane and faire, and the tovvel, after al vvas
ended, remained vvholie befpotted and defiled.

filed. Novv vvhat is more filthie then man conceiued in sinne? & vvhat is more cleane and bevvtiful, then our Sauiour Christ conceiued of the holie Ghost ? *My vvelbeloued is vvhite and vvel coloured* (saith the spovvse) *and chosen out emong thovvsands.* This most svveete and louing lord then so faire and so cleane, vvas content to receaue into him self al the spots and filthines of our sovvles, & leauing them cleane and free from those spots, he him self remained (as thou seeest him vppon the crosse) all bespotted and defiled vvith the same.

Cantic. 5.
10.

4

After this consider those vvoords vvith vvhich our Sauiour ended this historie saying . *I haue giuen you an example , that as I haue donne to you, so you doe also* . VVhich vvoords ar to be referred not onlie to this passage and president of humilitie; but also to al the other vvoorks and life of Iesus Christ : for so much as his vvhole life is a most perfect paterne of al al vertues, especiallie of those vvhich be in this place represented vnto vs, to vvit of humilitie & Charitie.

Ioan. 13.
15.

Of the institution of the most blessed Sacrament.

THAT vve may vnderstand somvvhat of this mysterie, it is to be presupposed, that no tounge created is able to expresse
the

the pasſing great loue, vvhich our Sauiour
Chriſt beareth tovvards the Catholique
Churche his ſpovvſe; & conſequentlie vnto
euerie one of thoſe ſovvles vvhich be in ſtate
of grace, for ſo much as euerie ſuch ſovvle is
alſo his ſpovvſe.

VVherefore vvhen this our moſt ſvveete   **1**
bridegrome minded to depart out of this
life, and to abſent him ſelf from the Church
his ſpovvſe, to the intent that this his abſence might not be to her anie occaſion to forget him, he left vnto her for a remembrance
this moſt bleſſed Sacrament, vvherein he
him ſelf vvould remaine, not ſuffering that
betvveene him and her there ſhould be anie
other pledge to renevve in her the remembrance of him, then euen him ſelf.

Moreouer this bridegrome in his long   **2**
abſence vvas deſirous to leaue ſom companie to his ſpovvſe, that ſhe might not
remaine ſolitarie and comfortles: and ſo
he left her the companie of this moſt bleſ-
ed Sacrament, vvherein he him ſelf remaineth reallie preſent, vvhich vvas in verie
deede the beſt companie that he could leaue
her.

At the ſame time alſo he vvould goe to   **3**
ſuffer death for his ſpovvſe, and to redeeme,
and enriche her vvith the price of his ovvne

              E   bloud:

bloud: and that fhe might, as often as fhe
vvould, enioy this treafure, he left her the
keys thereof in this moft bleffed Sacrament.
For as S. Chryfoftom faith: *So often as vvee com
to receaue the moft bleffed Sacrament, vve muft make
account that vve com to laie our mouthes to Chri-
ftes very fide, to drink of his moft pretious blovvd, &
to be partakers of this foueraine and diuine mifterie.*

4   This heauenlie bridegrome defired likevvife to be loued of his fpovvfe vvith an exceeding great loue, and therefore he ordeined this myfticall, and myfterious morfell
confecrated vvith fuch vvoords, that vvhoe-
foeuer receaueth it vvoorthilie, is foorthvvith touched and vvounded vvith this
loue.

5   Befides this our Sauiour vvould affure
his fpovvfe, and giue her a pledge of that
bleffed inheritance of eternal glorie, that
vvith the hope of this felicitie, fhee might
cheerefullie paffe throvvgh al the trovvbles
& aduerfities of this life. And that the fpoufe
might haue a firme and affured hope of this
felicitie, he left her heere in pledge this vn-
fpeakable treafure, vvhich is of as great value, as al that vvhich is there hoped for; and
this that fhe fhould not miftruft, but that
God vvil giue him felf vnto her in glorie,
                                    vvhere

vvhere fhe fhal liue in fpirite, feeing he denieth not him felf vnto her in this vale of
teares, vvhere fhe liueth in fleafh.

Moreouer our Sauiour purpofed at the   6
hovver of his death to make his teftament,
and to leaue vnto his fpovvfe fom notable &
vvorthie leagacie for her releife ; and fo he
left her this moft bleffed Sacrament, vvhich
vvas the moft precious, and moft profitable
bequeft that he could leaue vnto her, for fo
much as in the fame God left him felf.

To conclude, our Sauiour minded to leaue   7
vnto our fovvles fufficient prouifion, and
foode vvherevvith they might liue: becaufe
the fovvle hath no leffe neede of her proper
fuftenance, to mainteine her fpiritual life,
then the bodie hath of his foode, for mainte-
nance of his corporal life. For this caufe therfore, this vvife phifition our Sauiour Chrift
(vvho had alfo felt the pulfes of our vveaknes) ordeined this diuine Sacrament, and
for this hath he ordeined the fame in forme
of meate, that the verie forme, vvherein he
inftituted it, might declare vnto vs the effect
it vvoorketh, and vvith al the great necefsitie our fovvles haue of the fame, vvhich is
noeleffe then the neceffitie, that our bodies
haue of their propre foode.

*Tevvſdaie morning . Of our Sauiours praier in the
garden; his apprehenſion, and preſentation
before Annas.*

THIS daie thou haſt to meditate vppon
the praier of our Sauiour in the garden;
vppon his apprehenſion; and vppon his preſentation and euil vſage in the hovvſe of
Annas.

1   Conſider heere firſt hovv after that this
ſupper, ſo ful of miſterie vvas ended, our Saui
our vvent vvith his diſciples vnto the mount
Oliuet to make his praier , before he vvould
enter into the combat of his paſsion, thereby to teach vs , that in al the trovvbles and
tentations of this life vve muſt ſtill haue re-
courſe vnto praier , as it vvere to an holie
ancker, by vertue of vvhich the burden of
tribulation ſhal either be taken quite avvaye
from vs; or els vve ſhal haue ſtrength giuen
vs to be able to beare it , vvhich is an other
greater grace.

2   To accompanie him in this vvay our Sauiour tooke vvith him thoſe three of his beſt
beloued diſciples, to vvit S. Peeter, S. Iames
and S. Iohn , vvhich had ben vvitneſſes of
his transfiguration ; that the verie ſame perſons might ſee vvhat a far different ſhape he
tooke novv vppon him for the loue of men,
from

from that glorious shape, vvherein he had
sheyved him self vnto them, at his transfiguration . And becaufe they should vnderstand, that the invvard troubles of his
fovvle vvere noleffe, then began to be difcouered outvvardlie , he fpake vnto them
thofeforovvfulvvoords. *Mie foule is heauie euen* Matth.
to death; ftay heere, and vvatch vvith me.   26.38.

Our Sauiourvvhen he had fpoken thefe   3
vvoords, departed from his difciples a ftones
caft; and lying proftrat vppon the grovvnd,
he began his praier vvith verie great reue-
réce faying. *O father yf it be poſſible, let this cuppe*
paſſe from me; neuerthelcs not as I vvil, but as thou.
And hauing made this praier three times,
at the third time he vvas in fuch a great
agonie, that he began to fvveat euen dropps
of bloud, vvhich ranne dovvne alalong his
facred bodie, and trickled dovvne to the
grovvnd.

Confider novy our Sauiour in this do-   4
lovvrous cafe, and behold hovy there vvere
reprefented vnto him, al the cruel torments
vvhich he vvas to fuffer; and hovy appre-
hending in a moft perfect manner fuch
cruell paines as vvere prepared for his bodie
vvhich vvas the delicateft of al bodies; and
fetting before his eys al the finnes of the
vvhole vvorld, for vvhich he fhould fuffer,

and vvithall the great vnthankfulnes, and
ingratitude of fo manie fovvles, as he knevv
vvould neuer acknovvledge this benifit, nor
profit them felues of this fo greate, and fo
pretious remedie: his fovvle vvas vexed in
fuch fort, and his fenfes, and moft tender
flefh vvere fo troubled, that al the forces &
elements of his bodie vvere diftempered,
and his bleffed flefh vvas opened on euerie
fide, and gaue place to the bloud, that it
might paffe, and diftill throvvgh al the fame
in great abundance, and ftreame euen
dovvne to the grovvnd. Novv yf the flefh
fuffred thefe grieuous paines vvith onlie remembrance, and vvas in fo piteous a cafe, in
vvhat a dolefull ftate then, trovv ye, vvas
the fovvle that fuffred thofe paines directlie
in it felf?

5   Confider moreouer hovv vvhen our Sauiour had finifhed his praier, that counter-
faict frind of his came thither vvith that
hellifh companie, renouncing novv the
office of Apoftlefhip, and becomming the
ringleader and Captaine of Sathans armie.
Behold hovv vvithout al fhame he fet him
felf forvvards before al the reft, and comming to his good maifter, fold him vvith a
kiffe of moft traiterous frindfhip.

At the fame time our Sauiour faid vnto
them

them that came to lay hands vppon him: *Tovv ar com ovvt as it vvere to a theese, vvith svvordes and clubbes to apprehend me: I sate daily vvith you teaching in the temple, and you laide no hands on me . But this is your hovvre, and the povver of darknes* . This is a mysterie of great admiration. For vvhat thing is more to be vvoondered at, then to see the sonne of God, to take vppon him the shape, and image not onlie of a sinner , but euen also of a condemned person? *This* , saith he, *is your houre and the povver of darknes* . By vvhich vvoords is vnderstoode, that , from that time, that most innocent lamb vvas giuen vp into the povver of the Princes of darknes, vvhich be the diules , that by means of theire ministres they might execute vppon him al the cruelties and torments they could deuise.

*Matth.*26. 55.

Luc. 22. 53.

Luc. 22. 53.

Think thou then , o my sovvle , hovv much that diuine highnes abased it self for thee, sithence it arriued to the last extremitie of al miseries, vvhich is , to be giuen vp to the povver of diuels . And because this vvas the paine, vvhich vvas due to thy sinnes, it pleased him to put him self to this paine, that thou mightest remaine quite from the same.

So soone as these vvoords vvere spoken, 6

E 4　foorth-

foorthvvith al that hellifh rovvte and malicious rable of rauenous vvooolues affaulted this moft meeke and innocent lambe, fom haled him this vvay, fom that vvay, eche one to the vttermoft of his povver. O hovv vngentellie did they handle him? hovv difcourteouflie did they fpeake vnto him? hovv manie blovves and buffets did they giue him? vvhat crying & fhovvting made they ouer him? euen as conquerours vfe to doe, vvhen they haue obteined theire praie? They lay hold vppon thofe holie hands, vvhich a litle before had vvrought fo manie miracles, and dooe binde them verie ftraitlie vvith rovvgh & knottie cords, in fuch fort that they gavvle the fkinne of his armes, and make the verie blood to fpring out of them: and in this manner they leade him openlie throvvgh the common ftreates vvith great defpite and ignominie.

7 Confider novv vvel our Sauiour hovv he goeth in this vvay abandoned of his difciples, accompanied vvith his enimies; his pafe haftened, his breath fhortened, his colour changed, his face chafed and inflamed vvith his haftie going. And yet in al this euil intreating of his perfon, behold the modeft behauiour of his countenance, the comelie grauitie of his eys, and that diuine refemblance,

blance, vvhich in the middeſt of al the diſ-
courteſies in the vvoorld could neuer be ob-
ſcured.

Forthvvith accompanie thy Sauiour to   8
the hovvſe of Annas, and behold there hovv
vvhileſt he avvnſvvered verie courteouſlie
to the demaund, that the high prieſt made Ioan. 18.
vnto him concerning his diſciples and do-   19.
ctrine, one of thoſe vvicked caitifes that
ſtoode there by gaue him a greate blovve
vppon the face ſaying. *Anſvvereſt thou the high* Ioan. 18.
prieſt ſo ? Vnto vvhome our Sauiour avvn-   22.
ſvvered verie gentellie. *If I haue ſpoken yl,* Ioan. 18.
giue teſtimonie of euil ; but yſ vvel, vvhy ſtrikeſt 23.
thou me ?

Conſider then heere, o my ſoule, not onlie   9
the mildnes of this avvnſvvere, but alſo that
diuine face ſo marked and colovvred vvith
the force of the blovve, and that conſtant
looke of his eys ſo cleare and faire, vvhich
vvere nothing diſtempered vvith this ſo
ſhameful aſſault; and finallie that moſt holie
ſovvle, vvhich vvas invvardlie ſo humble &
readie to haue turned the other cheeke, yſ
the naughtie vvretched caitife had required
the ſame.

VVenſdaie

VVenſdaie morning. Of the preſentation of our Sa-
uiour before the high prieſt Cayphas: of the iniu-
ries he receaued that night; of Saint Peters
denial; and of his vvhipping at
the pillar.

THIS daie thou haſt to meditate vppon
the preſentation of our Sauiour before
the high prieſt Cayphas; vppon the iniuries
he receaued that night; vppon Saint Peters
denial of his maiſter; and vppon his vvhipping and ſcourging at the pillar.

I   Firſt conſider hovv from the firſt hovvſe
of Annas, they leade our Sauiour to the houſe
of Cayphas the high prieſt, vvhither reaſon
vvould that thou ſhouldeſt goe vvith him
to keepe him comvanie; & there ſhalt thou
ſee the ſonne of iuſtice, darkned vvith an e-
clipſe; and that Diuine face, vvhich the Angels deſire to behold, al defiled vvith ſpittel
moſt vnreuerentlie. For vvhen our Sauiour
being coniured in the name of the father, to
tel them vvhat he vvas, avvnſvvered to this
demaund, as it vvas meete he ſhould: thoſe
vvicked men, ſo vnvvoorthie to heare ſuch
an excellent and high avvnſvvere, and blin-
ded vvith the brightnes of ſo great a light,
aſſaulted him like madde dogges, and diſ-
gorged vppon him al theire malice & furie.

1.Petr. 1.
12.

There

There eache one to the vttermoſt of his
povver giueth him buffets & ſtrokes. There
they beſpit that diuine face vvith theiredi-
uiliſh mouths. There they blindfold his eys
and ſtrike him in the face , and ieſt at him
ſaying. *Prophecie vnto vs,ô Chriſt,vvhoe is he that* Matt. 26.
ſtrooke thee? O meruailous humilitie, & pa- 68.
tience of the ſonne of God! O bevvtie of the
Angels! vvas this a face to ſpit vppon! men
vſe,vvhen they muſt ſpit,to turne theire face
to the fovvleſt corner of the hovvſe:and vvas
there not to be found in al that pallace, a
fovvler place to ſpit in , then thy face, o
ſvveete Ieſus? O earth and aſhes, vvhie doſt
thou not humble thy ſelf at this ſo vvonderful example?

After this conſider vvhat trovvbles, and   2
paines our Sauiour ſuffred in al that dolefull
night: for that the ſouldiars, vvhoe had him
in cuſtodie,mocked & laughed him to ſcorne
as S. Luke ſaith, & vſed as a meane, to paſſe Luc. 22.
avvay the ſleepines of the night, to ſcoffe & 63.
ieſt at the Lord of maieſtie. Conſider novv,
o my ſovvle , hovv thy moſt ſvveete ſpouſe
is ſet heere as a marke, to al the arrovvs of
the ſtrokes and buffets they coulde giue him
there . O cruel night! O vnquiet night! in
vvhich thou,o my good Ieſus,tookeſt no repoſe at al , neither did thoſe reſt , vvhoe
ac-

accompted it a paſtime to vex and torment
thee. The night vvas ordained for this end,
that therein al creatures ſhould take their
reſt, and that the ſenſes, & membres vveried
vvith toyles & labours of the day might be
refreſſhed; and theſe vvickèd men vſe it as a
fit time to torment al thy membres and ſenſes, ſtryking thy bodie, afflicting thy ſovvle,
bynding thy hands, buffetting thy cheekes,
ſpitting in thy face, and lugging thee by the
eares, that thereby at ſuch time as all the
membres ar vvoont to take their reſt, they al
in thee might be trovvbled and payned. O
hovv far doe theſe mattins differ frō thoſe,
vvhich at the ſame time the quiars of Angels
ſoung to thee in heauen? There thy ſing holy, holy; but heere theſe caitifes cry: Put him
to death; put him to death: Crucifie him;
crucifie him. O ye Angels of paradiſe that
heard both theſe voices, vvhat thought ye,
vvhen ye ſavv him ſo ſpitefullie contemned
in earth, vvhome you vvith ſo great reuerence doe honour in heauen? vvhat thought
ye, vvhen you ſavv God him ſelf to ſuffer
ſuch deſpites, euen for thoſe that did ſuch
villanies vnto him? vvhoe hath euer heard of
ſuch a kind of charitie, that one vvould ſuffer death, to deliuer frō death the verie ſame
perſons, that procured & practiſed his death?
But

But aboue al, the paines and turmoiles of this trovvblefom night vvere increafed far more by the denial of S.Peter. For that familiar frind of our Sauiour; he that vvas elected and chofen to fee the glorie of his transfiguration; he vvhoe aboue al the reft vvas honoured vvith the principalitie and cheefe rule of the Chriftian Church; hee, I faie, firft before al others, not once, but three feueral times together, euen in the verie prefence of his lord and maifter, fvveareth & forfvveareth that he knovveth him not, and that he vvift not vvhoe hee is. O Peter is he that ftandeth there by thee fo vvicked a man, that thou accompteft it fo great a fhame onlie to haue knovven him? Confider that this is a condemnation of him by thee, before he be condemned by the high priefts: fithence thou giueft to the vvoorld to vnderftand by this thy denial, that he is fuch a manner of man, that euen thou thy felf doft accompt it as a great reproche & difhonour vnto thee, to haue as much as knovven him. Novv vvhat greater iniurie could be donne then this?

Our Sauiour then hearing this denial, turned back, and beheld Peter, & caft his eys vppon that fheepe, vvhich there vvas loft from him. O looke of meruailous force and vertue!

vertue! O silent and stil looke, but greatlie misterious and significatiue! Peter vnderstoode right vvel the language, and voice of this looke: for so much as the crovving of the cocke vvas not able to avvake him, but this vvas able. In deede the eys of our Sauiour dooe not onlie speake, but also vvoork, as it appeareth by the teares of S. Peter, vvhich yet gushed not so much from the eys of Peter, as they proceeded from the eys of Christ.

4   After al these iniuries cōsider vvhat scourgings, & vvhippings our Sauiour, suffred at the pillar. For the Iudge, perceauing that he could not pacifie the furious rage of those his most hellish enemies; determined to chastise him vvith such a seuere kind of punishment, as might suffice to satisfie the malitious ovvtrage of such cruel harts, that they being thervvith content, should cease to seeke after his death. Goe novv therefore, o my sovvle, & enter vvith thy spirite into Pilates consistorie, & carrie vvith thee great store of teares in a readines, vvhich shalbe needeful in that place, for that vhich thou shalt there both see and heare. Behold hovv those cruel & base tormentors doe strip our Sauiour of his garments vvith so great inhumanitie, he neuer so much as once opening his mouth, or speaking one vvoord to so manie

disdifcurtifies as they there vfed tovvards him.

Confider alfo vvhat haft they make to bynde that holie bodie to a pillar, that fo they might ftrike him more at theire pleafure, & vvhere, & hovv they beft lift. Behold hovv the Lord of Angels ftandeth there alone among the cruel tormentors, hauing on his part neither frinds, nor fuerties to help him, no nor fo much as eys to take côpafsion vppon him. Mark hovv forthvvith they begin vvith meruailous great crueltie to difcharge theire fcourges, & vvhips vppon his moft tender flefh, & hovv they laie on lafhes vppon lafhes, ftripes vppon ftripes, & vvoūdes vppon vvoundes. There thou mighteft quicklie fee that facred bodie fvvolen vvith vveales, the fkinne réted & torne, the bloud guffhing out, & ftreaming dovvne on euerie fide, throughout al parts of his bodie. But aboue al this, vvhat a pitiful fight vvas it to behold that fo great, & deepe open vvound betvvixt his facred fhovlders, vvhere cheefelie al theire lafhes and ftrokes did light?

After this behold hovv our Sauiour, vvhen they had ended to vvhippe him, coūered him felf, & hovv he vvent through al that place feeking his garmets in prefēce of thofe cruel tormétors, vvithout that anie mā offred him anie feruice, help, vvaffhing, or other fuch reliefe,

5

6

reliefe as ar vvont to be aforded to thofe that
be fo vvounded. Al thefe things no doubt ar
vvorthie of great feeling, thankfulnes and
confideration.

---

*Thurfdaie morning . Of our Sauiours Coronation
vvith thorns; of the vvords, Ecce Homo;
and bearing of the croffe vppon
his fhouldres.*

THIS daie thou haft to think vppon
the crovvning of our Sauiour vvith
thornes, hovv Pilate faid of him, *Ecce Homo*;
behold the man; and hovv he bare the croffe
vppon his fhoulders,

To the confideration of thefe moft doleful
paffages, the fpovvfe in the booke of Canticles inuiteth vs faying. *Goe forth, ô ye daughters
of Syon, & behold king Salomon vvith the crovvne,
vvith vvhich his mother crovvned him in the daie of
his efpovvfels, and in the daie of the ioifulnes of his
hart.* O my fovvle vvhat doeft thov? o my
hart vvhat thinkeft thou? O my toûge hovv
is it that thou art becom domme? O my
moft fvvete Sauiour, vvhen I open myne eys,
and behold this dolorous image, vvhich is
fet before me, my hart doth euen cleaue and
rent in funder for verie griefe. Hovv happeneth this o Lord? vvhat? did not the vvhippings vvhich thou fuffredft, and the death
vvhich

*Cantic. 3.
11.*

vvhich enſueth , and ſo great quantitie of
bloud alredie ſhed , ſuffice ; but that novv
alſo the ſharp thorns muſt, perforce, let out
the bloud of thy head, vvhich the vvhippes
and ſcourges before had pardoned ?

VVherefore, o my ſovvle, that thou maiſt   I
conceaue, and haue ſom feeling of this ſo
doleful paſſage , ſet firſt before thine eys the
former ſhape of this lord , and vvithal the
excellencie of his vertues, and then incontinentlie turne thy ſelf to behold in vvhat
pitiful ſort he is heere . Conſider therefore
the greatnes of his bevvtie, the modeſtie of
his eys , the ſvveetenes of his vvoords , his
authoritie , his meekenes , his mild behauiour, and that goodlie countenance of his
ſo ful of reuerence . And vvhen thou haſt
thus beholden him, and delited thy ſelf to ſee
ſuch a perfect foorme , turne thine eys and
behold him in this pitiful plight , clad vvith
an old purple garment to be ſcorned ; holding in his hand a reede for roial ſcepter,
that horrible diademe of thornes on his
head ; his eys hollovv and vvanne , his countenance dead , and his vtter ſhape vvholie
disfigured , and begored vvith blovvd , and
defiled vvith ſpittel, vvherevvith his face
vvas al beſmeered and beraide . Behold him
in al parts invvardlie and ovvtvvardlie ; his

F   hart

hart pearced through, and through vvith
forovvs, his bodie ful of vvoundes, forfaken
of his difciples, perfecuted of the Ievves, fcor
ned of the foldiars, contemned of the high
priefts, bafelie reiected of the vvicked king,
accufed vniuftlie, & vtterlie deftiture of the
fauour of all men.

2   Think alfo vppon this, not as a thing paft,
but as prefent; and not as though it vvere
an other mans paine, but thine ovvne. Imagin thy felf to be in place of him that fuf-
freth, & think vvhat thou vvouldeft feele, yf
in fo fenfible & tender a part as is thy head,
they fhould faften a nomber of thornes,
and thofe alfo verie fharp, vvhich fhould
pearce euen to the fkulle. But vvhat fpeake
I of thornes? yf it vvere but onlie the pric-
king of a pinne, thou couldeft hardlie fuffer
it; novv vvhat, thinkeft thou, did that moft
tender and delicate head of our Sauiour feele
vvith this fo ftraunge kind of torment?

3   VVhen they had thus crovvned, and
fcorned our Sauiour, the Iudge tooke him
by the hand in fuch euil plight as he vvas,
and leading him out to the fight of the furious people, faid vnto them, *Ecce homo.*
Behold the man, as much as yf he faid. If
for enuie you fought his death, behold him
heere in fuch fort, that he is not to be enui-
ed at,

at , but rather to be pittied . VVere you
afraied left he vvould haue made him felf
a king? behold him heere fo disfigured, that
he fcarcelie feemeth to be a man . Of thefe
hands fo faft bound , vvhat feare you ? of
this man fo vvhipped and fcourged, vvhat
demaund you more? By this thou maift vnderftand, o my fovvle, in vvhat fort our Sauiour came then forth , feeing the Iudge
beleeued , that the pitiful plight in vvhich he
vvas, might fuffice to breake the harts of
fuch cruel enimies . VVhereby thou maift
vvel perceaue hovv vnfeemelie a thing it is,
that a Chriftian man haue no compafsion of
the paines & forovvs of our Sauiour Chrift,
feeing they vvere fuch as vvere fufficient, as
the Iudge vvas fullie perfuaded , to mollifie
thofe fo fierce and fauage harts.

But vvhen Pilate favv that thofe punifhments executed vppon that moft holie
and innocent lambe , vvere not able to affvvage the furie of his enemies, he entred
into the iudgment hall, and fate him dovvne
in his tribunall feate, to giue final fentence
in that caufe . The Croffe vvas novv prepared and readie at the gate', and that dreadful banner vvas difplaied high in the ayer
threatning the death of our Sauiour. And
after that the cruel fentence vvas giuen and

F 2   pub-

publified, the enimies added thereunto an
other crueltie, vvhich vvas to charge vppon
thofe fhouldres, fo rent and torne vvith
vvhips and fcourges receiued before, the
heauie tree of the Croffe. Al vvich notvvithftanding, our merciful Sauiour refufed not
to carie this burthen vvhereuppon vvere
laid al our finnes, but embraced the fame
vvith fingular charitie and obedience for
the loue he bare vnto vs.

5   After this the innocent Ifaac vvent to the
place of facrifice vvith that fo heauie burthen
vppon his vveake fhoulders, great multi-
tudes of people folovving after him, and
manie pitiful vvoomen that accompanied
him vvith theire teares. VVhoe vvould not
haue vvept moft bitterlie, feeing the king
of Angels to goe fo faintlie vvith fuch a
vvaightie burthen, his knees trembling
vnder him, his bodie crovvching, his eys fo
modeft, his face al bloudie, vvith that
guirland of thornes in his head, and vvith
thofe fhameful and opprobrious exclamations and outcries vvhich they gaue
againft him.

6   In the meane feafon, o my fovvle, vvithdravv thine eys a little from this cruel fight,
and vvith al fpeede, vvith lamentable fighs,
vvith larmeful eys, goe tovvards the hovvfe
of

of the bleſſed virgin , and vvhen thou art
com thither , caſting thy ſelf doune at her
feete, begin to ſpeake to her vvith a doleful
voice ſaying. O ladie of Angels, O Queene
of heauen , Gate of paradiſe , Aduocatrice
of the vvorld, Refuge of ſinners , Health
of iuſt parſons, Ioie of Sainċts , Miſtres of
vertues, Mirrour of cleanenes , Tytle of
chaſtitie, Patterne of patience , and Example of al perfection : vvoe to me , o bleſſed
ladie , that haue liued to ſee this preſent
hovver. Hovv can I liue hauing ſeene vvith
mine eys that vvhich I haue ſeene ? vvhat
neede more vvoords? I haue left thy onlie
begotten ſonne , and my lord in the hands
of his enimies vvith a Croſſe vppon his
ſhoulders, to be crucified vppon the ſame.

VVhat vnderſtanding is able to comprehend , hovv deepelie this ſorovv pearced
the bleſſed virgins hart ? Her ſovvle began
heere to vvax faint, and her face, and al the
parts of her virginlie bodie, vvere couered
ouer vvith a deadlie ſvveate, vvhich vvas
ſufficient to haue ended her life, yf the diuine diſpenſation had not reſerued her for
greater pains, and for a greater crovvne.

Novv the holy virgen goeth to ſeeke her
ſonne, the great deſire vvhich ſhe hath to ſee
him, reſtoring vnto her againe the ſt ength
F 3.   vvhich

vvhich forovv had taken from her. She
heareth a far of the claffhing of armour,
the trovvpes of people, and the ovvtcries
vvhich by his enimies vvere thundered
againſt him. Incontinentlie alſo ſhe ſeeth
the gliſtering ſpears and halbards, vvhich
vvere holden vppe a loft. She approcheth
neerer and neerer vnto her deerelſe beloued
ſonne, and openeth her eys, vvhich vvere
dimmed vvith forovv, to ſee, if ſhe poſsibly
might, him vvhom her ſovvle ſo exceedinglie loued. O loue and feare of this bleſſed
virgin Maries hart! On one ſyde ſhee defired to ſee him, on the other ſhe vvas vnvvilling to ſee him ſo miſerablie disfigured.
At the length, vvhen ſhe vvas com vvhere
ſhe might ſee him, then thoſe tvvo lights
of heauen did behold one an other, and their
harts vvhere pearced through vvith their
eys, and they vvounded vvith their mutual
ſight their pitiful ſovvles. Theire toungs
vvere becom domme, and yet the hart of
that moſt ſvveete ſonne ſpake to the hart of
his mother, and ſaid vnto her, vvherefore
cameſt thou hither my doue, my beloued,
and my ſvveete mother? Thy forovv in-
creaſeth mine, and thy tormentes be a torment to me, depart my deare mother and
returne home: it is not decent for thy virginlie

ginlie shame-fastnes and puritie, to be in companie of murderers and theeues.

These and otherlike vvoords ful of compassion and pitie, vvere spoken in those pitiful harts, and in this manner they passed ouer that irksom, and paineful vvay euen vnto the place of the Crosse.

Fridaie morning. Of the Crosse, and the seuen vvoords vvhich our Sauiour spake vppon the same.

THIS day thou hast to meditate vppon the misterie of the Crosse, and vppon the seuen vvoords vvhich our Sauiour spake.

Avvake novv, o my sovvle, and begin to think vppon the misterie of the Crosse, by vvhose fruite is repared the hurt of that poisened fruite, of the forbidden tree. Consider first hovv vvhen our Sauiour vvas com to this place, those cruel enimies, to make his death more shamefull, stripped him of al his apparel, euen to his innermost garment, vvhich vvas vvholie vvouen through out vvithout anie seame. Behould novv heere vvith vvhat meekenes this most innocent lamb suffreth him self to be thus stripped, vvithout opening his mouth or

F 4 speaking

speaking anie vvoord againſt them that
vſed him in ſuch ſort; but rather vvith a
good vvil conſented to be ſpoiled of his
garments, & vvith ſhame remaine naked,
that by the merite of this nakednes, and
vvith the ſame, the nakednes in vvhich
vve vvere fallen throvvgh ſinne, might be
far better couered, then vvith the leaues of
the fig-tree.

§

Som holie fathers reporte that the tor-
mētors to pluck of our Sauiours garments,
tooke of moſt cruellie the crovvne of thornes vvhich he had vppon his head; and that
hauing ſtripped him they ſet it on againe,
& faſtned the ſharp thornes to the braine
vvhich vvas an exceeding great griſe: And
ſurelie it is to be thought that they vſed this
crueltie againſt him, hauing vſed manie
others, and thoſe alſo verie ſtrange in al
the proceſſe of his paſsion: eſpeciallie ſeeing
the holie Euangeliſt ſaith, that thy did vnto
him vvhatſoeuer they vvould. And as his
garment ſtucke faſt to the vvoundes of his
ſcourges, and the bloud vvas novv congea-
led and faſtned vnto his garment, at vvhat
time thy ſtripped him, they haled it of vvith
ſuch furious haſt and force (as thoſe caitiſſes
vvere far from al pitie and mercie) that they
renevved al the vvoundes of his vvhippings,
in ſuch

in such ruefulvvise: that that great vvound
of his shoulders distilled bloud on al partes.

Consider novv heere, o my sovvle , the **2**
excellencie of the goodnes and mercie of
God, vvhich shevveth it self so euidentlie in
this misterie. Behold hovv he that clotheth
the heauens vvith clovvdes , and the fields
vvith flovvers & bevvtie, is heere spoiled of
al his garments. Consider the cold vvhich
that holie bodie suffred, standing as it stoode
spoiled, & naked not onlie of his garments,
but also of his verie skinne and flesh , vvith
so manie gapes, and vvide holes of open
vvoundes throughout the same. And yf S.
Peter being clothed and shodde, felt cold the
night before, hovv far greater cold suffred
that most delicate and tender bodie, being
so naked and vvounded as it vvas?

Consider after this hovv our Sauiour vvas **3**
nayld vppon the Crosse, & the paine vvhich
he suffred at that time, vvhen those great and
square nailes pearced through the most sensible and tender parts of his bodie , vvhich
vvas of al bodies most delicate. And consider
also vvhat extreme griefe it vvas to the blessed virgin, vvhen she savv vvith her eys, and
heard vvith her eares the mightie and cruel
hard strokes vvhich vvere laid on so thick, &
iterated one after an other vppon his diuine

mem-

members. For certainelie those hammers & nailes passed through the hands of the sonne but they vvounded and pearced the verie hart of the mother.

4

Consider hovv forthvviththey hoysed vp the Crosse on high, & vvent about to ráme it in the hole, vvhich they had made for that purpose, & hovv, such vvere those cruel ministers, at the verie time of rearing it vp & placing it, they let it fal vvith a iump into the hole vvith al the vveight thereof: and so that blessed bodie vvas sore shaken and iogged in the ayre, and thereby his vvounds of the nailes vvere enlarged, vvhich vvas a most intollerable paine.

Novv then o my svveete Sauiour and Redeemer, vvhat hart maie be so stonie hard that vvil not riue a sunder for griefe, sith this daie the verie stones them selues vvere ryuen cósidering that vvhich thou suffredst vppon the Crosse? The sorous of death, o Lord, haue enuironed thee; & the vvaues of the sea haue ouervvhelmed thee. Thou art mired in the depth of the bottomles goulfes, and findest nothing vvhere vppon to staie thy self. Thy father hath forsaken thee; vvhat hope maist thou haue of men? Thy enimies crie out against thee, thy frinds breake thy hart, thy sovvle is afflicted, and for the loue thou bea-

rest

rest to me, thou admittest no comfort. Mie
sinnes, o Lord, vvere vndoubtedlie verie
greate, and thy penance vvel declareth it. I
see thee, o my king fastened to a tree, & there
is nothing to susteine thy bodie but three
yron nailes: of those thy sacred bodie hangeth vvithout anie other stay or comfort.
VVhen the vveight of thy bodie staieth vppon thy feete, then ar the vvounds of thy
feete more vvydened, and torne vvith the
navls vvherevvith they ar pearced. And
vvhen the svvaie of thy bodie staieth vppon
thy hands, then ar the vvounds of thy hands
more rent vvith the poise of thy bodie. Novv
thy holie head tormented, and vveakened
vvith the crovvne of thornes, vvhat pillovv
hath it to rest vppon? O hovv vvel might
thy armes (most blessed and excellent virgin)
be heere emploied to supplie this office! But
alas, thy armes maie not serue for this present, but the armes of the Crosse. Vppon
them must that sacred head recline it self
vvhen it vvil repose, and yet the ease he shal
receaue thereby, shal be but onlie to driue &
stick those thornes more fast into his braine.

The sorovvs of the sonne vvere much increased by the presence of his mother, vvith
vvhich his hart vvas no les crucified vvithin, then his holie bodie vvithout. Tvvo
crosses

5

croffes be heere prepared for thee, o good
IESVS, this daie; the one for thy bodie,
and the other for thy fovvle. The one is of
paffion, the other of compaffion. The one
pearceth thy bodie vvith nailes of iron, the
other pearceth thy moft holie fovvle vvith
nailes of forovve; vvhoe is able to declare o
good IES VS, vvhat griefe it vvas to thee
vvhen thou diddeft confider the great an-
guifhes of the moft holie fovvle of thy mother, vvhich thou knevveft fo certainlie vvas
there crucified vvith thee? vvhen thou fa-
vveft that pitiful hart of her pearced, and
thruft through vvith the fyvoord of forovv?
vvhen thou diddeft open thy blovvdie eys,
and beheldeft her diuine face, vvhollie ouer
caft vvith palenes and vvannes of death; and
thofe angvvifhes of her fovvle, vvhich caufed not her death, and yet vvere greater to
her then death it felf; and thofe riuers of
teares vvhich guffhed out from her moft
cleare eys, and heardeft thofe deepe fighs
and fobbes, vvhich burft out of her facred
breft, being enforced vvith the vehemencie
of griefe and forovv?

Novv vvhat breft (faithS. Bernard) maie
be fo of iron, vvhat bovvels fo hard, that
they be not moued to compafsion, o moft
fvveete mother, confidering the teares and
paines

paines vvhich thou diddeſt endure at the
foote of the Croſſe, vvhen thou ſavveſt thy
moſt deere ſonne ſuffer ſo grieuous, ſo long,
and ſo opprobrious and ſhameful torments?
vvhat hart can think, vvhat toung can expreſſe thy ſorrovv, thy teares, thy ſighes, and
the cleauing a ſunder of thy hart, vvhen
ſtanding in this place, thou ſavveſt thy beloued ſonne vſed in ſuch cruel ſort, and yet
couldeſt not help him? yvhen thou beheldeſt
him naked, and couldeſt not clothe him;
parched vp vvith thirſt, & couldeſt not giue
him to drink; iniuried, and couldeſt not
defend him; diffamed as a malefactour, and
couldeſt not anſvvere for him; his face ſo defiled vvith ſpittel, and couldeſt not make it
cleane; finallie his eyes guſhing out teares,
and couldeſt not drye them, nor receaue
that laſt gaſpe vvhich came out from his ſacred breſt, nor ioyne thy face vvith, his ſo
knovven and ſo beloued, and in ſuch manner dye imbraced vvith him. In this time
thou diddeſt vvel proue in thy ſelf, that the
prophetie vvas fulfilled, vvhich that holie
old Simeon had foretold thee, before he died, ſaying, that a ſvvord of ſorovv ſhould
pearce thy hart.

But o moſt pitiful virgen, vvherefore
vvouldeſt thou, o bleſſed ladie, increaſe thy
ſorovv

forovv vvich the fight of thyne ovvne eys?
vvherefore vvouldeft thou find thy felf
prefent this daie in this place? It is not a
thing decent for one fo retyred, as thou art
vvoont to be, to appeare in common places;
It becommeth not a motherlie hart to fee
her children dye, although it ftoode vvith
their honour and reputation, and they dyed
in their bead; and comeft thou then to fee
thy fonne die by iuftice, & amongft theeues
vppon a croffe? But novv feeing thou haft
refolued to furpaffe and ouercom al motherlie affection, and that thou vvilt honour this
mifterie of the croffe, vvherefore doeft thou
approche fo neere vnto the fame, that
thou muft carie avvay in thie mantle, a
perpetual memorie and remembrance of
this thy forovv? Thou canft not aford thy
fonne anie comfort or remedie, but vvel
thou maift vvith thy prefence increafe and
augment his torment.

In deede this onlie vvanted to the increafe of his forovvs, that in the time of his
agonie, in the laft inftant and conflict of
his death, euen vvhen the laft fighs raifed vp
his tormented breft, he fhould then caft
dovvne his eys altogeather dazeled and
dimmed, & fhould behold thee ftanding at
the foote of the croffe. And becaufe he being

neere

neere to the end of his life had his senses so
vveakened and feebled, and his eyes so ob-
scured vvith the shadovv of death , that he
could not see a far of, thou madest thy self so
neere, to th'end he might knovv thee, and
see those armes, in vvhich he had ben receaued and caried into Egipt, so faint and broken: and those virginal brests, vvith vvhose
milk he had ben nourisshed, becom euen a
sea of sorrovv. Behold o ye Angels these
tvvo figures , yf peraduenture you maie
knovv them. Behold o ye heauens this crueltie, and couer your self vvith mourning
for the death of your Lord: let the cleere
ayre becom obscure and dark , that the
vvoorld see not the naked bodie of your
Creator. Cast vvith your darknes a mantel
vppon his bodie, that profane eys behold
not the ark of the testament yncouered. O
ye heauens vvhich vvere created so bright
and faire ! o thou earth clothed vvith such
varietie and beavvtie ! yf you did hide your
glorie in this so greate paine ; yf you that be
insensible , did after your manner feele the
same, vvhat then did the bovvels and virginal brest of the blessed mother? O al you,
saith shee, that passe by the vvaie, consider
and behold yf there be anie sorovv like vnto
mie sorovv. Trulie there is no sorovv like
                                        vnto

vnto thie forovv, becaufe in al the creatures
ofthe vvoorld there is no loue like vnto thy
loue.

6

After this thou maift confider thofe feuen
vvoords, vvhich our lord fpoke vppon the
Crofse, of vvhich the firft vvas. *Father pardon
them, for they knovv not vvhat they dooe.* The fecond vvas to the good theefe: *This daie fhalt
thou be vvith me in paradife.* The third vvas to
his moft bleffed mother; *VVoman behold thy
fonne.* The fourth vvas: *I am a thirft.* The fift
vvas: *My God, my God vvhy haft thou forfaken
me?* The fixt vvas: *It is finifhed.* The feuenth
vvas: *Father into thy hands I commit my fpirite.*

Mar. 23.
34.
Mar. 23.
43.
Ioan. 19.
27.
Ioan. 19.
28.
Matt. 27.
46.
Ioan. 19.
30.
Mar. 23.
46.

Confider novv, o my fovvle, vvith hovv
great charitie he cōmended in thefe vvoords
his enimies vnto his father; vvith hovv
greate mercie he receaued the thife vvhich
confeffed him; vvith vvhat bovvels he commended his pitiful mother to the beloued
difciple; vvith hovv greate thirft and drith
he fhevved hovv much he defired the faluation of men; vvith hovv lamentable a voice
he povvred out his praier, and vttered his
tribulatiō before the face of almightie God;
hovv he performed fo perfectlie, euen to the
verie end, the obedience of his father; and
hovv finallie he commended vnto him his
fpirite, and refigned him felf vvholie into his
most

moſt bleſſed hands.

Heerehence it appeareth, hou in eche one of theſe vvoords, remaineth incloſed ſom ſingular document, and inſtruction of vertue . In the firſt, is cōmended vnto vs Charitie tovvards our enimies. In the ſecond, pitie and mercie tovvards ſinners. In the third dutie and reuerence tovvards our parents. In the fouerth , zea'e and deſire of our neighbours ſaluation . In the fift, praier in time of tribulations, and vvhen vve ſeeme to be forſaken of God. In the ſixt, the vertue of Obedience and Perſeuerance. And in the ſeuenth a perfect reſignation into the hands of God, vvhich is the ſumme and principal of al our perfection.

Satturdaie morning. Of the pearcing our Sauiours ſide; of his taking dovvne from the croſſe; of the pitiful bevvailing of our ladie; and of Chriſtes burial.

THIS daie thou haſt to meditate vppon the pearcing of our Sauiours ſide vvith a ſpeare; of his taking doune from the croſſe; together vvith the lamentation of our lady, and the office of the burial.

Conſider then , hovv after that our Sauiour had giuen vp the ghoſt vppon the croſſe, and thoſe cruel miniſters had accompliſſhed

G   their

their desire, vvhich longed so much to see
him dead, yet vvith al this the flame of theire
furie vvas not quenched: because that, notvvithstanding such things as had past, they
resolued to reuenge and fiesh them selues
more vppon those holie reliques vvhich remained, parting and casting lottes vppon
his garments, and pearcing his sacred brest
vvith a cruel speare.

O ye cruel ministres! O ye harts of iron!
Seemed that so litel to you vvhich his bodie
suffred being aliue, that ye vvould not pardon it euen after it vvas dead? vvhat rage of
enmitie is there so great, but that it is appea-
sed, vvhen it seeth his enimie dead before
him? Lift vp a litle those cruel eys of yours
& behold that deadlie face, those dimmeeys,
that failing countenance, that palenes and
shadovv of death: for although you be more
hard then either iron or adamant stone, yea
though ye be more hard then your ovvne
selues, yet in beholding him you vvil be pacified.

2   After this commeth the minister vvith a
speare in his hand, and vvith great force
thrusteth the same through the verie naked
brest of our Sauiour. The crosse shooke
in the aire, vvith the force of the stroke;
and from thence issued vvater and bloud,
                                              vvhere

vvherevvith ar healed the sinnes of the
vvorld. O riuer that runneſt out of paradiſe,
and vvatereſt vvith thy ſtreames all the
vvhole face of the earth ! O vvound of this
pretious ſide, made rather vvith feruent loue
tovvards mankind, then vvith the ſharp
iron of the cruel ſpeare! O gate of heauen !
vvindovve of paradiſe! place of refuge! tovv-
er of ſtrength! ſanctuarie of iuſt perſons! ſe-
pulchre of pilgrims! neſt of cleane doues, &
floriſhing bed of the ſpovvſe of Salomon.
Al haile o vvound of this pretious ſyde, that
vvoundeſt al deuout harts; ſtroke that ſtrikeſt the ſovvles of the iuſt; roſe of vnſpeak-
able bevvtie; rubie of ineſtimable price; en-
trance into the hart of Chriſt; teſtimonie of
his loue; and pledge of euerlaſting life.

Next to this conſider, hovv the very ſame
daie in the euening, there came thoſe tvvo
holie men Ioſeph and Nicodemus, vvhoe
reared vp their ladders vnto the croſſe, and
tooke dovvne the bleſſed bodie of our Sauiour into their armes. The holie virgin then
perceauing, that the torment of the croſſe
vvas novv ended, and that the holie bodie of
our Sauiour vvas comming tovvards the
earth, ſhe prepareth her ſelf to giue him a
ſecure hauen in her breſt, and to receaue him
from the armes of the Croſſe, into her ovvne

armes. And fo fhe requefteth vvith great
humilitie of thofe noble men , that for fo
much as fhee had také no leaue of her fonne,
nor receaued the laft embracings of him vppon the croffe, at the time of his departure,
they vvould novv fuffer her to approche
neere vnto him, and not increafe her difcom-
fort on euerie fide, yf, as the enimies had before taken her fonne from her, being yet a-
liue, fo her frinds vvould take him from her
being novv dead.

4   Novv vvhen the bleffed virgin had him
in her armes, vvhat tounge is able to expreffe that , vvhich fhe then felt? O ye Angels of peace, vveepe vvith this holie virgin;
vveepe ye heauens; vveepe ye ftarres of heauen; and al creatures of the vvorld accompanie the lamentation of the bleffed virgin
Marie. The bleffed mother embraceth the
torne bodie, fhee clippeth it faft to her breft,
(her ftrength feruing her to this thing onlie)
fhe putteth her face betvveene the thornes
of the facred head; fhe ioineth countenance
vvith countenance; the face of the moft holie
mother, is imbrued vvith the bloud of the
fonne; and the face of the fonne, is bathed
vvith the teares of the mother. O fvveete
mother, is this peraduéture thy moft fvveete
fonne? Is this he vvhome thou conceauedft
vvith

vvith so greate glorie, & broughtest foorth vvith so great ioy? vvhat is novv becom of thy former ioyes? vvhither is thy vvonted gladnes gone? vvhere is that mirrour of bevvtie, in vvhich thou diddest behold thy self?

Al those that vvere present, vvept vvith her. Those holie matrones vvept. Those noble gentlemen vvept. Heauen and earth vvept, and al creatures accompanied the teares of the virgin.

The holie Euangelist also vvept, and embracing the bodie of his maister said: O my good lord & maister, vvhoe shalbe my teacher from this time forvvards? To vvhome shal I resort vvith my doutes? vpon vvhose brest shal I rest mie self? vvhoe shal impart to me the secreats of heauen? vvhat straunge change and alteration is this? The last euening thou sufferedst me to rest vppon thy holy brest, giuing me ioye of life; and novv dooe I recompence that so greate benifit, vvith holding thee dead on my brest. Is this the face, vvhich I savve transfigured vppon the mount Thabor? Is this that figure, vvhich vvas more cleere then the sonne at middaie?

Likevvise that holie sinner Marie Magdalen vvept, and embracing the feete of our

G 3   Sa-

Sauiour said . O light of myne eyes and remedie of my sovvle , yf I shal see my self
vvearied vvith sinnes, vvhoe shal receaue
me ? vvhoe shal cure my vvounds ? vvhoe
shal ansvvere for me ? vvhoe shal defend
me againſt the Phariſees ? O hovv far othervviſe held I theſe feete, and vvaſſhed them,
vvhen thou receauedſt me ? O my svveete
hart-roote, vvhoe could bring to paſſe that
I might novv die vyith thee ? O life of my
ſovvle hovv can I ſaie that I loue thee, ſeeing
that I remaine aliue, vvhen I haue thee dead
before mine eys?

In like manner did al that holie companie vveepe and lament, vvatering & vvaſh-
ing that holie bodie vvith teares . But novv
vvhen the hovver of his burial vvas com,
they vvynd his holie bodie in a cleane linnen ſheete: they bynde his face vvith a nap-
kin ; & laying the bodie vppon a beere, they
goe to the place of the monument, and there
they laie in that pretious treaſure . The ſe-
pulchre vvas couered vvith a ſtone, and the
hart of the bleſſed mother vvith a clovvde
of heauines and forovve. There once againe
ſhe taketh leaue of her ſonne. There ſhe beginneth a freſhe to feele her heauie ſolitarines . There ſhe ſeeth her ſelf novv diſpoſ-
ſeſſed of al her good . Finallie there her hart
remai-

remaineth buried, vvhere her treasure vvas left.

Sonnedaie morning. Of the descending of our Sauiour into Limbus, of his appearing to our ladie, to S. Marie Magdalen, to the disciples; and of his Ascension.

THIS daie thou maist meditate vppon the descending of our Sauiour to Limbus; of his appearing to our blessed ladie, to S. Marie Magdalen, to the disciples; and of his glorious Ascension.

First of al consider, hovv exceeding greate the ioy & comfort vvas, vvhich those holie fathers in Limbo receaued, through the visitation and presence of theire Redeemer, and vvhat thankes and praises they gaue him for this saluation, so exceedinglie desired and hoped for. Those that returne from the east India into Spaine, saie of them selues, that they esteeme al the paines, and trauailes of their voiage past by sea, verie vvel imploied, vvhen they consider the extreme ioy, vvhich they receaue at the daie of theire returne to their countrie. Novv yf this sayling, & absence from theire countrie of one or tvvoe yeares, be of force to cause so great ioye, vvhat contentement and pleasure vvould the absence of three, or fouer thovvsand yeares, vvoorke in thofe that vvere to receaue fo great faluation, and to take hauen in the land of fuch as liue for euer?

2

Confider likevvife the ioy, vvhich the bleffed virgin this daie receaued in the fight of her fonne, vvhich vvas rifen : for certaine it is, that as fhee vvas the onlie perfon vvhich moft felt the paines of his paffion and death, fo fhe vvas the onlie, that moft vvas partaker of the ioy of his Refurrection.

Novv vvhat invvard comfort had fhe, vvhen before her, fhe beheld her fonne aliue and glorious, accompanied vvith all thofe holie fathers vvhich vvere rifen vvith him? vvhat did fhe? vvhat faid fhe? of vvhat máner vvere her embracings? her kiffes? the teares of her pitiful eys? and her defires to be alvvais vvith him, yf it might be graunted her?

3

Confider the ioy of thofe holie Maries, & efpeciallie of her, vvhich perfeuered vveeping before the fepulchre, vvhen fhe favve the beloued of her fovvle, and caft her felf dovvne at his feete, and fovvnd him rifen and liuing, vvhome fhe fought and defired to fee, although he had ben dead. And confider vvel, that next to his bleffed mother, he appeared firft to this vvoman, vvho moft loued him, moft perfeuered, moft vvept, and

and moſt carefullie ſought him ; thereby to
make thee knovv for certaine, that thou
ſhalt alſo find God, if thou ſeeke him vvith
the ſelf ſame teares and diligence.

Conſider after vvhat ſort he appeared to **4**
the diſciples, vvhich vvent tovvards Emaus,
in forme of a pilgrime ; & behold hovv gracious, and courtious he ſhevveth him ſelf
vnto them in his vvoords; hovv familiarlie
he keepeth them companie; hovv ſvveetlie
he diſguiſeth him ſelf that they knovv him
not ; and finallie hovv louinglie he diſcouered him ſelf vnto them, and left them vvith
paſſing invvard comfort and contentement.
Let thy ſpeech and talk be alſo ſuch as vvas
this of theſe men, and confer vvith invvard
ſorovv and feeling that, vvhich they confer-
red (vvhich vvas of the totments and paines
that Chriſt had ſuffered) and perſvvade thy
ſelf aſſuredlie, that thou ſhalt not vvant his
preſence and companie, yf thou procure
to haue alvvaies this in thy remembrance
and memorie.

Touching the miſterie of the Aſcenſion; **5**
conſider firſt, hovv our Sauiour differred &
prolonged his mounting vp into heauen, for
the ſpace of fortie daies, in vvhich he appeared oftentimes to his diſciples, teaching
them, and ſpeaking vvith them of the
kingdom

kingdom of God . In such manner that he
vvould not ascend vp into heauen , nor depart from them, vntil he had left them such,
as they might be able vvith spirite, to ascend
into heauen vvith him . VVhereby thou
maist vnderstand, that oftetimes the corporal presence of Christ (that is the sensible consolation of deuotion) leaueth those, that be
novv able vvith spirite to flie on high , and
be more secure and free from peril and danger . In vvhich thing the prouidence of almightie God maruailouslie discouereth it
self, and the manner vvhich he obserueth in
dealing vvith his at sundrie times: that is, he
cherisheth the vveake and feeble; he exer-
ciseth the valiant & stronge; he giueth milk
to the little ones : he vveaneth such as be
greate; he comforteth some ; he proueth o-
thers; and so dealeth vvith eche one, according to the degree of his profit , & aduaun-
cement. VVhereof it folovveth, that neither
he vvhich is fauoured , hath cause to becom
presumptuous; seeing that cherishing is an
argument of vveakenes: nor he vvhichis left
discomforted , to be dismaied ; seeing this is
oftentimes a signe of strength.

6   In the presence of his disciples , and they
beholding him , he vvent vp into heauen;
because they vvere to be vvitnesses of these
misteries

misteries: and none can better beare vvitnesse of the vvoorks of God, then he vvhich knovveth them by experience. Yf thou erneftlie desire to knovv hovv good almightie God is, hovv svveete, and hovv pleasant tovvards his, hovv greate the vertue and efficacie of his grace is, of his loue, of his prouidence, and of his confolations, enquire of thofe that haue proued it, and they vvil giue sufficient teftimonie of it.

He vvas alfo defirous that they fhould fee him goe vp into heauen, that thereby they might folovv him vvith theire eys & vvith theire fpirite, that they might feele his abfence, that his departure might make them retired and folitarie, vvhich vvas a moft fit preparation to receaue his grace. Helifeus requefted Helias to giue him his fpirite; and the good maifter anfvvered him. Yf thou canft fee me, vvhen I depart from thee, thou fhalt obtaine thy demaund. So they in deede fhalbe heyres of the fpirite of Chrift, vvhome force of loue fhal make to feele the abfence of Chrift: they vvhich fhal feele his departure, and remaining in this banifhment, fhal continuallie figh for his prefence. So felt that holie man, this abfence, vvhoe faid. Thou departedft from me, o my comforter, and thou tookeft not thy leaue of me.

4. Reg. 2.

Going

Going on thy vvaie, thou didest giue thy blessing to thine, and I savve it not. The Angels promised that thou vyouldest returne, and I hard it not.

Novv vvhat solitarines, vvhat feeling, vvhat cries, vvhat teares vvere those of the most blessed virgin, of the beloued disciple, of S. Marie Magdalen, & of al the Apostles vvhen they savv him goe from them, & depart out of their sight vvhoe had stolen from them their harts? yet, notvvithstanding all this, it is vvriten, that they vvent back into Ierusalem vvith great ioye, because they loued him exceedinglie. For the self same loue, vvhich made them feele so much his departure, made them on the other side reioice of his glorie; & true loue seeketh not so much it self, as that vvhich it loueth.

Luc. 24, 52.

7   It remaineth to consider, vvith hovv great glorie, vvith vvhat ioye, vvith vvhat exclamations and praises, this noble triumpher vvas receaued in that excellent citie: vvhat vvas the feast, and entertainement vvhich they made him: vvhat it vvas to behould men, & Angels there ioyned together, and al in companie to goe tovvards that noble citie, to fill vp those seates, vvhich so manie yeares had ben voide; & that most blessed humanitie of our Sauiour, to mount
aboue

aboue all, & to fit at the right hand of God
the father? All this deferueth to be dulie confidered, that vve maie vnderftand, and fee
hovv vvel our labours be imploied for the
loue of God; & hovv he, vvhich humbled
him felf, and fuffered more then all other
creatures, is novv aduanced, & exalted a-
boue them all: that here-hence the louers of
true glorie, maie knovv the vvaie vvhich
they muft follovv to obtayne the fame,
vvhich is to defcend, thereby to afcend;
and to put them felues vnder the feete of all
others, thereby to be exalted aboue all.

OF SIXE THINGES THAT MAIE
concurre in the exercife of praier.

CHAP. IV.

HESE be, good Chrifti-
an reader, the meditati-
ons in vvhich thou maift
exercife thy felfe, in all the
daies of the vveeke, that
fo thou vvant not matter,
vvhereof to thinke. But here it is to be noted, that fome things maie goe before this
meditation, and fom others follovv after it,
vvhich be annexed vnto the former, and as
it vvere neighbours vnto them.

For

For firſt, before vve enter into meditation, it is requiſite that vye prepare our hart vnto this holie excerciſe, vvhich is as to tune a viell, before vve plaie vppon it.

After preparation folovveth the reading of that matter, vvhich vve be to meditate vppon that daie, according to the diſtribution of the daies of the vveeke, as hath ben ſaid before. VVhich reading is vndovvtedlie neceſſarie for ſuch, as ar beginners, vntill a man dooe knovv, vvhat he ovvght to meditate vppon. After he maie proceede vnto meditation.

Next to meditation there maie folovv out of hand a deuoute giuing of thankes for the beniſits vvhich vve haue receaued, vvith an offering vp of al our life, and of the life of our Sauiour Chriſt, The laſt part is the Petition vvhich is properlie called praier, in vvhich vve demaund all that, vvhich is behoucful as vvel for the ſaluation of our ſelus, as of our neighbours, and of al the vvhole Catholike churche.

Theſe ſix things maie be exerciſed in praier, vvhich things, emong other commodities and porſits, bring this alſo, that they yeeld vnto a man more plentie of matter, vvhere vppon to meditate, ſetting before him all theſe diuerſities of meats, that in
caſe

cafe he can not eate of one, he maie eate of
an other, and that vvhen he hath made an
end of meditation in one matter, he maie
enter into an other; and there find other
matter, vvherein to continevv his meditation.

I knovv right vvel, that nether all thefe
partes, nor this order is alvvaies neceffarie,
yet this manner vvil ferue for nouices, and
young beginners; that fo they may haue
fom order, & direction vvherby to gouerne
them felues at the beginning. And therefore of anie thing that fhalbe here treated, I vvould not that anie man fhould
make a perpetual, or general rule: becaufe
my intent is not to make anie lavv, but to
fhevv an introduction, thereby to direct
nouices and beginners, and to put them in
this vvaye: in vvhich courfe after that they
fhalbe once entred, then the very vfe and
experience, and much more the holy gholt
vvil teach them the reft, that they haue to
dooe herein.

N O VV

112   THE FIRST TREATISE
OF PREPARATION VVHICH IS
requisite before praier.

CHAP. V.

 T shal novv be requisite
for vs, to treate particularlie of euerie one of these
parts aforesaide, & first of
the Preparation, vvhich
goeth before the others.

Being in the place of praier, kneeling or
standing, thy armes stretched out in manner of a crucifixe, or prostrate vppon the
grovvnd, or sitting (yf thou canst not settel
thie self in anie other sort) after thou hast
made the signe of the Crosse, thou must recollect thie imagination, & vvithdravve the
same from all things of this life, and liftvp
thy mind to heauen, considering that our
Lord beholdeth, and looketh vppon thee.
Thou must also stand there vvith such attention and reuerence, as yf thou hadst God
there reallie present before thine eys, and
vvith a general repentance of thy sinnes (yf
thie praier be in the morning) thou maist saie
the general confession *Confiteor Deo, &c.* or
(yf thy meditation be in the euening) thou
maist examine thy conscience, touching all
that

that vvhich, thou haſt thought, ſpoken, or
donne, or heard in that daie, as alſo, hovv
forgetful thou haſt ben of our lord ; and re-
penting thy ſelf of all the defects cōmitted
that daie, and of al thoſe of thy life paſt, and
humbling thy ſelf before the maieſtie of
almightie God, in vvhoſe ſight thou ſtan-
deſt, thou maiſt vtter theſe vvoords of the
holie Patriarch.

I vvil ſpeake to my lord, although I be but duſt Geneſ. 18.
& aſhes : and vvith the ſubſtance and matter 27.
of theſe fevv vvoords, thou maiſt, for ſum
little time, entertaine thy ſelf, conſidering
vvel vvhat thou art, and vvhat God is, that
ſo thou maiſt vvith more reuerence, humble
thy ſelf before ſo great a maieſtie, as is that
of almightie God. For thou art a bottomleſſe
depth of infinite ſinnes and miſeries : and
God is an infinite deepenes of al riches and
greatnes : and being in this conſideration,
thou muſt dooe him al due reuerence, and
and humble thy ſelf before his ſupreme
maieſtie.

VVith this alſo, thou muſt humblie beſeeche this lord to giue thee grace, that thou
maiſt ſtand there vvith ſuch attention and
deuotion, vvith ſuch invvard recollection,
and vvith ſuch feare and reuerence, as it behoueth thee to haue before ſo ſoueraine a
　　　　　　　H　　　　maieſtie,

maiestie, and that thou maist so passe ouer this time of praier, that thou maist com from the same vvith nevv desires and force, to doe al such things as appertaine to his seruice. For the praier, vvhich yeeldeth not this fruite, is to be esteemed verie vnperfect and of small valevv.

OF READING.

CHAP. VI.

FTER the preparation is ended, there folovveth Reading of that thing, vvhere vppon thovv art to meditate in time of praier. VVhich Reading ought not be donne lightlie & hastilie, but vvith deliberation and attention, applying thereunto not onlie thy vnderstanding, to conceiue such things as thou readest, but much more thy vvil, to tast those things that thou vnderstandest. And vvhen thou findest anie deuout passage, staie somvvhat longer vppon it, thereby to haue som greater feeling of that, vvhich thou hast read.

Let not the Reading be ouer-long, that so thou maist haue more time for meditation,

tion, vvhich is of so much more profit, by
hovv much more it vvaigheth, and entreth
into the consideration of things, vvith more
leasure and affection . Neuertheles, vvhen
thou findest thy hart so distracted, that it
cannot enter into praier, then thou maist
staie somvvhat the longer in Reading, or
ioine Reading and meditation together, by
reading first one point, & meditating vppon
it, and then an other, and an other in like
sort. For in so dooing, vvhen the vnderstanding is once bound to the vvoords of the
reading, it hath not occasion to vvander a-
brode so easilie, into diuers thoughts and
imaginations, as vvhen it goeth free and at
libertie. And yet better it vvere to striue in
casting of such thoughtes, and to perseuer
and vvrastle against them (as the Patriarche
Iacob did all the night long) continuing in
the vvork of praier : that in the end, vvhen
the vvrastling is donne, vve maie obtaine the
victorie, our lord giuing vs deuotion, or som
other greater grace, vvhich is neuer denied
to those, that labour and fight faithfullie.

OF

CHAP.   VII.

 TRAITE after reading
folovveth meditation vp-
pon the point vvhich
vvee haue read . And this
meditatió is fomtimes vp-
pon things , vvhich may
be figured vvith the Imagination; as at all
the paſſages of the life and paſſion of our Sauiour Chriſt; of the laſt iudgement; of hel; or
of Paradiſe. Som other times it is of things,
vvhich doe apperteine rather tō the vnderſtanding, then to the imagination ; as is the
conſideration of the benifits of almightie
God : of his goodnes and mercie , or of anie
othe: his perfections. This kind of meditation is called *Intellectual* , and the other *Imaginarie*. And vve ar vvoont to vſe both the
one , & the other manner in theſe exerciſes,
according as the matter of the things doth
requi.e.

Novv vvhen the med tation is *Imaginarie*,
vve muſt then figure, and repreſent euerie
one of theſe things, in ſuch vvife as it is, or
in ſuch vvife as it might perhaps paſſe , and
make

makeaccounte, that in the verie same place vvhere vve be, al the same passeth in our presence, that by meanes of such a representation of these things, the consideration and feeling of them maie be more liuelie in vs. But to goe and meditate such things, as passed, eache in his oune place, is a thing vvhich doth comonlie vveaken, and hurt the head.

And for this verie cause likevvise, a man must not fixe his imagination ouer much vppon the things, of vvhich he meditateth, that so he vvearie not is head.

But for as much as the principall matter of meditation, is the holie pasion of our Sauiour Iesus Chrift, it is to be vnderstoode, that in this misterie maie be confidered fiue principal points, or circumstances, vvhich concurre in the same: to vvit, vvhoe he is that suffereth: vvhat he suffreth; for vvhome he suffereth; in vvhat manner he suffereth: And for vvhat end he suffereth.

Touching the firft point, vvhich vvas, vvhoe hee is that suffereth: I aunsvvere that he vvhich suffereth is; the Creator of heauen and earth; the onlie sonne of God; the highest goodnes, and vvisdom that can be imagined; the most innocent and most holie sonne of the blessed virgin Marie.

Concerning the second point, to vvit

H 3   vvhat

vvhat he suffereth: I aunsvvere that he suffereth most grieuous pains, as vvel in his soule as in his bodie . For in his soule he suffered so greatangvvish & affliction, as no hart is able to comprehend it; cõsidering the ingratitude of men, tovvards this so singular and high a benifit: The compassion of his most innocent and blessed mother: The sinnes of the vvorld that vvere present, past, and to com, for all vvhich he suffered. And in his bodie he endured cold, heat, hunger, vvearines. vvatchings, iniuries, betraying, he vvas sould of his disciple, he did svveate drops of bloud, he vvas spitte vppon, buffeted, so oftentimes bound, forsaken, euil spoken of, falstie accused, vvhipped, scorned, appareled as yf he had bene a foole, crovvned vvith thornes, lesse esteemed then Barabbas, vniustlie condemned, he caried his ovvne crosse vppon his shoulders, he vvas crucified betvvene tvvoe theeues, he did drink easell & gall, and finallie he died a most opprobrious , & reprocheful death vppon the mount Caluarie, in time of greatest solemnitie.

The third point to be considered, is for vvhome he suffered: & euident it is, that he suffred for mankind disobedient & vngrateful, created of nothing, vvho of him self can dooe nothing, knovveth nothing, nor is anie
thing

thing vvorth: for a creature of vvhome he ne
uer had, nor neuer vvas to haue anie neede.
For a creature vvhich had offended, & vvas
to offend and difobey him fo manie times.

The fourth point to be confidered, is in
vvhat manner he fuffered: vvhere vve fhall
fee, that he fuffred vvith fuch great patience
and meekenes, that he vvas neuer offended
nor angrie vvith anie bodie: vvith fo great
humilitie, that he made choice of the moft
contemptible death that vvas vfed in thofe
daies: vvith fo great readines and alacritie,
that he vvent foorth to meete his enimies;
vvith fo great charitie, that he called his
frind him, that betraied and fould him; healed his eare that tooke him; regarded vvith
eyes of mercie him, that had denied him;
and praied for thofe that crucified him.

The fift point to be confidered, is vvherefore and to vvhat end he fuffereth: vvhere
it is manifeft that he fuffered to fatisfie the
iuftice of almightie God, and to appeafe the
vvrath of his father; to accomplifh the pre-
dictions and propheties of the Patriarches
and Prophetes: to deliuer vs from the thral-
dom of hell, and to make vs capable of
heauen; to fhevv vs the vvaie to heauen
vvith his perfect Obedience: and to con-
found the diules, vvhoe by reafon of theire

H 4   pride

pride haue lost that, vvhich men dooe gaine through theire humilitie.

OF THANKESGIVING.

CHAP. VIII.

A F T E R meditation folovveth thankefgeuing, of vvhich a man muſt take occaſicn of the meditation paſt, and giue thankes vnto our lord, for the benifit he hath donne vnto him in the ſame ; as for example, yf the meditation vvas of the paſſion, he muſt thanke our lord that he hath redeemed vs vvith ſo great paines. And if it vvere of our ſinnes ; for that he hath expected vs ſo long time to dooe penance; yf it vvere of the miſeries of this life , for that he hath deliuered vs from ſo manie of them; yf of the departing out of this vvoorld , and of the hovver of our death; for that he hath deliue ed vs from the daungers of it, and expected vs , and giuen vs life to dooe penance ; and yf it vvere of the glorie of paradiſe, for that he hath created vs to be partakers of ſo great a felicitie : and ſo likevviſe yve maie dooe in the reſt.

And vvith theſe benifits thou muſt ioine al the

all the other benifits, of which vve haue
fpoken before, vvhich be the benifit of
Creation, Conferuation, Redemption, Vocation, and Glorification: and fo thou fhalt
giue thankes to our lord, for that he hath
made thee to his likenes and image, and
hath giuen the memorie, to remember him;
ynderftanding, to knovve him; and vvil to
loue him; and for that he hath giuen thee
an angel, to keepe thee from fo manie daungers and perils, and from fo manie mortal
finnes, and alfo from death, thou being in
finne, vvhich vvas no leffe benefit, then to
deliuer thee from euerlafting death: and for
that he made thee to be borne of Chriftian
parents, and gaue thee holie baptifme, and
the ein his grace, and promifed thee his
glorie, and receaued thee fo his child.

Alfo vvith thefe benifits, thou muftioine
other general and particular benifits, vvhich
thou knovveft to haue receaued of our lord;
and for thefe and al others, as vvel publique
as priuate, thou muft yeeld him as hartie
thankes as poffible thou maift, and inuite
al creatures, as vvel in heauen as in earth,
that they affift and help thee, to dooe thy
durie in this, and vvith this fpirite and defire thou maift faie fomtimes that Canticle:
Benedicite omnia opera Domini Domino, or els
the

Pſal. 102 the pſalme : *Benedic anima mea Domino , &*
omnia quæ intra me ſunt nomini ſancto eius. Bene-
dic anima mea Domino , & noli obliuiſci omnes re-
tributiones eius. Qui propitiatur omnibus iniquita-
tibus tuis, qui ſanat omnes infirmitates tuas. Qui re-
dimit de interitu vitam tuam , qui coronat te in mi-
ſericordia & miſerationibus.

OF OFFERING.

CHAP. IX.

THIS being donne , that
is , vvhen a man hath ge-
uen thankes to our lord
vvith al his hart for al
theſe benifits, then foorthvvith the hart naturallie
breaketh out into that affect of the Prophet
Dauid ſaying; *VVhat ſhall I yeeld vnto our Lord*
Pſal. 515. *for all thoſe things vvhich he hath beſtovved vppon*
12. *me?* And this deſire a man in ſom ſort ſatis-
fieth, vvhen he geueth, and offereth vp to
almightie God that, vvhich of his part he
hath , and is able to giue him.

And for this end, he ought firſt to offer vp
him ſelf to God, for his perpetual ſklaue, re-
ſigning and laying him ſelf vvholie in his
hands, that his diuine maieſtie dooe vvith
him, as it ſhal beſt pleaſe him : and iointlie
he

he muſt offer vp to him all his vvoords, his
vvoorks, his thoughts, and his paines, that
is, vvhatſoeuer he doeth and ſuffereth, that
ſo al maie be to the glorie and honour of his
holie name.

Secondlie, he muſt offer vp to God the
father, the merites & vvoorkes of his ſonne,
and all the paines, vvhich in this vvoorld
he ſuffered for obedience of him, euen from
the manger vntil the croſſe ; for ſo much as
they al be our ſubſtance, & heritage vvhich
he left vs in the nevv teſtament, by vvhich
he made vs his heires of al theſe ſo greate
treaſures. And in like manner as that vvhich
is giuen me, is no leſſe mine, then that
vvhich I haue goten by mine ovvne paines
and labour; ſo the merites of Chriſt, & the
right vvhich he hath geuen me, ar no leſſe
mine, then yf I had ſvveate and laboured
for them my ſelf. And therefore a man maie
vvith as much right, offer this ſecond preſent as the firſt, laying dovvne by order al
our Sauiours vvoorks and paines, and al the
vertues of his moſt holie life, his Obedience,
his Patience, his Humilitie, his Charitie,
vvith al the reſt ; becauſe this is the moſt
riche, and moſt pretious offer that maie be
offered.

OF

CHAP. X.

Mmediatlie after that vve haue offered vp vnto almightie God, this so riche a present, vve maie then vvith great securitie, in vertue of the same, demaud or him vvhatsoeuer fauours & grace. And first let vs demaunde vvith great affection of Charitie, and vvith desire of the glorie of God, that al nations and people of the vvorld maie knovv, praise and adore him, as theire onlie true God, and lord, saying, euen from the bottom of our hart, these vvords of the Prophet. *Let all people* Psal. 66. *confesse thee, o God, let all people confesse thee.*
4.

Let vs praie also for the Catholike Church, and for al the Prelates of the same, such as be the Pope, Cardinals, Bisshops, and other inferior ministres and Prelates; that our lord vvil gouerne them, and giue them light, in such sort, that they maie bring all men to the knovvledge, and obedience of theire Creator. VVe must likevvise praie (as S. Paul counseleth vs) *for* 1. Timoth. *kings, and for al those that be in dignitie, that* 2. 2.

(through

(thorough theire prouidence) vve maie liue a
quiet and peaceable life. in al puritie and chastitie,
because this is acceptable before God our Sauiour,
vvhoe desireth that all men be saued, and com to the
knovvledge of the truth.

Let vs also praie our lord for al the members of his mistical bodie ; for the iust , that
he vvil conserue them in theire goodnes;
for sinners , that it maie please him to conuert them ; for the dead , that he vvil merci-
fullie deliuer them, out of the great paines
of purgatorie , and bring them to the rest of
euerlasting life . Let vs praie also for al such
as bee poore, sicke , in prison, in captiuitie
&c. that God, through the merites of his
sonne , vvil help and deliuer them.

After that vvee haue thus demaunded
for our neighbours , let vs forthvvith aske
for oure selues. Novv vvhat vve ought to
desire for our selues, the particular neede of
eche one vvil teach him, if yet he knovv him
self. Let vs also vvith this demaund pardon,
and amendment of our sinnes, by the merites and paines of our Sauiour ; and especiallie let vs requeft his ayde , and assistance
against al those passions and vices, to vvhich
vve feele our selues most inclined , and of
vvhich vve be most tempted ; and let vs
discouer al these our vvounds to this hea-
                              uenlie

uenliephifition, that by this meanes he vvil
vouchfafe to heale, and cure them vvith
the ointment of his grace.

After this make an end, vvith demaun-
ding the loue of God; and in this demaund
ftaie, and occupie thy ielf for the moft part
of the time, cefiring ourlord vvith moft
hartie affection and defire, to graunt thee
this vertue, for fo much as in it confifteth al
our good, and fo thou maift faie as folovveth.

AN ESPECIAL PETITION OF THE loue of God.

BOVE all this giue me, O
lord thy grace, that I may loue
thee vvith all my hart, vvith
all my fovvle, vvith all my
forces, and vvith all my en-
trailes, euen in fuch fort, as thou defireft.
O all mie hope, all mie glorie, al mie refuge,
and al mie ioie! O the moft beloued of beloueds, O florifhing fpovvfe, O fvveete
fpovvfe, O honifvveete fpovvfe! O comfort
of my hart, O life of my fovvle, and the
pleafant repofe of my fpirite!

Prepare, o my God, prepare, o mie lord,
in me an acceptable dvvelling place for thie
felf, that accoding to the promife of thie
holie

holie vvoord, thou com to me, and repose in me; mortifie in me, vvhatsoeuer displeaseth thy sight, and make me a man according to thie hart; vvound, o lord, the most invvard part of my sovvle, vvith the dartes of thie loue, and make me drunke vvith the vvine of thy perfect charitie.

O vvhen shall this be? vvhen shall I please thee in al things? vvhen shall al that diein me, vvhich is contrarie to thee? vvhen shall I be altogeather thine? vvhen shall I leaue to be mine ovvne? vvhen shall nothing els liue in me, but thou? vvhen shall I loue thee most feruentlie? vvhen shal the flame of thie loue vvholie burne me? vvhen shall I be altogeather melted, and pearced through vvith the vvoonderful efficacie of thy svveetenes? vvhen vvilt thou take me hence by force, and drovvne me, transport me and hide me in thy self, vvhere I maie neuer more be seene? vvhen vvilt thou free me from all these impediments and distractions, and make me one spirite vvith thee, that I maie not anie more depart from thee?

O deerebeloued, deerebeloued, deerebeloued of my sovvle, o svveetenes of my harte; heare me, o lord, not for my merites and deserts, but for thy infinite

goodnes

goodnes and mercie. Teache me, lighten
me, direct me, and assist me in al things;
that I maie dooe nothing, nor saie nothing,
but that vvhich is agreeable to thie sight.
O mie God, mie vvelbeloued, mie deerest
hart, and the verie good of mie sovvle! O
mie svveete loue, o my great delite, o mie
strength! help me, o mie light, and guide
mee tovvards thee.

O God of mie bovvels, vvherefore giuest
not thou thie self to thie poore creature?
Thou fillest the heauens and the earth, and
leauest thou mie hart emptie and void?
Seeing thou clothest the lilies of the field,
giuest meate to the little birds, and feedest
the vvoormes of the earth, vvherefore doest
thou forget me, vvhoe haue forgoten all o-
thers for thie sake? To late haue I knovven
thee, o infinite goodnes! To late haue I
loued thee, o bevvtie so auncient, and so
nevv. VVoe to the time, that I loued thee
not: vvoe to mee, since I knevv thee not.
Blinde vvas I, that I savve thee not. Thou
vvast vvithin me, and I vvent seeking thee
abrode. But novv, although I haue found
thee late, suffer not, o lord, for thie diuine
mercie, that I euer leaue thee.

And because one of the things, vvhich
most pleaseth thee, and most vvoundeth thy
hart,

hart, is that a man haue eys vvherevvith to
behold thee, giue me, o lord, thofe eys,
vvith vvhich I maie fee thee; to vvit, eyes
fimple of a doue; eyes chaft and fhamefaft;
eyes humble and louing; eyes deuout, and
geuen to teares; eyes attentiue, & difcreete
to knovv thy vvill, and fulfil the fame;
that vvhen I looke vppon thee vvith thefe
eyes, I may be feene of thee vv:th thofe
eyes, vvith vvhich thou diddeft vievv S. Peeter, vvhen thou madeft him to bevvaile his
finne; vvith vvhich thou dideft behold that
prodigal child, vvhen thou receauedft him,
& gaueft him a kiffe, of peace; vvith vvhich
thou dideft behould the publicane, vvhen
he durft not lift vp his eyes to heauen; vvith
vvhich thou diddeft behold Marie Magdalen, vvhen fhe vvafhed thy feete vvith the
teares of her eyes; finallie vvith thofe eyes,
vvith vvhich thou dideft behold the fpoufe
in the Canticles, vvhen thou faideft vnto
her. *Hovv bevvtiful art thou, o mie dearling, hovv* Cantic. 4.
bevvtiful art thou? Thie eyes ar as the eyes of doues; 1.
that pleafing thee vvith the eyes and beu-
tie of mie fovvle, thou giue them thofe
pledges of vertues and graces, vvith vvhich
they maie appeare alvvaies faire, and
bevvtiful in thie prefence.

O moft high, moft merciful, moft gracious

I   Tri-

Trinitie the father, the sonne and the holy
Ghost, one onlie true God, teach me, direct
me, and help me, O lord, in al things. O almightie father, for the greatnes of thy infinite povver fasten, & establish my memorie
vppon thee, and fill the same vvith holie
and deuout desires. O most holie Sonne, for
thy euerlasting vvisdom clarifie, and illuminate my vnderstanding, and bevvtifie
the same vvith knovvledge of the highest
veritie, and of mine ovvne extreme basenes.
O holie Ghost, the loue of the father and
the sonne, for thy incōprehensible goodnes
ground in me thy vvill, and kindle the same
vvith so great fiar of loue, that no vvaters
maie be able to quenche it. O most blessed
Trinitie, my onlie God, and al my good!
o that I vvere able to praise thee, and loue
thee, as all the angels doe praise and loue
thee! O that I had in me the loue of all the
creatures in the vvoorld, vvith hovv good
a vvil vvould I aford it thee, and povvre it
out into thee? albeit neither this vvere sufficient to loue thee in such vvise, as thou
deseruest. Thou onlie canst loue thy self
vvoorthilie, and vvoorthilie praise thy self;
because thou alone doest comprehende thy
incomprehensible goodnes, and so thou
onlie canst loue the same as it deserueth: so
that

that onlie in that diuine breſt of thy moſt gracious maieſtie, the iuſtice and lavve of true loue is entirelie obſerued.

O virgin Marie! virgin Marie! virgin Marie! moſt holie virgin, mother of God, Queene of heauen, ladie of the vvhole vvoorld, veſtrie of the holie Ghoſt, lilie of puritie, roſe of patience, paradiſe of delites, mirrour of chaſtitie, patterne of innocencie, praie for me poore baniſhed creature and pilgrime, and make me partaker of thy moſt aboundant charitie. O al ye happie Sainꞓts, and ye other bleſſed ſpirites, that dooe ſo burne in the loue of youre Creator, and in particular ye Seraphines, vvhoe enflame the heauens, and the earthe vvith your loue, abandon not this my poore and miſerable hart, but rather purge the ſame, as the lippes of Eſaie, from al ſort of ſinne, and burne it vvith the flame of your moſt feruent loue, that it maie loue this onlie lord, ſeeke him onlie, make his abode and repoſe in him onlie, and this for euer and euer. Amen.

CHAP. XI.

A L that vvhich hitherto hath ben ſaid, ſerueth to yeeld vs matter of conſideration, vvhich is one of the principall partes of this ſpiritual affaire, conſidering that ſuch, as haue ſufficient matter of conſideration, be but the leſt number of ſo manie people; & ſo for vvant of matter, vvhereupon to meditate, manie there be, that abandon this kinde of exerciſe. Novv vve vvil ſet dovvne breefelie ſomvvhat touching the manner, and forme vvhich in it maie be obſerued. And albeit the cheefe maiſter of this vvoork, be the holie Ghoſt, yet experience hath tavvght vs, that ſom aduiſes be requiſite and neceſſarie in this part: becauſe the vvaie to goe tovvards God is hard, & hath neede of a guide, vvithout vvhich very manie goe long time loſt and a ſtray.

The first aduise.

LET then the first aduise be this, that vvhen ve set our selues to consider anie of the aforesaide things, in theire times and exercises appointed, vve must not so binde our selues vnto it, that vve esteeme it ill donne, to goe from that to som other thing, vvhen vve finde therein more deuotion, more tast, and more profit. For as in conclusion al this serueth for deuotion, so that vvhich maketh most to this purpose, is to be taken for the best. Hovvbeit a man ought not to dooe this vppon verie light occasions, but vvhen he perceiueth euident commoditie to com thereby.

The second aduise.

THE second aduise is, that a man labour to eschevv, in this exercise, superfluous speculation of the vnderstanding, and procure to handle this affaire rather vvith affections, and feelings of the vvil, then vvith discourses and speculations of the vvitte. VVherefore they vndovvtedlie take not the right course, vvhoe in time of praier, giue them selues to meditate vppon diuine mi-

I 3   steries,

steries, in such vvise, as yf they studied to
preache them : vvhich manner is rather to
make oure spirite to vvander more abrode,
then to recolleƌ it ; and to goe more out of
it self, then to be in it self. Therefore vvhoe
mindeth to dooe vvel in this matter, let him
com vvith the hart as it vvere of an old
vvoman ignorant, and humble, and rather
vvith a vvil disposed and prepared to feele,
and to be affeƌed tovvards the thinges of
God, then vvith an vnderstanding purified,
and attentiue to search and examine them;
because this is a thing proper to those, that
studie to get knovvledge, and not to those,
that praie and thinke vppon God, thereby
to lament and moorne.

The third aduise.

THE former aduise teacheth vs hovv
vve ought to quiet our vnderstanding,
and commit al this busines to oure vvil ; but
this present aduise prescribeth boundes, and
limites to the same vvil, that it be not to excessiue, nor to vehement in her exercise.
VVherefore it is to be vnderstoode, that the
deuotió vvhich vve seeke to obteine, is not
a thing that may be goten by force of armes
(as som parsons think, vvhoe by eccessiue
                                        sigh-

sighings, and enforced sobbings, procure to
vvring out teares and compassion, vvhen
they think vppon the passion of our Sauiour) for such force drieth vp the hart, and
maketh the same more vnable to receaue
our lords visitation, as Cassianus affirmeth.
Moreouer, those things ar vvont to preiudice, and hurt the health of the bodie, yea
somtimes they leaue the sovvle so astonied,
and agast by reason of the litell taft she
hath there receaued, that she is loth to returne againe to this exercise, as to a thing,
vvhich she hath tryed by experience to
haue ben verie paineful, and irckfome ynto
her.

Let a man therefore content him selfe,
vvith doing sincerelie vvhat lieth in him,
that is, that he esteeme him self to be present at that, vvhich our Sauiour hath suffered, beholding (vvith a sincere and quiet
eye, vvith a tender and compassionate hart,
& prepared for vvhat foeuer feeling it shall
pleafe our lord to giue him) that vvhich
he suffered for him, and fo difpose him felf
rather to receiue fuch affections, as the
mercie of God shall aford him, then to
vvring them out vvith teares. And vvhen
he hath donne this, let him not vexe him
felf anie more for anie other thing, though

I 4   it be

it be not graunted him as he defireth.

The fourthe aduife.

OF all thefe aduifes a forefaid, vve maie
gather vvhat manner of attention
vve ought to haue in praier, for that in this
exercife, it is cheefelie expedient, to haue our
hart not heauie, nor dul, but liuelie, attent,
and lifted vp on high. But as it is heere neceffarie on the one fide, to haue attention
and recollection of hart, fo it behoueth on
the other fide, that this attention be tempered and moderated, that it neither hurt our
health, nor hinder oure deuotion. For fom
there be, that doe vvearie theire head vvith
ouer much violence, vvhich they vfe to be
attentiue vnto thofe things, vvherevppon
they meditate, as vve haue faid before. And
againe there be others, vvhoe to auoide this
inconuenience, ar in theire meditation verie
flack and negligent, and verie eafie to be
caried avvay vvith euerie vvinde. Novv to
efchevv thefe tvvo extremities, it is expedient that vve vfe fuch a meane, that vve
dooe neither vvith ouermuch attention
vvearie our head, nor vvith to much carelefnes and negligence fuffer our thoughts to
goe vvandering vvhither foeuer they vvil.
So

So that like as vve are vvont to saie to him
that rideth vppon a frovvard kicking horse,
that he hold the reines of his bridle as he
ought, that is neither to hard, neither to
slacke, that the horse neither turne back-
vvard, nor runne to headlong forvvard; euen
so must vve endeuoure that our attention
in our praier be moderate, not forced vvith
carefulnes, nor vvith violent labour and
traueil.

But noyv especially vve must be vvel
vvarie, that in the beginning of meditation vvee dooe not trouble, and vvearie our
head vvith to much attention: for vvhen
vvee doe so, our forces commonlie vvant vs
to goe forvvards therein, as it happeneth to
a traueller, vvhen he maketh to great hast
in going, at the beginning of his iourneye.

The fifte aduise.

BVT among al these aduises the princi-
pallest is, that he that praieth be not
dismaied, nor geue ouer his exercise, vvhen
he feeleth not foorthvvith that svveetenes
of deuotion, vvhich he desireth. It is requisite to expect the coming of our lord, vvith
longanimitie and perseuerance; for that it
greatlie appertaineth to the glorie of his
maie-

maieſtie, to the baſenes of our condition, and to the importance of the affaire vvhich vve haue in hand, that oftentimes vve attend, and vvatche at the gates of his ſacred palaice.

Novv, vvhen thou haſt after this ſort expected for a certaine time, in caſe our lord ſhal then com vnto thee, giue him moſt hartie thankes for his comming; and yf it ſeeme vnto thee that he com not, humble thy ſelf then before him, and acknovvledge, that thou art not vvoorthie to receaue that thing, vvhich is not giuen thee; and be content that thou haſt there made a ſacrifice of thy ſelf, denied thine ovvne vvil, crucified thy appetite, ſtriued vvith thy ſelf, & donne at the leaſt vvhat thou couldeſt of thine ovvne part.

And in caſe thou haue not adored our lord vvith ſenſible adoration, according to thy deſire, it is ſufficient that thou haſt adored him in ſpirite and in truth, according as his vvil is to be adored. And truſt me aſſuredlie, that this is the moſt daungerous paſſage of al this nauigation, and the place vvhere trevv deuoute perſons ar prooued & tried, and that yf thou eſcape vvel out of this daunger, thou ſhalt haue proſperous ſucceſſe in al the reſt.

Th

The sixte aduise.

THIS aduise is not much differing from the a foresaid, nor of lesse necessitie then it; and it is, that the seruante of God dooe not content him self, vvith vvhat soeuer little taft he findeth in his praier, as some vse to dooe, vvhoe vvhen they shedd a feavve teares, or feele a little tendernes of hart, persvvade them selues, that then they haue accomplished and performed theire exercise But this is not enough for the obteining of that thing, vvhich heere vve seeke for. For like as a little devv or sprinkling of vvater, is not sufficient to cause the earth to bring forth fruite (vvhich doth no more but onlie alay the duft, and vvet the vppermoft parte of the grovvnd) but it is needeful to haue so much vvater, that it maie enter into the innermoft part of the earth, & there soke, and vvater through the same: euen so is it requisite to haue here abūdance of this devv, and vvater of heauen, to bring foorth the fruite of good vvoorkes.

And therefore vve ar counseled, not vvithout great reason, that vve take as long time for this holie exercise, as vve maie. And better it is to haue one long time for the fame, then tvvo short times: for yf the time be short, al is spent almoft in settling

ling the imagination , and in quieting the
minde : and then vvhen vve haue quie-
ted the fame , vve rife from our exercife,
euen vvhen vve fhould begin it . And def-
cending more in particular to limite this
time , I am of opinion, that vvhat foeuer
is leffe than one hovvre and a halfe , or tvvo
hovvres , is to fhort a time for praier : becaufe that oftentimes there is fpent more
than halfe an hovver , in tempering our inftrument , that is , as I faid before , in quieting our imagination : and fo al the reft of
the time is requifite for the enioying of the
fruite of praier . True it is , that vvhen vve
goe to this exercife of praier, after fom other
holie exercifes , our hart is then better difpofed for this affaire ; and fo , like drie
vvoode , is verie apte to conceiue more
quicklie in it felf this heauenlie fiar.

Likevvife earlie in the morning our meditation may be the longer , becaufe then
our hart is much better difpofed for this
exercife, then at anie other time . Hovvbeit
in cafe that a man haue little time , by reafon of his manifolde bufines , yet let him
not omit to offer vp his mite vvith the
poore vvidovve in the temple : for yf he
faile not of his devvtie herein , throvvghe
his ovvne negligence, he that prouideth
for all

for al creatures according to their necessitie,
vvil not vvant to prouide likevvise for him.

ACording vnto this forefaide aduise,
vve vvil giue an other verie like,
vvich is; that vvhen oure fovvle is visited
either in praier, or out of praier, vvith anie
speciall visitation of our Lord, vve suffer
it not to passe avvaie in vaine, but take the
commoditie and benifite of that occasion,
that is offered vnto vs. For certaine it is,
that vvith this vvinde, a man shall saile
more in one hovver, than vvithout it in
manie daies.

And so vve reade that the holie father
S. Francis did, of vvhome S. Bonauenture
vvriteth, that he had such a speciall care in
this point, that in cafe our lord did visite
him vvith anie speciall visitation, vvhile
he vvas traueiling by the vvaie, he caufed
his companions to goe before, and he staied
alone behinde, vntil he had made an end
of chevving, and digesting that svveete mor-
fel, vvhich vvas there sent vnto him from
heauen. VVhosoeuer they be that dooe not
foe, ar vvont comonlie to be chastised vvith
this punishmēt, that theye find not almightie God, vvhen they seeke him; becaufe he
found not them, vvhen he fought for them.

THE SECOND

PART OF THIS FIRST

TREATISE,

VVHICH SPEAKETH OF deuotion.

VVHAT THING DEVO-
tion is.

CHAP. I.

T HE greateſtlabour, that ſuch perſons endure as geuethem ſelus to praïer, is the vvant of deuotion, vvhich oftentimes they feele in the ſame ; for vvhen this faileth not , there is nothing more ſvveete, nor eaſie then to praie . For this cauſe, ſeeing vve haue alredie treated of the matter of praier , and of the manner vvhich maie be obſerued therein ; it ſhall be expedient that vve treate novv of ſuch things , as help and further vs to deuotion, and alſo of thoſe that hinder vs, and of the temptations vvhich be moſt common to deuout perſons , and of certaine aduiſes,
                                    vvhich

vvhich be verie neceſſarie for this exerciſe.
But firſt it ſhal be much to the purpoſe, to
declare vvhat thing deuotion is, that ſo
vve maie vnderſtand before, hovv great
a ievvel that is, for vvhich vvee traueill.

Saint Thomas ſaieth that deuotion is
a certaine vertue, vvhich maketh a man
quicke and readie to al vertue, and vvake-
neth him, and diſpoſeth him to doe good
vvoorks vvith facilitie and eaſines. VVhich
definition of deuotion, ſhevveth manifeſtlie
the great neceſſitie and profit of this vertue,
becauſe in the ſame is conteined much
more, then manie can thinke of. VVherefore it is to be vnderſtoode, that the greateſt
hinderance vvhich vve haue to liue vvel,
is the corruption of our nature, vvhich came
vnto vs by ſinne, from vvhich procedeth
a great inclination that vve haue to dooe
yll. And theſe tvvo things make the vvaie
of vertue difficultous, and hard vnto vs,
vvhere as vertue, of her ovvne nature, is the
moſt ſvveete, bevvtiful, and amiable thing
that is in the vvoorld.

Novv againſt this difficultie and heauines, the diuine vviſdome of almightie God
hath prouided a moſt fit, and conuenient
remedie, to vvit the vertue and ayde of deuotion. For euen as the north-vvinde ſcat-
tereth

tereth and dissolueth the clovvdes, and
leaueth the aire bright and cleare; so true
deuotion shaketh of from our sovvle al this
heauines and difficultie, and leaueth her
aftervvards disposed, and redie to dooe al
good : because this vertue is in such manner
vertue, that it is also a speciall gift of the
holie ghost, a devy of heauen, a succour &
visitation of God, obtained by the meanes
of praier, vvhose condition is to fight
against this difficultie, to shift of this sluggishnes, to giue this readines, to illuminate
the vnderstanding, to force the vvill, to
kindle the loue of God, to quenche the
flames of yll desires, to breede lothsomnes of
the vvoorld, and hatred of sinne, and then
to giue a man nevv feruor, a nevv spirite, a
nevv force, & breath to dooe good vvorks.

Iudic. 16.   In such sorte that like as Sampson, vvhen
he had his haire, had more strength then all
the men of the vvoorld, and vvhen he had
his haire cut of, became feeble and vveake,
as other men ar: so is also the sovvle of a
Christian man passing strong, vvhen he
hath deuotion, but vvhen deuotion faileth,
she beccmmeth exceding vveake. And so
this is the greatest commendation that maie
be giuen to this vertue, that she being but
onlie one, is as it vvere a prick and spurre
to all

to all others . And therefore vvhoesoeuer
earneftlie defireth to vva ke in the vvaie
of vertues, let him not goe vvithout thefe
fpurres; for he fhal neuer be able , vvithout
them, to get his euill beaft out of the mire.

Of that vvhich hath ben faide, it feemeth
manifeft, vvhat thing true and fubftantial
deuotion is . For in deede deuotion is not
that tendernes of hart , nor confolation,
vvhich thofe dooe fomtimes feele , that
exercife praier ; but it is th's readines, and·
corrage to dooe good vvoorks ; vvhereof
it often folovveth , that the one is found to
be in vs , vvithout the other, vvhen it pleafeth God to proue fuch as be his. True it is,
that this deuotion and readines, doth oftentimes merite and deferue to haue that confolation;as on the other fide, the felfe fame
confolation and fpiritual g ft , increafeth
fubftantiall deuotion. And for this caufe,
the feruants of God maie vvith much reafon
defire, and afke thefe comfortes and confolations , not for the fvveetenes vvhich
they feele in them ,but in this refpect , that
they be caufe of the increafing of this deuotion; vvhich maketh vs fo fit to vvoorke
vvel; as the Pophet faith. *I haue runne* (o lord) Pfal. 118.
the vvaie of thy commandements , vvhen thou did- 32.
deft enlarge my hart,to vvit, vvith the comfort

K   of thy

of thy confolation , vvhich vvas caufe of this my fvviftnes. Novv, here vvee minde to treate of the meanes, by vvhich vve maie obteine this deuotion : and becaufe this vertue is the fpurre of al other vertues , therefore to treate of the meanes, by vvhich deuotion is gotten , is to treate of the meanes, bv vvhich vve obteine all other vertues.

OF NINE THINGS, VVHICH
help vs greatlie to atteine vnto deuotion.

CHAP. II.

VT novv , the things, vvhich help vs to obteine deuotion, be manie. For firft, it maketh much to the purpofe, to take thefe holie exercifes verie earneftlie & hartilie , vvith a determined , and refolued mind to doöe all that , vvhich is neceffarie for the obteining of fo pretious a ievvel, be it neuer fo difficultous or hard: for it is moft certaine, that there is nothing of importance, vvhich hath not his difficultie : and fo likevvife it happeneth in this affaire, at the left to fuch as be nouices and young beginners.

Second-

Secondlie, it helpeth alfo much to keepe the hart from all kinde of idle and vaine thoughts, from al ftraunge affections and inordinate defires, from all difturbance, & paffionate motions, for fo much as it is eui-cent, that eche one of thefe things letteth deuotion, and that it is no leffe requifite, to keepe the hart vvel tempered for praier, than to keepe an inftrument vvil tuned for playing on it.

Thirdlie, it helpeth alfo greatlie, to keepe our fenfes recollected, fpeciallie our eyes, our eares, our tounge : becaufe that by our tounge vve poure out our hart, and by our eyes & eares, vve fill the fame vvith diuers imaginations of things, vvhich trovvble the peace & quietnes of the fovvle. VVherefore it is faide vvith great reafon, that a man giuen to contemplation, muft be deafe, blinde, and dumme, for that hovv much leffe he is occupied in ovvtvvard affaires, the more fhal he be recollected vvithin him felfe.

Fourthlie, Solitarines helpeth alfo to de-uotion, for fo much a the fame doeth not onlie take avvaie occafions of diftractions from our fenfes, and from our hart the oc-cafions of finnes, but alfo it inuiteth a man to abide vvithin him felf, and to deale

K 2   vvith

vvith God, and vvith him felf alone, being
moued thereunto through the opportunitie of the place, vvhich admitteth no other
companie but this.

Fiftlie, fomtimes the reading of fpiritual
and deuoure bookes helpeth much, becaufe
they giue vs matter of confideration, they
recollect the hart, they avvaken deuotion,
& make a man vvillinglie to think of that,
vvhich hee found to be fo fvveete : and
moreouer that is alvvaies reprefented to
the memorie, that aboundeth in the hart.

Sixtelie, it much helpeth to haue a continual memorie of almightie God, to be alvvaies in his prefence, and to vfe thofe fhorte
praiers, vvhich S. Auguftine calleth iacula-
torie, or in manner of dartes, for that thefe
praiers keepe the hovvfe of the hart, and
maintaine the feruor of deuotion, as hath
ben faide before : and fo a man finde h him
felf at al times readie, and in ordre to praie.
This is one of the cheefeft documents of
fpiritual life, and one of the greateft remedies
for fuch, as haue not time, nor place to giue
them felus to praier : and vvhofoeuer fhal
haue alvvaies this care, he fhal profit much
in little time.

Seuenthlie, it helpeth to be continual,
and to perfeuer in good exercifes, at the
times

times and places ordeined, efpeciallie at night, or in the morning, vvhich be the times moft conuenient for praier, as al holy fcripture teacheth vs.

Eightlie, aufteritie and abftinence of the bodie, fober diet, lying hard, hearcloth, difcipline or vvhipping, and fuch like things help alfo much, becaufe al fuch things, as they rife out of deuotion, fo likevvife they avvaken, maintaine, and nurrifhe the roote from vvhence they firft grevv, vvhich is deuotion.

Finally, the vvoorkes of mercie help much, becaufe they giue vs hope to prefent our felues before God; they accompanie oure praiers vvith oure feruice, fo that oure praiers be not drie demaunds; and deferue that the praier be mercifallie heard, vvhich proceedeth from a merciful hart.

OF NINE THINGS THAT hinder praier.

CHAP. III.

S there be fom things that help and further deuotion, fo likevvife fom others there be that hinder the fame, emongft vvhich the firft is our finnes,

K 3   not

not onlie thofe that be mortal, but alfo venial finnes, becaufe thefe, albeit they dooe not extinguifh charitie in vs, yet dooe they flack and make cold the feruor of Charitie, vvhich is as it vvere deuotion it felf; and therefore it is reafon to auoide them vvith al care and diligence, yf not for that they dooe vs harme, at the left becaufe they hinder vs from dooing good.

Secondlie, the remorfe of confcience, vvhich proceedeth of the felf fame finnes, is a great let, vvhen it is ouergreat, becaufe it maketh the fovvle vnquiet, heauie, difmaied, and vveake to dooe anie good exercife.

Thirdlie, vvhatfoeuer greefe or difguft of minde, or inordinate afflection doth alfo hinder; becaufe the taft and fvveetenes of a good confcience, and of fpiritual comfort, can not ftand together vvith fuch things.

Fourthlie, too manie cares ar a great let, vvhich be thofe flies of Egypt, that difquiet our foule, and doe not fuffer her to take that fpiritual fleepe, vvhich is vvont to be taken in praier, but there, more then at anie other time, dooe difturbe her, and turne her from her exercife.

Fiftlie, ouermanie affaires be alfo a great hinderance, for that they take avvaie the
time,

time, and choke the ſpirite, and ſo leaue a man vvithout hart, to attend to almightie God.

Sixtlie, pleaſures and ſenſual conſolations dooe likevviſe hinder, becauſe they make ſpiritual exerciſes to ſeeme vnſauerie. And moreouer, he that is much delited vvith the conſolations of the vvoorld, deſerueth not thoſe of the holy Ghoſt, as S. Bernard ſaith.

Seuenthlie, the pleaſure in too much eating & drinking, & much more in ſumptuous bankets, ar no ſmal let, becauſe theſe be an euil diſpoſition for ſpiritual exerciſes, & holy vigils; for vvhen the bodie is heauie and charged vvith to much meate; the ſovvle is verie yl diſpoſed to flie on high.

Eightlie, the vice of curioſitie, as vvel of our ſenſes, as of our vnderſtanding, that is, a deſire to heare, ſee, and vnderſtand nouelties, is alſo a hinderance, becauſe al theſe things robbe time, diſquiet the ſovvle, and diſtract her diuers vvaies, and ſo be a let to deuotion.

Finallie, the interruption and breaking of theſe holy exerciſes, is an other hinderance, I meane, vvhen they be not left for ſom holy cauſe, or iuſt neceſſitie, for ſomuch as the ſpirite of deuotion is verie delicate,

K 4   vvhich,

vvhich, vvhen it is once departed either it
turneth no more, or at the lest vvith great
difficultie . And therfore, euen as young
plantes require theie ordinarie vvatering,
vvhich yf they vvant, they forthvvith fade
and drie vp , so likevvise falleth it out in deuotion, vvhen it vvanteth the vvatering of
deuout consideration.

Al this hath ben here spoken of so breefly , to the end it might better be kept in
memorie; the declaration vvhereof, euerie
one, that vvil, maie see by practise and long
evperience.

OF THE MOST COMMON TEN-
tations, vvhich be vvont to vvearie such
as geue them selues to praier;
and of theire remedies.

CHAP. IV.

I T shal not be amisse novv
to treate of the tentations,
most common to such per-
sons, as geue them selus to
praier, and of theire remedies; vvhich tentations be
for the most part these that folovve . The
vvant of spiritual consolations. The vvarre
of importunate thoughts. The thoughts
of blas-

of blafphemie and infidelitie. The miftruft
of going forvvard . The prefumption of
hauing greatelie profited .   Thefe be the
moft common tentations that ar in this
vaie, the remedies of vvhich be thofe that
folovve.

---

*The firft remedie , againft vvant of fpi-
ritual confolations.*

FIRST, the remedie for him that vvanteth fpiritual confolations , is , that for
this he leaue not the exercife of his accuftomed praier, although it feeme vnto him vn-
fauourie, and of fmall fruite , but rather put
him felf in the prefence of almightie God, as
guiltie and culpable , and examining his
confcience, ferche vvhither peraduenture he
loft this fauour through his ovvne fault:
and praie our lord vvith greate confidence
that he pardon him , and fhevv him the in-
eftimable riches of his patience and mercie,
in fuffering and forgeuing one, that can doe
nothing els but offend him.

In this fafhion fhal he dravv profit of his
drynes, taking occafion to humble him felf
the more , vvhen he feeth hovv much he
offendeth, and to loue God the more, confidering hovv much he forgiueth him . And
albeit

albeit he find not taſt in theſe exerciſes , let
him nŏt forſake them; becauſe it is not requi
ſite that that thing be alvvaies ſauourous,
vvhich muſt be profitable : at the leſt vviſe
this vve finde by experience, that as often
as a man perſeuereth in praier, vvith ſom
litel attention and care, dooing in this the
beſt that he is able, at the end he commeth
from thence comforted and ioyful, vvhen
he ſeeth, that of his part, he did vvhat laie
in him. It is not much to continue much in
praier, vvhen there is much conſolation.
Much it is, that vyhen there is ſmal deuotion, our praier then be much , and much
more the humilitie, and patience, and perſeuerance in dooing vvel.

It is alſo requiſite at ſuch times, to behaue
our ſelues vvith more ſollicitude and carefulnes, then at other times, vvatching vppon the gard of our ſelues, and examining
vvith good attention our thoughts ,
vvoords and deedes. For ſeeing that in this
time vve vvant ſpiritual ioie and comfort,
vvhich is the principal oare to rovve in this
nauigation, it is needeful to ſupplie vvith
care and diligence, that vvhich vvanteth of
grace . And vvhen thou ſeeſt thy ſelf in this
caſe, thou muſt make accoumpt (as S. Bernard ſaith) that the vvatches that guarded
thee,

thee, ar afleepe, & that the vvalles that defended thee, ar fallen dovvne. And therfore al
hope of thy faluation confifteth novv in
vveapons, feeing that the vvalls can no
more defend thee, but the fvvoord and dex-
teritie in fighting. O hovv greate is the
glorie of the fovvle, that fighteth in this
fort, that vvithout a fhield, defende h her
felf, vvithout vveapons, fighteth, vvithout
ftrength, is ftrong, and finding her felf alone
in the combat, taketh courage and a good
hart for her companions?

This is the principal tovvch-ftone, vvith
vvhich the finenes of frinds is vvoont to be
proued, vvhether they be true or noe.

---

*The fecond remedie, againft impor-
tunate thoughts.*

AGAINST the tentation of importunate thoughts, vvhich ar vvoont
to moleft vs in the time of praier, the remedie is to fight againft them manfullie, and
vvith perfeuerance, albeit this refiftance
muft not be vvith too much labour, and
anxietie of fpirite, becaufe this affaire confifteth not fo much in force, as it doth in
grace and humilitie. And therefore, vvhen
a man findeth him felf in this fort, he
ought

ought, vvithout anxietie (becaufe this is no fault, or els verie light) to turne him felf to God, and vvith al humilitie and deuotion fay to him in this manner.

Thou feeft heere, o lord, vvhat a one I am; and vvhat could be expected of this dungehill, but fuch euil fent? vvhat could be looked for of this ground, vvhich thou hadft curfed, but thiftles & brambles! This is the fruite vvhich it can yeeld, if thou, O lord, make it not cleane. And hauing faid thus, let him turne to goe forvvards, as he had begonne, and looke vvith patience for the vifitation of our lord, vvhich neuer vvanteth to thofe that be humble. But yf notvvithftanding all this, thefe thoughts vnquiet thee, and thou neuertheles vvith perfeuerance dooe refift them, and dooe vvhat lieth in thee, thou muft think for certaine, that thou fhalt vvinne much more by this manner of refiftance, then yf thou diddeft enioie God vvith all contentment.

The third remedie againſt tentations of blaſphemie.

FOR remedie of tentation of blafphemie, it is to be noted, that as noe kind
of ten-

of tentation is more combresom then this, so none is lesse dangerous; & so the remedie is to make no account of these tentations, for so much as sinne consisteth not in feeling of anie thing, but in consenting therevnto, and in taking pleasure of it, vvhich heere vve see is not, but rather the contrarie, & therefore this may rather be called a paine then a fault: because the farther of that a man is, to receaue ioy of these tentations, the farther of also he is, to commit anie fault in them. And therfore the remedie, as I said, is to make no accoumpt of them, neither to feare them: for vvhen vve haue to much feare of them, the feare it self avvakeneth them & stirreth them vp.

The fourth remedie against tentations of Infidelitie.

A GAINST tentations of Infidelitie the remedie is, that a man calling to minde on th'one side his ovvne basenes, & on th'other the greatenes of almightie God, he think of that vvhich God hath commaunded him, and be not curious in searching his vvoorks, forasmuch as vve see, that manie of them exceede our vnderstanding. And therefore he, that desireth to

enter

enter into this sanctuarie of Gods vvoorks, must enter vvith much humilitie and reuerence, & carie vvith him the eys of a simple doue, not of a malitious serpent; and the hart of an huble scholler, not of a rash iudge. Let him becom as a little child, for to such God doth reuele his secretes. Let him not be careful to knovv the *vvherefore*, that is the reason of Gods vvoorks; let him shut the ey of his vnderstanding, and haue open onlie the ey of faith, because this is the instrument, vvith vvhich vve ought to feele the vvoorks of God. To knovv the vvoorks of men, the ey of humane vnderstanding and vvisdom, is indeede very good, but to vnderstand the vvoorks of God, there is nothing more improportionate then is that eye. And because this tentation is ordinarilie very noisome, therefore the remedie of it, is the same of the former tentation, vvhich is, not to esteeme of it, for somuch as this tentation is rather a paine, then a fault, for in that thing there can be no fault, in vvhich the vvil taketh no pleasure, but is contrarie vnto it, as before hath ben declared.

The

The fift remedie , against tentations of diffidence
and presumption.

AGAINST the tentations of diffidence and presumption , vvhich be çotrarie vices, it behoueth vs to haue diuers remedies . For diffidence or miftruft the remedie is to confider, that this gift of praier is not to be obteined , onlie by thine ovvne ftrength and force, but by the grace of God, vvhich is gotten fo much the fooner , by hovv much a man more miftrufteth his ovvne propre forces , and trufteth onlie in the goodnes of God, by vvhich all things are poffible.

For prefumption the remedie is to confider, that there is no more euident token, that a man is far off from all goodnes , then to thinke that he is verie neere it. Behold thy felf alfo, as in a glaffe , in the life of thofe that be Sainēts , and of other excellent and vertuous perfons , that yet liue in this vvoorld, and thou fhalt eafilie fee, that in comparifon of them , thou art no other then a little dvvarfe , in comparifon of a mightie greate giant ; and fo yf thou be not fenfeles thou vvilt not prefume of thy felf.

                                                The

*The sixt remedie, against excessiue desire of spiritual
tast and consolation; and against the contempt
of such as haue them not.*

AN other tentation is, an ouergreedie
desire to haue consolations and spiritual feelings; and a contempt of others, that
haue them not. And so for remedie of this
tentation, I mind to set dovvne, vvhat end
euerie one ought to have in these spiritual
exercises. To vvhich purpose it is to be
knovven, that forasmuch as this communication vvith God is so svveete and delectable, as the vviseman saith, herehence it riseth
that manie persons dravven by the force of
this vvoonderful svveetenes, vvhich is far
surpassing vvhatsoeuer can be said of it, com
by this meanes to God, & giue them selues
to spiritual exercises, as vvel of reading,
as also of praier, and often vse of the Sacraments, for the greate tast vvhich they feele
in these things : in such sort, that the principal end, vvhich moueth them to this, is the
desire of this maruelous svveetenes. This in
deede is a greate, and vniuersal deceipt,
vvherein manie fal: forvvhereas the principal, and cheefe end of al our vvoorks, ought
to be to loue and seeke almighrie God, this
is ra-

is rather to loue, and seeke a mans ovvne
self, to vvit his ovvne tast and contentement, then God.

And that vvhich is more, of this deceipt
there folovveth an other, no lesse then it,
vvhich is, that a man iudgeth of him self
and others, according to these gustes and
feelings, and esteemeth that euerie one hath
so much lesse, or more perfection, hovv
much more, or lesse gust he hath of God,
vvhich is an exceeding great deceipt.

Novv, against these tvvo deceipts, let
this aduise and general rule be obserued, to
vvit, that euerie one knovv and vnderstand,
that the end of al these exercises, and of al
spiritual lyfe, is the obedience of Gods commaundements, and the fulfilling of his diuine vvil and pleasure, for the vvhich it is
necessarie, that our ovvne vvil die, to the
end that so the vvil of God may liue and
raigne in vs, seeing th'one is so contrarie
to the other.

But for so much as so great a victorie, as
this, can not be gotten vvithout great fauours, and comforts of God; therfore principallie it behoueth vs to exercise praier,
that by it vve may obteine these fauours,
and feele these comforts, and so bring this
affaire to a good end. And in this sort, and

L   to this

to this effect vve may demaund, and procure thofe pleafures of praier , as vve faid
before, as Dauid demaunded them vvhen

Pfalm. 51.
14.
he faid. *Reftore vnto me the gladnes of thy faluation, and confirme me vvith the principall fpirite.*

Novv , according to this , a man maie
eafilie vnderftand, vvhat ought to be th'end,
that he muft haue in thefe exercifes ; and
heerehence likevvife he fhall knovv , by
vvhat he muft efteeme , and meafure as vvel
his ovvne forvvardnes and profit , as alfo
that of others ; vvhich is , not by the feelings, that he hath receaued of God, but by
that vvhich for Gods fake he hath endured,
as vvel in doing the vvill of God, as in denying his ovvne vvill . In fo much that the
Sainéts faie right vvel, that the true proofe
of a man , is not the guft of praier , but the
patience of tribulation, the denying of him
felf, and the fulfilling of the vvill of God,
albeit for this end , as vvel praier greatlie
helpeth, as alfo the feelings and confolations
that be geauen in the fame.

Novv , conformablie to this , he that defireth to fee . hovv much he hath profited in
this vvay of God , let him confider, hovv
much he grovveth euerie daie in invvard,
and ovvtvvard humilitie ; hovv he fuppor-
teth the iniuries , donne to him by others:
hovv

hovv he beareth other mens vveakenes;
hovv he succoreth the necessities of his
neighbours; hovv he hath compassion, & is
not offended at other mens defects; hovv
he findeth him self to hope in God in time
of tribulation; hovv he ruleth his toung:
hovv he keepeth his hart; hovv he dounteth
his bodie, vvith all the appetites and senses
thereof; hovv he supporteth him self in
prosperities and aduersities: hovv he helpeth and prouideth for him self in all things,
vvith maturitie and discretion. And aboue
all this, let him consider, yf he be dead to
the loue of honor, of pleasure, and of the
vvoorld; and according to that, vvhich he
hath profited in this, or disprofited, so let
him iudge him self, and not according to
that, vvhich he feeleth, or feeleth not of
God. And therefore he ought alvvaies to
haue an eye, and this also the cheefest, to
mortification, and an other to praier,
because this verie same mortification, cannot be perfectlie obteined, but by the help
of praier.

THE

THE SECOND
TREATISE OF VO-
CAL PRAIER.

OF THE VTILITIE AND
necessitie of vocal praier.

CHAP. I.

LBEIT vocall praier
be in deede of greate
fruite, and profit at all
times, and for all kind of
states and persons, yet
particularlie it serueth for
such, as dooe not geeve
them selus vvel to th'exercise of meditation,
vvhereof vve haue vvriten in the former
treatise. For to such, as hath ben alredie
said, vocall praiers doe serue verie much, &
more particularlie for those, that dooe not
vnderstand laten. For vvhome this treatise
shal serue as a deuocionarie, in vvhich they
maie exercise and stirre vp theire deuotion.
And for this also, the doctrine of the former
treatise maie serue, in vvhich those things,
ar handled, that help deuotion, and those
also,

alfo , that hinder the fame ; that by this meanes a man maie procure the one , and quite him felf of the others that be contrarie, and fo vvith th'one and other treatife, furtherand augmenthis deuotion.

And after that he fhall haue fom daies cōtinued thefe praiers, yf he find conuenienttime, he maie exercife him felf in mentall praier, thatis in thofe confiderations, vvhichhaue ben fet dovvne in the meditations of the former treatife ; that in this manner vve maie goe by little , and little mounting vp from that vvhich iseafie , to that vvhich is more difficultous andhard.

This little preamble then prefuppofed, vve vvil begin to laie dovvne heere certaine praiers, amongft vvhichthefe feuen , that folovv, fhall haue the firft place, and eche of them ferueth to obtaine fom particular vertue, andgrace of our lord, as by them fhall appeere. And thefe feuen praiers maie be diuided , according to the feuen daies of the vveeke, that is , to eche daie his praier; and after that thefe be ended, a man maie exercife him felf in others, as his deuotion fhall require.

A PREAMBLE TO THE PRAIERS
that folovv, treating of the preparation, and
mind, vvith vvhich they muſt
be made.

CHAP. II.

prou.23.1

WHEN *thou ſhalt ſitte* (ſaith the vvise man) *to eate vvith a Prince, conſider diligentlie thoſe things, that ar ſet before thy face:* that thereby thou maiſt knovv vvhat thou oughteſt to prepare for thy parte. And conformablie to this document, let him that commeth to treate vvith almightie God in praier, firſt of al fixe his eys vppon our lord, vvith vvhome he goeth to treate, and conſider vvith greate attention, vvhat, and vvhoe he is; becauſe ſuch a one as he is, vvhome he repreſenteth to him ſelf, ſuch a hart & affects it behoveth that he haue tovvards him. Let him then lift vp his eyes on high vvith al humilitie, and behold God ſitting in the throne of his maieſtie, aboue al vvhatſoeuer is created, and let him conſi-
Apocal.
19. 16.
der hovv this is he, vvhoe hath vvriten *in his garment, and in his thigh, king of kings, and lord of lords;* & alſo hovv he is infinitelie perfect,
beau-

beautiful, glorious, good, merciful, iust, terrible, and admirable; likevvise hovv he is a most kind father, a most liberall benefactor, and a most genteel Redeemer and Sauiour. And after that he hath considered him in this sorte let him forthvvith think vvith vvhat vertues, and affects he ought of his part to be ansvverable to these titles; and he shall find, that for asmuch as he is God, he deserueth to be adored, because he is infinitelie perfect and glorious, to be praised; because he is good and beautiful, to be beloued; because he is terrible and iust, to be feared; because he is lord and king of all things, to be obeyed; in respect of his benifits, he deserueth infinite benedictions, and thanks; because he is our Creator and Redeemer, he deserueth that vve offer him al that vve ar, seeing all is his: and because he is our helper and Sauiour, it behoueth that of him onlie vve seeke remedie for all our necessities.

These and such other like actes of vertues, ovveth a reasonable Creature to those titles, and greatenes of his Creator. These be the vertues, and these the affects, vvith vvhich vve must of our part be ansvverable, and honour this lord, vvhoe as he is all things, so vvill he be vvorshipped and respected

L 4   pected

pected vvith all thefe affects and feelings;
vvhich, although thev be vertualiie exercifed and found in all thofe vvoorks, vvhich
be donne for his loue, yet more excellentlie
thev be exercifed in praier.

And this is one of the greateft prerogatiues that praier hath, being made as it ought
to be, that in the fame be found the acts of
al thefe moft noble vertues, Faith, Hope,
Charitie, Humilitie, Religion, Feare of
God, and other fuch, as vve fhall euidentlie fee in the praiers folovving, vvhich
conteine all this, and therefore it behoueth,
that they be greatlie efteemed of, and exercifed vvith much deuotion and repofe of
mind.

THE

THE FIRST PRAIER, FOR THE
firſt daie of the vveeke, vvhich ſerueth to ſtirre
vp in our ſovvle a holie feaxe of God, by
conſidering thoſe things that induce vs thereunto.

CHAP. III.

F that publican of the *Luc.* 18.
ghoſple, vvas not ſo bold 13.
as to lift vp his eys to heauen, but ſtanding a far of,
did ſtrike his breſt and ſaid,
God be merciful to me a ſinner:
and yf that holy vvoman a ſinner, vvas not *Luc.*7.37.
ſo hardy as to preſent her ſelf before the face
of our lord, but going behind him, did caſt
her ſelf dovvne at his feete, and vvith the
teares of her eys, obteined pardon of her
ſinnes; and yf the holie Patriarch Abraham, *Genes.* 18.
deſyring to ſpeake vnto thee, ſaid, *I vvil* 27.
ſpeake vnto my lord, albeit I be duſt and aſhes: yf
theſe, I ſaie, vvere ſo lovvlie & humble,
vvhen they preſented them ſelues before
thy maieſtie, being yet ſuch perſons as they
vvere, vvhat ſhall one ſo poore & miſerable a ſinner, as I am, doe? vvhat ſhall durt
and aſhes dooe? vvhat ſhall the bottomles
deepnes of all ſinnes and miſeries dooe?
                                    But

But because I am not able, o lord, to obteine that feare and reuerence, vvhich is due vnto thy maiestie, vvithout casting mine eyes vppon the same; giue me leaue that I may be so bould as to lift vp mie bleare eyes, in such sort, that the brightnesse of thy glorie, doe not dasel the vveakenes of my sight. And for so much as the beginning of true vvisdome, is the feare of thy holy name, vvith this, o lord, haue I a desire to beginne novv.

Giue me then grace, o my lord, my God, and vouchsafe to povvre into my soule the gift of feare, by the meanes of thy holy spirite; for vvithout it, al the considerations, that I am able to alleage heere, vvil little auaile me; because to this feare thou didst *Luc. 12. 4* exhort vs, vvhen thou didst saie. *Be not afraid of them that kill the body, and after this haue no more to doe. But I vvil shevv you vvhome ye shall feare: feare him vvho after he hath killed, hath povver to cast into hel, yea I say to you, feare him.* This self same the holie Church teacheth *In festo S. Michaelis.* vs, vvhen she saith. *Be not afraid in the presence of nations. But adore and feare ye God in your harts, because his Angel is vv.th you to deliuer you.* Let my sovvle then, o lord, and my hart feare thee, seeing in thee, vvhoe art al things, there is no les reason vvhere-

vvherefore to feare thee, then to loue thee. For as thou art in deede infinitelie merciful, fo art thou infinitelie iuſt, & as the vvoorks of thy mercie be innumerable, fo be alfo the vvoorks of thy iuſtice, and, that vvhich is much more to be feared, the veſſels of vvrath be vvithout comparifon moe, then the veſſels of mercie; for fomuch as thofe that be damned, ar fo manie; & thofe that be ſaued, fo fevve. Let me then, o lord, feare thee, for the greatnes of thy iuſtice, for the deepenes of thy iudgments, and for the highnes of thy maieſtie, for the immenſitie of thy greatnes, for the number of my ſinnes and offences, and aboue al, for the continual reſiſtance againſt thy holy infpirations. Let me feare thee, and tremble before thee, before vvhofe face the povvers doe tremble, the pillers of heauen, yea and al the vvhole compaſſe of the earth doe quake. VVhoe then, O king of nations, vvil not feare thee? vvhoe vvil not tremble at thofe vvoords, vvhich thou thy felf haſt ſpoken by thy Prophet. *Vvil you not then feare me, and before mie face vvil you not be foroyvful? vvhoe haue fet the fands a bound to the fea, and an eternal commaundement vvhich he ſhal not paſſe? and they ſhal be moued and ſhal not be able, and his vvaues ſhall fvvelle, and ſhall not paſſe ouer it.* Ierem. 5. 22.

Yf

Yf then al the creatures of heauen & earth, doe in this manner obey and feare thee, for the greatnes of thie maiestie, vvhat shall I doe, most vile sinner, dust and ashes? yf the Angels tremble, vvhen they adore thee, and sing thie praises, vvherefore doe not mie lippes and mie hart tremble, vvhen I am so bold as to doe this office? O miserable vvretch that I am! hovv is mie sovvle becom so hard? hovv ar the fountaines of mine eys dried vp, that they povvre not out abūdance of teares, vvhen the seruant speaketh vvith his lord, the creature vvith his Creator, man vvith God, he that vvas made of slime and cley, vvith him that made al of nothing? more I vvould saie, but I am not able, because I can not doe al that I desire. *Thou, o lord, fasten vvith thie feare mie flesh;* let mie hart reioice, that it may feare thy holy name.

Let me also feare thee, o lord, for the greatnes of thie iudgments, vvhich thou hast shevved from the beginning of the vvoorld vntil this daie. A greate iudgment vvas the fall of that Angel, so principall and so beautifull. A greate iudgment vvas the fall of all mankind, for the fault committed by one. A greate iudgment vvas the punishment of the vvhole vvoorld, by the

Psal. 118.
120.

Isai. 14.
2. Petr. 2.
Gen. 3.

Gen. 7.

vvaters

vvaters of the diuge . A greate iudgment
vvas the election of Iacob, & the reprobation of Esau; the forsaking of Iudas, and
the vocation of S. Paul ; the reprobation
of the Ievves , and the election of the Gen-
tiles; vvith other suchlike vvounders, vvhich
dailie passe ouer mens heads and yet ar vn-
knovven to vs . And aboue al this , a most
dreadfull iudgement it is , to see so manie
nations vppon the face of the earth, to be
in the countrey & shadovv of death, and
in the darknes of infidelitie , going from
one darknes to an other, and from temporal paines to eternal torments . Let me
then feare thee, o lord, for the greatnes of
these iudgments, seeing I knovv not, as yet,
vvhither I shalbe one of these forsaken, or 1. Pet. 4.
noe. For *yf the iust shall scarse be saued, the sinner* 18.
and vvicked vvhere shall he appeare? yf that innocent man Iob , trembled at the furie of
thie vvrath, as at the violence of the sour-
ging vvaues, hovv shal not he be afraid
& tremble, that seeth him self so far of from
this innocencie ? yf the Prophet Ieremie
trembled being sanctified in the vvombe,
and found no corner vvere to hide him self,
because he vvas full of the feare of thie anger, vvhat shall he dooe, that came from
his mothers vvombe vvith sinne, and hath
since

since that time committed so manie, and so
gteat sinnes? Let me feare thee also, o lord,
for the innumerable multitude of mie sinnes, vvith vvhich I must appeare before
thy iudgment, vvhen before thie face there
shall com that burning fiar, and round a-
bout thee a boisterous tempest; vvhen thou
shalt assemble heauen and earth together,
to iudge thy people. There, then, before
so manie thovvsands of nations, shal be discouered my vvickednes; before so manie
quiars of Angels, shal be diuulged my sinnes, not onlie those committed by vvoords
and vvoorks, but those also committed by
thoughts. VVhere I shall haue as manie for
my iudges, as haue gone before me by example of good vvoorkes; and so manie shall be
vvitnesses against me, as haue giue me presi-
dents of vertues. And yet expecting this
iudgment, I cease not to giue bridell to my
vices, but rather more & more I lie rotting,
and corrupting in the dregges of my sinnes;
stil glutonie maketh me vile, pride maketh
me vaine, couetousnes maketh me niggesh,
enuie consumeth me, murmuration teareth
me in peeces, ambition puffeth me vp, anger
trovvbleth me, lightnes of maners dravveth
me out of my self, sluggishnes benumeth
me, heauines casteth me dovvne, and fauour
lifteth

lifteth me vp. Thou feeft heere the companions, vvith vvhich I haue liued frō the daie of mie childhood, vntil this prefent time; thefe be the friends, vvith vvhome I haue cōuerfed; thefe the maifters, that I haue obeied; thefe the lords, vvhich I haue ferued, *Enter not* therfore, o lord, *into iudgment vvith thy feruant, becaufe no man liuing fhall be iuftified before thee:* for vvhoe is he that fhal be found iuft, yf thou vvouldeft iudge him vvithout pitie? for this then, o lord, proftrating my felf at thy feete, vvith an humble and contrite fpirite, I vvil vveepe vvith the Prophet, and faie. *Lord rebuke me not in thy furie; nor chaften me in thy vvrath. Haue mercie vppon me, lord, becaufe I am vveake; heale me, lord, becaufe mie bones ar trovvbled. And mie fovvle is verie much trovvbled; but thou, lord, hovv long? Be thou conuerted, lord, and deliuer my fovvle; faue me for thy mercie. Becaufe there is none in death, that is mindful of thee; and in hel, vvhoe vvill confeffe vnto thee? I haue laboured in my figh, I fhall euerie night vvafh mie bed; vvith my teares fhall I vveat mie couche. Mine eye is troubled vvith furie, I am vvaxen old among al mine enimies.* Glorie be to the father, and to the fonne, and to the holie ghoft; As it vvas in the beginning, and novv, and euer, and vvoorld vvithout end. Amen.

Pfal. 142. 2.

Pfalm. 6.

THE

THE SECOND PRAIER, FOR THE
second daie, of the praifes of God.

CHAP. IIII.

I N this exercife of feare and penance; it behoued me, o lord, to fpend all mie life; feeing I haue fo iuft caufe vvherefore to feare, and vvherfore to lament. Yet notvvithftanding al this, as the greatnes of thie glorie obligeth vs, to vvorfhip & reuerence thee; fo like vife doth it binde vs to praife and glorifie thee, becaufe to thee onlie is due a hymne, and praife in Sion, thou being in deede, as thou art, a paffing great deepenes of al perfections, and a maine fea of vvifdom, of omnipotencie, of beuvtie, of riches, of greatnes, of fvveetenes, of maieftie; in vvhome be all the perfections, and bevvties of all creatures in heauen and in earth, and thofe alfo all in the higheft degree of perfection. In comparifon of vvhich, al bevvtie, is foulnes; all riches, ar pouretie; al povver, is vveakenes; al vvifdom, is ignorance; all fvveetenes, is bitternes; and finallie all, vvhatfoeuer vve fee in heauen and in earth, is much les before

fore thee, then is a little candel, in comparison of the sunne.

Thou art vvithout deformitie, perfect; vvithout quantitie, great; vvithout qualitie, good; vvithout vveaknes, strong; vvithout place, al vvheresoeuer thou vvilt; in vertue, omnipotent; in goodnes, highest; in vvisdom, inestimable; in thy counsels, terrible; in thy iudgments, iust; in thy thoughts, most secreat; in thy vvoords, true; in thy vvoorks, holy; in thy mercies, abundant; vvith sinners, most patient; and vvith those that be penitent, most pitiful. Therfore, o lord, for such a one I dooe confesse, and acknovvledge thee; for such a one I dooe praise thee, & glorifie thy holy name. Giue thou me light in my hart, and vvoords in my mouth, that my hart may think of thy glorie; and my mouth be ful of thy praises. But for somuch as *praise is not beautiful in the* *Eccl.* 15. 9. *mouth of a sinner*, I request all the Angels of heauen, and al the creatures of the vvoorld, that they together vvith me praise thee, and supplie in this behalfe my faults; inuiting them to this, vvith that glorious canticle, vvhich those holy children did sing vnto thee, amiddest the flames of fiar in the fornace of Babilon saying. *Blessed art thou, o lord* *Daniel.* 3. *god of our fathers, and praised, and superexalted*

M   *for*

for euer . And bleſſed is the holie name of thie glorie, and praiſed , and ſuperexalted for euer . Bleſſed art thou in the holie temple of thie glorie, and ſuperpraiſed, and ſuperglorious for euer . Bleſſed art thou in the throne of thie kingdom , and ſuperpraiſed , and ſuperexalted for euer. Bleſſed art thou that beholdeſt the deapths , and ſitteſt vppon the Cherubines , and praiſed , and ſuperexalted for euer . Bleſſed art thou in the firmament of heauen, & praiſed, and glorious for euer . All the vvoorks of our lord , bleſſe our lord, praiſe and exalt him for euer . Angels of our lord, bleſſe our lord , praiſe and ſuperexalt him for euer. Heauens bleſſe our lord , praiſe and ſuperexalt him for euer. All vvaters that be aboue the heauens, bleſſe our lord, praiſe and ſuperexalt him for euer. All ver-tues of our lord, bleſſe our lord, praiſe and ſuperexalt him for euer. Sunne and moone bleſſe our lord, praiſe and ſuperexalt him for euer . Stars of heauen bleſſe our lord , praiſe and ſuperexalt him for euer . All raine and devve bleſſe our lord , praiſe and ſuperexalt him for euer . Al ſpirits of God bleſſe our lord, praiſe and ſuperexalt him for euer . Fiar and heate bleſſe our lord, praiſe and ſuperexalt him for euer. VVinter and ſommer bleſſe our lord, praiſe and ſuperexalt him for euer. Moiſtures and hore froſt bleſſe our lord, praiſe and ſuperexalt him for euer . Froſt and cold bleſſe our lord , praiſe and ſuperexalt him for euer. Yſe and ſnovve bleſſe our lord , praiſe and ſuperexalt him for euer. Nights & daies bleſſe our lord, praiſe and

and superexalt him for euer. *Light and darknes blesse our lord, praise and superexalt him for euer. Lightnings and clovvdes blesse our lord, praise and superexalt him for euer. Let the earth blesse our lord, let it praise and superexalt him for euer.* Mountaines and hillocks *blesse our lord, praise and superexalt him for euer. All things that spring vppon the earth blesse our lord, praise and superexalt him for euer.* VVelles *blesse our lord, praise & superexalt him for euer. Seas & riuers blesse our lord, praise & superexalt him for euer.* VVhales, *& all things that be moued in the vvaters, blesse our lord, praise and superexalt him for euer. All byrds of the arre blesse our lord, praise and superexals him for euer.* Children *of men blesse our lord, praise & superexalt him for euer.* Let Israel *blesse our lord, let him praise & superexalt him for euer.* Priests *of our lord, blesse our lord, praise and superexalt him for euer. Seruants of our lord, blesse our lord, praise and superexalt him for euer.* Spirites *and sovvles of iust men, blesse our lord, praise and superexalt him for euer. Holie and humble of hart, blesse our lord, praise and superexalt him for euer.* Glorie be to the father, and to the sonne, and to the holie ghost: as it vvas in the beginning, and novv, and euer, and vvoorld vvithout end, Amen.

M 2   THE

THE THIRD PRAIER, FOR THE
third daie, to giue thanks to God for
his benifits.

CHAP. V.

I LIKE-vvise giue thee thanks, o lord, for all the benifits & fauours, vvhich I haue receaued of thee, since the time that I vvas cōceiued, vntil this present daie, & for the loue, vvhich from al eternitie thou hast borne me, vvhen euen from the same, thou didst determine to create me, to redeeme me, to make me thine, & to giue me al that, vvhich hitherto thou hast geauen me, for somuch as al that I haue, or may hope to haue, is thine. Thine is my bodie, vvith al the parts and senses of the same; thine is my sovvle, vvith al her habilities and povvers; thine be al the hovvers and minutes, that hitherto I haue liued; thine is the streangth and health, vvhich thou hast geauen me; thine is heauen, and the earth vvhich susteineth me; thine is the sunne and the moone, the stars and the feelds, the fovvles and the fishes, the beasts and al other creatures, vvhich at thy commaundement serue me. Al this, o my lord, is thine,
and

and for the fame I geaue thee as mane
thanks, as I am able to giue thee . Neuertheles, much greater thanks I yeeld thee,
that thou thie felf haft vouchfafed to becom
mine , feeing that for my remedie, thou
haft offred and geauen all thie felf; in fo
much that for me thou vvaft clothed vvith
fleafh; for me thou vvaft borne in a ftall;
for me thou vvaft reclined in a manger; for
me thou vvaft fvvadled in poore cloutes; for
me thou vvaft circumcifed the eight daie:
for me thou didft flie into Egypt ; for me
thou vvaft in fo diuers forts tempted, perfecuted, yl vfed, fcourged, crovvned vvith
thornes, difhonoured, iudged to death, and
nailed vppon a croffe ; for me thou dideft
faft, praie, vvatch, vveepe, and fuffer the
greateft torments and outrages , that euer
vvere fuffed . For me thou didft ordeine,
and dreffe the medicines of thy facraments,
vvith the liquor of thie pecious blovvd,
and principallie the cheefeft of all the Sacraments, vvhich is that of thie moft facred
bodie (vvherein thou, o mie God, art conteined) for mie reparation, for mie mainte-
nance, for mie ftrength , for mie delices, for
a pledge of mie hope , and for a teftimonie
of thie loue . For al this I yeeld thee as
great, and as manie thanks as I can giue

M 3   thee

thee, saying, from the bottom of mie hart,
with the Prophet Dauid, Blesse o mie sovvle
our lord, and al those things that ar vvithin me,
his holie name. Blesse o mie sovvle our lord, and
forget not all his fauours. VVhoe hath pitie of all
thy iniquities, and healeth all thy diseases. VVhoe
deliuereth from death thy life, vvhoe crovvneth the
in mercie and compassions. VVhoe filleth thy desire
in goods, thy youth shal be renued as that of an
eagle. Our lord is dooing mercie, and iudgment to
all that suffer iniurie. He made his vvaies knovven
to Moises, to the children of Israel his vvils. Our
lord is merciful and pitiful, long-suffering, and
veriemerciful. He vvil not be angrie for euer, neither for euer vvil hee threaten. He hath not dealt
vvith vs according to our sinnes, neither according
to our iniquities hath he revvarded vs. Because according to the height of heauen from earth, hath
be confirmed his mercie vppon those that feare him.
As far as the east is distant from the vveast, hath he
made far from vs our iniquities. Euen as a father
hath compassion of his sonnes, our lord hath had
compassion of such as feare him, because he knovveth our vvoorkmanshippe. He remembred that
vve ar dust; a man as the grasse, so ar his daies, as
the flouer of the filde, so shall he fade. Because his
spirite shall passe avvaie in him, and shall not remaine, and shall not knovve anie more his place.
But the mercie of our lord from euer, and euen for
euer

Psal. 102.

euer vppon thosethat feare him. And his iustice vppon the sonnes of sonnes, to those that keepe his testament. And ar mindfull of his cōmandements, to fulfil them. Our lord hath prepared his seate in heauen, and his kingdom shall ouerrule all. All Angels blesse our lord, that be mightie of porver, and dooe his vvoord, to obey the voice o' his speeches. Blesse ye our lord al his vertues; you his ministres that dooe his vvill. Blesse our lord all his vvoorks, and in euerie place of his soueraigntie, blesse thou, o mie sovvle, our lord. Glorie be to the father, and to the sonne &c.

THE FOVVERTH PRAIER, FOR the fouerth daie, of the loue of God.

CHAP. VI.

AND yf vve be so greathe bound to our benefactours by reason of theire benifits, yf euerie benefit be as it vvere a fiarbrand, and a prouokement to loue, and yf according to the great quantitie of vvoode, the fiar is also great that is kindled in it; hovv great then should the fiar of loue be, that ought to burne in my hart, seeing the vvoode of thy benifits is so greate, and

M 4　　so ma-

so manie the prouokements that I haue of
loue? yf al this vvorld visible & inuisible be
for me; ought not, by al reason, the flame,
of loue that should rise thereof, to be as
greate as it? And speciallie I ought to loue
thee, because in thee onlie, ar to be found al
the reasons and causes of loue, that be in al
creatures, and those also in the highest degree of perfection. For yf vve speake of
goodnes, vvhoe is more good then thou? yf
of beautie, vvhoe is more beautiful then
thou? yf of svveetnes and benignitie, vvhoe
is more svveete and bening then thou? yf
of riches and vvisdome, vvhoe is more riche
and more vvise then thou? yf of loue, vvhoe
hath euer loued more, then he that so much
suffered for our sakes? yf of benifits, vvhose
is al that vve haue, but thine? yf of hope,
of vvhome dooe vve hope to haue vvhatsoeuer vve neede, yf not of thie mercie? yf
to our parents vve naturallie ought to beare
great loue, vvhoe is more our father, then he

Math. 23.
9. that saith. *Cal none father to your self vppon
earth, for one is your father, he that is in heauen?*
Yf the bridegromes ar beloued vvith soe
great loue, vvhoe is the bridegrome of my
fovvle, but thou; and vvhoe filleth the bo-
some of my hart, and of my desires but thou?
yf the last end, as the Philosophors say, is
beloued

beloued vvith infinite loue ; vvhoe is my
beginning, & my laſt end but thou ? vvhēce
came I, and vvhither goe I to repoſe, but
to thee? vvhoſe is that vvhich I haue, and of
vvhome muſt I receaue that vvhich I neede,
but of thee ? finallie yf likeneſſe be cauſe
of loue, to vvhoſe image and reſemblance
vvas mie ſovvle created, but to thine? This
is euidentlie knovven by her manner of
operation , for vvhere there is like manner
of operation, there is alſo like manner of
being : and this, o lord , is ſo betvvixt thee
and man ; for no other thing is that vvhich
the Philoſophers ſaie, that *art doth imitate na-*
ture, and nature art, but to ſaie that man doth
vvoork as God, and God as man . VVhere
then there is ſo great likelihood in vvoor-
king, there is alſo in being. If therfore this
title, and eche one of the reſt by it ſelf, be
ſo ſufficient a motiue of loue; vvhat a motiue behoueth that to be, that procedeth of
all theſe titles together ? Trulie that vantage vvhich the vvhole maine ſea hath , in
reſpect of eche one of thoſe riuers that enter into it , the ſame it behoued alſo that
this loue ſhould haue, in reſpect of al other
loues.

Yf then , o mie lord and mie God, I haue
ſo manie cauſes to loue thee, vvherfore ſhal
I not

I not loue thee vvith all my hart, & vvith all
my bovvels? O all my hope! o the most beloued of all beloueds! O florishing spovvse!
svveete spovvse! honie-svveete spovvse! O
my louing beginning, & my highest sufficie-
encie, vvhen shal I loue thee vvith al my forces, & vvith all my soule? vvhen shal I be a-
greeable to thee in al things? vvhen shall all
that die, vvhich in me is contrarie to thee?
vvhen shal I be vvholie thine? vvhen shal I
leaue to be mine ovvne? vvhe shal nothing
beside thee liue in me? vvhen shall all the
flame of thy loue burne me? vvhen vvilt
thou rauish, drovvne, and transport me into
thee? vvhen vvilt thou take avvaie all impediments & disturbance, & make me one spirite vvith thee, in such sort, that I may neuer
more depart from thee? Ah good Lord,
vvhat doth it cost thee to doe me so great
good? vvhat doest thou quite of thy house?
vvhat dost thou lose of thy substáce? vvherfore then, o lord, thou being a sea of infinite
liberalitie & clemencie, doest thou reteine
in thine anger thy mercies tovvardes me?
vvherfore shal my vvickednes ouercom thy
goodnes? vvherfore shal my faults be a grea
ter occasion to códemne me, then thy goodnes to saue me? if in steede of sorovv & penance, it please thee to accept of it, I am so
much

much difcontented to haue offended thee,
that I vvould rather haue endured a thovvfand deaths, then haue committed anie one
offence againft thee. If in fteede of fatisfa-
&tion thou pleafe to take it, behold here this
my miferable bodie; execute, o lord, vppon
it al the furie of thy vvrath, vvith this condition, that thou doe not depriue me of thie
loue. I requeft not at thie hands gold nor
filuer, I demaund not of thee heauen nor
earth, nor anie other thing created, becaufe
all this can not fatiate me vvithout thee,
and all to me is but pouertie, vvithout thie
loue. Loue I defire, loue I requeft at thie
hands, loue I demand thee, for thie loue dooe
I fufpire, graunt me thie loue, and it fuffifeth
me. VVherfore, o lord, doeft thou fo much
differre me this fauour? vvherfore doeft thou
fee me languifh daie and night, and doeft
not fuccor me? Hovv long o lord vvilt thou
forget me? hovv long vvilt thou turne thie
face avvaie from me? hovv long fhall mie
fovvle goe vvauering vvith fo great anxietie and defire? Behold me, o mie lord, and
haue mercie vppon me. I demaund not of
thee that copious portion, vvhich is giuen
to children; I vvil content mie felf vvith
one onlie little crumbe of thofe, that come
from thie table. Heere then I prefent mie
felf

felf as a poore, and hungrie little vvhelp before thy riche table; heere I ftand beholding thee in theface and confidering hovv thou doeft eate, and doeft giue to eate to thy children, vvith the repaft of thy glorie. Heere I ftand changing a thovvfand formes, and figures in my hart, and this to bend dovvne thy hart, that thou take compaffion of me. The things of this vvoorld, o lord, doe not fil me, thee onlie I long for, thee I feeke, thy face, o lord, I defire, & thy loue vvil I alvvaies demand, and fing vvith thy Prophet. *I vvil loue thee o lord my fortitude; our lord is mie ftaie, and my refuge, and he that deliuereth me. My God, my helper, & I vvil hope in him; my protector, and the horne of my faluation, and my receauer. Praifing I vvil cal vppon our lord, and from my enemies I fhal be fafe.* Glorie be to the father and to the fonne, &c.

Pfalm. 17.

THE FIFT PRAIER, FOR THE
fift daie, of hope in God.

CHAP. VII.

 ETHER doth all this, onlie bind me to loue thee, but alfo to put all my hope in thee alone, for in vvhome ought I to haue

haue hope, if not in one that so much loue'h
me, and in one that hath donne me so much
good, and in one that hath suffred so much
for me, and in one that hath so oftentimes
called me, expected me, tolerated me, for-
geauen me, and deliuered me from so manie
euils? In vvhome ought I to hope, but in
him that is infinitelie merciful, pitiful, louing, gentle, suffering and pardoning? In
vvhome ought I to hope, but in him that is
my father, and my father almightie, father
to loue me, and almightie to remedie me;
father to vvish me vvel, and almightie to
doe me good; vvhoe hath more care and
prouidence of his spiritual children, then
anie carnal father of his natural children.
Finallie in vvhome ought I to hope, but in
him, that almost in al his holie scriptures,
repeateth nothing more, then commaun-
ding me that I approche to him, and hope
in him, and promiseth me a thovvsand fauours and revvards yf I doe so; giauing me
for paune of al this his veritie and his vvord,
his benifits bestovved vpdon me, his torments endured for me, and his bloud vvhich
he hath shed in confirmation of this truth,
vvhat is there then, that I maie not hop:
of so good a God, and so true; of a God that
hath so much loued me, that he vouchsafed
to be

to be clod vvith fleaſh for me; and ſuffered
ſcourging, pinching, and buffeting for me;
& finallie of a God, that did let him ſelf die
vppen a Croſſe for me; and encloſed him
ſelf in a ſacred hoſt for me? Hovv can he flie
from me, vvhen I ſeeke him, vvhoe hath ſo
ſought me, vvhen I fled from him? Hevv
can he denie me pardon, vvhen I ſeeke it at
his hands, vvhoe hath commaunded me
that I requeſt it of him? Hovv can he denie
me remedie, vvhich novv coſteth him nothing, vvhoe procured me the ſame, vvhen
it did coſt him ſo deerelie? for altheſe rea-
ſons then, I vvil confidentlie hope in him,
and vvith the holy Prophet, in al my tribulations and neceſſities I vvil hartilie ſing.

Pſal. 26.   *Our lord is mie light, and mie ſaluation, vvhome*
ſhal I feare? Our lord is the protector of mie life,
at vvhome ſhal I tremble? yf armies ſhal
ſtand againſt me, my hart, ſhal not feare.
If vvar ſhal riſe againſt me, in him
vvil I hope. Glorie be to
the father, and to
theſonne, &c.

THE SIXT PRAIER FOR THE SIXT
daie, of Obedience.

CHAP. VIII.

VT for afmuch as hope is
not fecure vvithout Obe-
dience (according to that
vvhich the Pfalmift faith,
Sacrifice ye facrifice of iuftice, Pfal.4.6.
and hope ye in our lord) giue
thou me, o my God, that vvith this hope in
thy mercie, I ioine the obedience of thy holy commaundements, feeing that I no leffe
ovve thee this Obedience, then all other
vvhatfoeuer vertuous affects; becaufe thou
art my king, my lord, my Emperour, to
vvhome the heauen, the earth, the fea and
al creatures obey, vvhofe commaundements
and lavves they haue hitherto kept, and
vvil obferue for euer. Let me then, o lord,
obey thee more then they al, for fomuch as
I am more obliged thereunto then they.
Let me obey thee, o my king, and obferue
entirelie all thy moft holie layves. Reigne
thou in me, o lord, and let not the vvoorld
reigne in me anie more, nor the Prince of
the vvoorld, nor mie flefh, nor mine ovvne
propre vvill but thine. Let all thefe tyrans
depart

depart out of me, that be vsurpers of thy
seate, theeues of thy glorie, corrupters of
thy iustice, and doe thou onlie, o lord, commaund and ordeine, and let onlie thou, and
thy sceptre be acknovvledged, and obeyed:
that so thy vvil maie be donne in earth,
as it is fulfilled in heauen. O vvhen shall
this daie be! O vvhen shall I see my self free
from these tyrans! O vvhen shall there be
heard in my sovvle none other voice, but
thine! O vvhen shal the forces, and pykes of
mie enimies be so subiected, that I find no
contradiction in my self, to fulfil thy holy
vvil and pleasure! O vvhen shall this boi-
strous & tempestuous sea be so calme, vvhen
shall this heauen be so faire and vnclovvdie,
vvhen shall mie passions be so quiet and
mortified, that there be neither vvaue, nor
clovvde; nor noise, nor anie other perturba-
tion, that maie alter, and chaunge this peace
and obedience, and hinder this thie kingdom in me? Giue thou me, o lord this obedience, or to saie better, this soueraignt e
ouer mie hart, that in such sort it maie obey
me, that in al things I maie subiect the same
to thee : and being in this subiection, I
maie saie vvith al mie hart as the Prophet
said *Set me o lord for a lavv, the vvaie of thy iusti-*
fications, and I vvil search it out alvvaies. Giue me

Psal. 118.
33.

vnder-

vnderstanding, and I vvil seeke thie lavv, and vvil keepe it vvith al mie hart. Guide me in the pathe of thy commaundements, because I haue desired the same. Incline my hart to thy testimonies, and not to auarice. Turne avvay mine eys that they see not vanitie, in thy vvaie quicken me. Glorie be to the father, and to the sonne, and to the holie ghost, &c.

THE SEVENTH PRAIER, FOR THE
seuenth daie, in vvhich a man offereth him self,
and al things that he hath, to God.

CHAP. IX.

VEN so as I am bound, o lord, to obey thee, am I also bound to resigne, and offer my self into thy hands, because I am a together thyne, & thyne by so manie and soe iust titles. Thyne, because thou hast created me, and giuen me this being that I haue : thyne, because thou doest maintaine me in this being, vvith so manie benifits and fauours of thy prouidence : thyne, because thou hast redeemed me out of captiuitie, & hast bought me, not vvith gold nor siluer, but vvith thine ovvne bloud; and thine, because so manie other

N   times

times thou haſt redeemed me, hovv manie
times thou haſt dravven me out of ſinne. Yf
then by ſo manie titles & claimes I be thine,
and yf thou for ſo manie reſpects be mie
king, mie lord, mie Redeemer, and mie de-
liuerer, heere I turne to reſigne into thie
hands thie ſubſtance, vvhich I my ſelf am;
heere I offer mie ſelf to be thie ſclaue and
captiue; heere I giue vp the kaies and o-
mage of mie vvill, to th'end that hencefor-
vvard I be no more mine ovvne, nor of
anie other, but thine; that I liue not, but
for thee; nor doe no more mine ovvne vvill,
but thine, in ſuch ſort, that I nether eate, nor
drinke, nor ſleepe, nor doe anie other thing,
vvhich is not according to thee, and for
thee. Heere doe I preſent mie ſelf to thee,
that thou diſpoſe of me, as of thine ovvne
ſubſtance, as it beſt pleaſeth thee. Yf it like
thee that I liue, that I dye, that I be in health,
that I be ſick, that I be riche, that I be poore,
that I be honoured, that I be diſhonoured,
to all I offer mie ſelf, and reſigne my ſelf
into thie hands, and I diſpoſſeſſe me of mie
ſelf, that I be novv no more mine ovvne,
but thine, in ſo much, that vvhat is thine by
iuſtice and right, be alſo thine by mie vvill.
But vvhoe, o lord, can doe anie of theſe
things vvithout thee? vvhoe can make as
                                    much

much as one steppe vvithout thee ? Giue
me therfore grace, o lord, to doe that vvhich
thou commaundest, and commaund vvhatfoeuer it pleafeth thee. Remember, o lord,
that thou thy felf haft commaūded vs moft
inftantlie, that vve fhould afk thee, faying:
*Afke, and it fhal be giuen you; feeke and you fhal
finde; knocke and it fhal be opened to you.* Thou   Matth. 7.
alfo thie felf haft faid by thy Prophet . *A God*   7.
iuft, and fauing there is not befides me. Be conuer-   Ifaiæ.45.
ted to me, and you fhal be faued , al the ends of the   21.
earth. Yf then thou thy felf, o lord , doeft cal
vs, doeft inuite vs, and doeft hold open thine
armes, to the end that vve com to thee,
vvherefore fhould vve not hope, that thou
vvvilt receaue vs in them? Thou art not , o
lord, as men ar , vvhoe becom poore by
giuing, and therfore ar fo troubled, vvhen
ought is demaunded of them. Thou art not
fo, becaufe as thou becommeft not poore in
th'one , thou art not offended in th'other;
and therefore to afk of thee , is not to importunate thee , but to obey thee (feeing
thou haft commaunded vs to afk of thee) to
honour thee , and to glorifie thee : for by
dooing this, vve proteft that thou art God,
and the vniuerfal lord, and giuer of al things;
of vvhome vve ought to demaūd al , feeing
that of thee dependeth al vvhatfoeuer. And

hence it is, that thou thy self doest demaund
vs this sort of sacrifice, aboue al others saying. *Cal vppon me in the date of tribulation, I vvil
deliuer thee, and thou shalt honour me.* I then
being moued through this thy gracious
commaundement, doe com to thee, and
beseeche thee, that thou vvilt vouchsafe to
giue all this, that I ovve vnto thee; to vvit
that I maie so adore thee, so feare and reuerence thee, so praise thee, so giue thee thanks
for al thy benifits, so loue thee vvith al my
ha t, so settle al mie hope and confidence
in thee, so obey thy hoïe cōmaundements,
so offer & resigne mie self into thy hands,
and so vnderstand hovv to request thee
other fauours, as it behoueth me to doe
for thy glorie, and for my saluation. I beseeche thee also, o lo d, to gra nt me pardon of my sinnes, & true contrition & confession of them al, & to giue me grace, that
I maie no more offend thee in them, nor in
anie other; and chcefelie I demaund of thee
strength and vertue to chasten mie flesh, to
refraine mv toung, to mortifie the appetites
of my hart, & to recollect the thoughts of
my imagination, that I, being altogether
so renued and reformed, may deserue to be
a liuing temple, and thy aboce. Giue me
likevvie, o lo d, al those vertues, by vvhich
this

Psal. 49.
15.

this thy dwelling place maie be not onlie purified and cleanfed , but alfo adorned and decked, fuch as be the feare of thy holie name ; a moft ftedfaft hope ; a moft profound humilitie; moft perfect patience ; a cleare difcretion : pouretie of fpirite; perfect Obedience; continual ftrength & diligence in al trauails, apperteining to thy holie feruice; and aboue al, a moft inflamed charitie towards my neighbours, and towards thee . And for afmuch as I deferue none of al thefe things, be mindful, o lord, of thy mercie, which prefuppofeth our miferie, to be put in execution. Be mindful, that thou defireft not the death of a finner, as thy felf haft faid, but that he be conuerted an l liue. *Ezech.33. 11.*

Be mindful, that thy onlie begoten fonne came not into this world , as he him felf faid, to feeke thofe that be iuft, but finners. *Math. 9. 13.*

Be mindful , that whatfoeuer he did, and fuffred in this world, from the daie that he was borne, vntill he gaue vp the ghoft vppon the Croffe, he fuffred it not for him felf, but for me ;which all, I offer vp to thee in facrifice, for my neceffities and offenfes; and for his fake, and not for myne owne, doe I befeeche thee of mercie . And for afmuch as of thee it is faid, that thou wilt honour the father in his fonnes , honour

N 3   him.

him, by dooing good to me. Be mindfull, that I haue recourse to thee, that I enter through thy gates, and that to thee, as to a true physition and lord, I present my neceßities, and vvounds; and so vvith this spirite vvill I cal vppon thee, vvith that praier vvhich the Prophet Dauid made, saying.

Psal. 85. Incline, o lord, thyne eare, and heare me; because I am needie and poore. Keepe my sovvle, because I am holy; saue, o my God, thy seruant, that hopeth in thee. Haue mercie vppon me, o lord, because to thee haue I cried al the day; make glad the sovvle of thy seruant, because to thee, o lord, haue I lifted vp my sovvle. Because thou, o lord, art svveete and milde; and of much mercy to all those that cal vppon thee. Vnderstand, o lord, vvith thy eares my praier; and listen to the voice of my request. In the day of my tribulation haue I cried vnto thee; because thou hast heard me. There is none like to thee amongst the Gods, o Lord; and there is none according to thy vvoorkes. All the nations that thou hast made shal com and adore before thee, o lord; and shall glorifie thy name. Because thou art great, and dooing vvoonders; thou onlie art God. Guide me, o lord, in thy vvay & I vvill vvalke in thy veritie; let my hart reioice that it may feare thy name. I vvil confeße to thee o lord my God, in al my hart: and I vvil glorifie thy name for euer. Because thy mercie is great vppon me; and thou hast deliuered my sovvle, out
of the

of the deepeſt hell. Glorie be to the father, and to the ſonne. &c.

A PRAIER TO THE HOLY GHOST

CHAP. X.

HOLY Ghoſt, the comforter, that in the holy daie of Pentecoſt diddeſt com doune vppon the Apoſtles, and fill theire holy breſts vvith charitie, grace, and vviſdom: I beſeeche thee, o lord, for this vnſpeakeable liberalitie and mercie, that thou vvilt fil my ſoule vvith thy grace, and all mie entrails vvith the vnſpeakeable ſvveetenes of thy loue. Com, o moſt holy Spirite, and ſend vs from heauen ſom one beame of thy light. Com, o father of the poore, o giuer of gifts, o light of harts. Com, o beſt comforter, ſvveete gheſt of ſovvles, and theire ſvveete refreſhing. Com to me, o cleanſer of ſinnes, & phiſition of diſeaſes. Com, o ſtrength of vveakelings, & remedie of thoſe that ar fallen. Com, o maiſter of the humble, and deſtroier of the proude. Com, o ſingular glory of thoſe that liue, and only ſaluation of thoſe that die. Com, o my God, and prepare me for thee, vvith the riches

N 4 of thy

of thy gifes and mercies. Make me drunk,
vvith the gift of vvisdom; inlighten me,
vvith the gift of vnderstanding; gouerne
me vvith the gift of counsel; encourage me,
vvith the gift of strength; teach me, vvith
the gift of science, vvound me, vvith the gift
of pietie; and pearse my hart, vvith the gift
of feare.

O most svveete louer of those that be
cleane of hart, kendle & burne al my bovvels, vvith that most svveete fiar of thy loue,
that they al being so burned, maie be ra-
uished & dravven to thee, vvhich art my
last end, and the depth of all goodnes. O
most svveete louer of cleane soules, for so
much as thou knovvest, that I of my self
am able to doe nothing, extend thy pitiful
hand vppon me, and make me leaue my
self, that so I may be able to passe vnto thee.
And to this end, o lord, beate doune, mortifie, annihil, and vndoe in me vvhatsoeuer it
shal pleae thee, that thou make me vvholy
according to thy vvil, that so al my life be a
perfect sacrifice, to be altogether consumed
in the fiar of thy loue. O that som one could
aford me this, that thou vvouldest admit
me to so great good! Behold, that this thy
poore and miserable creature, daie and night
suspireth to thee. My sovvle hath thirsted
after

after the liuing God, vvhen shal I com and
appeare before the face of al graces? vvhen
shal I enter into the place of that vvonderful tabernacle, euen to the face of my God?
vvhen vvilt thou fill my sovvle, vvith the
ioye of thy diuine countenance? vvhen shal
shee be satiated vvith thy diuine presence?
O fountaine of eternal brightnes, turne to
enclose me in that depth, vvhence I proceeded, vvhere I may knovv thee, as thou didst
knovv me, and loue thee, as thou didst loue
me, and see thee for euer, in the companie
of al Saincts. Amen.

A PRAIER VVHILES VVEE HEARE
masse, or at anie other time, taken out of diuers
places of S. Austen.

CHAP. XI.

MOST merciful, & su-
preame creator of heauen
and earth, I the most vile
of al sinners, together
vvith thy holy Church,
offer vp to thee this most
pretious sacrifice, of thy onlie begoten
sonne, for al the sinnes of the vvoorld. Behold, o most merciful king, him that suffereth,

reth, and gentellie remember for vvhome he suffereth. Is not this peraduenture, o lord, thy sonne, vvhome thou diddest deliuer to death, for the remedie of an vngrateful seruant?

Is not this peraduenture the author of life, vvhich being lead as a sheepe to the slaughter, disdeigned not to suffer such a cruel kind of death? Turne, o lord my God, the eys of thy maiestie, vppon this vvoork of vnspeakeable pietie. Consider thy svveete sonne, stredched out vppon the vvoode of the Crosse, and his most innocent handes gushing out bloud, and be thou content to pardon those euils, vvhich my hands haue committed. Consider his naked brest, pearced vvith that cruel iron of the speare; and renue mee vvith that sacred fountaine, vvhich I beleeue to haue runne from thence. Behold those most holy feete, vvhich neuer past through the vvay of sinnes, novv pearced vvith those hard nails, and let it please thee to direct my feete, in the vvay of thy holie commaundements. Doest not thou perchaunce, o most pitiful father, consider the head of thy most louing sonne fallen doune, & his vvhite neck bovved dovvne vvith the presence of death? Consider, o most merciful Creator, in vvhat plight the
bodie

bodie of thy beloued fonne remaineth, and
haue mercie vppon the feruant, vvhich
he hath redeemed. Behold hovv his naked
breſt remaineth all vvhite; hovv his bloudie fide remaineth all redde: hovv his bovvels extended remaine drie; hovv his
bevvtiful eys remaine dimme, hovv his
kinglie preſence and figure remaineth pall
and vvanne; hovv his armes ſtretched out
remaine ſtiffe; hovv his knees like alabaſtre
remaine hanging, & hovv the ſtreames of
that diuine bloud vvaſh his pearced feete.
Behold, o glorious father, the mangled
membres of thy moſt louing fonne, and remember the miſeries of thy poore feruant.
Behold the torments and paines of our Redeemer, and forgiue the offenſes of the redeemed. This is our faithful Aduocate before thee, o father almightie. This is that
high prieſt, vvhich hath no neede to be
ſanctified vvith other bloud, feeing he ſhi-
neth embrued vvith his ovvne. This is the
holy facrifice agreable and preſent, offred
and receaued in the fauour of ſvveetenes.
This is the lamb vvithout ſpotte, vvhich
heald his peace before thoſe, that did ſheare
him; vvhich being charged vvith ſtripes,
defiled vvith ſpittle, and iniuried vvith reproches, did not open his mouth. This is
he

he, vvhich hauing committed no sinne
suffered for our sinnes, and cured our
vvounds vvith his vvounds.

Novv vvhat hast thou donne. o most
svveete Lord, that thou vvast so iudged?
vvhat hast thou comitted, o most innocent
lamb, that thou vvast so dealed vvithall?
vvhat vvere thy faults, & vvhat the cause of
thy codemnation? Trulie, o lord, I am the
vvound of thy paine, I am the occasi n of
thy death, and the cause of thy condemnation. O meruailous dispensation of God! He
sinneth that is euil, and he is punished that
is good: he offendeth that is guiltie. and he
is vvounded that is innocent: the seruaunt
committeth the fault, and the lord paieth
for it. Hovv far, o sonne of God, hovv far
hath thy humilitie abased it self? hovv far
hath thy charitie extended it self? hovv far
hath thy loue proceeded? Hovv far hath
thy compassion arriued? I haue committed
the offense, and thou endurest the punishment. I haue donne the sinnes, and thou
suffrest the torments. I am he that vvaxed
provvd, & thou art humbled. I am the disobedient, and thou art becom obedient, euen
to death, and so paiest the fault of my diso-
bedience. Behould heere, o king of glorie,
behould heere thy pietie, and my impietie;

thy

thy iuſtice, and my vvickednes. Conſider
therefore novv, o eternall father, hovv thou
oughteſt to haue mercie vppon me, ſeeing
that I haue offered thee ſo deuoutlie, the
moſt pretious offer that could be offred thee.
I haue preſented to thee thy moſt louing
ſonne, & ſet betvvixt thee & me this faithful aduocate. Receiue vvith a cheerefull
coūtenance the good paſtor, & conſider the
ſtraied ſheepe, vvhich he beareth vppon his
ſhoulders. I beſeeche thee, o king of kings,
by this holie of holies, that I may be vnited
to him in ſpirite, ſeeing he diſdained not,
to be vnited to me in fleſh: and I humblie
requeſt thee, that by the means of this praier, I may deſerue to haue him for my helper,
for ſo much as of thy meere grace, vvithout
that I deſerued it at thy hands, thou haſt
giuen me him for my Redeemer.

A DEVOVT PRAIER TO OVR
blessed Ladie.

CHAP. XII.

GLORIOVS and hap-
pie virgin, more pure then
the Angels, more bright
then the starres, hovv shall
my praier appeare before
thee, seeing the grace that I
merited through the passion of him vvhich
redeemed me, I haue lost it thorough the
vvickednes of mine ovvne fault? But yet,
although I be so great a sinner, knovving
my request to be iust, I vvil make bold to
beseeche thee, that thou vvilt heare me.
O my Queene and Ladie, I humblie request
thee to praie thy sacred sonne, that for his
infinite goodnes and mercie, he pardon me
vvhatsoeuer I haue donne against his vvill
and commaundement. And yf this may not
be graunted me, in respect of my vnvvor-
thines, yet let me obtaine it, to the end that
that perish not, vvhich he hath created to
his Image & likenes. Thou art the light of
darknes. Thou art the mirrour of Sainɔ̌ts.
Thou art the hope of sinners. All generations praise thee; all those that be afflicted
call

call vppon thee; all thofe that be good behold thee; all creatures reioice in thee; the
Angels in heauen vvith thy prefence; the
fovvles in purgatorie vvith thy comfort;
the men vppon earth vvith thy hope. All
call vppon thee, and thou doeft a vvnfvvere
to all, and praie for all. Novv vvhat fhal I
doe, vnvvorthie finner that I am, to obtaine thy fauour, for fo much as my finne
troubleth me, my demerite afflicteth me,
and my malice maketh me fpeachles. I befeeche thee, o moft pretious virgin, for that
thy fo greeuous and mortallforovv, vvhich
thou diddeft feele, feeing thy beloued fonne
going vvith the Croffe vpon his fhoulders,
to the place of his death, that thou vvilt
mortifie all my paffions and tentations, that
I lofe not thorough mie vvickednes, that
vvhich he redeemed vvith his bloud. Put alvvaies in my thought thofe pitiful teares,
vvhich thou diddeft fhedde, vvhen thou
diddeft fee the vvounds, and the bloud
of thy bleffed fonne; that thorough the
contemplation of them, there runne fuch
quantitie of teares out of myne eyes, that
they may be fufficient, to vvafh avvay all
the fpottes of my finnes. For vvhat finner
vvill be fo bold, as to appeare vvithout
thee before that eternal Iudge, vvhoe although

though he be mild in his suffering, yet is he iust in his punishment; for so much as neither revvard is denied for doing good, nor paine eschevved for doing euil. VVhoe then shal be so iust, that in this iudgment he shal not haue neede of thy helpe? vvhat shal becom of me, o blessed virgen, yf I vvin not by thy intercession that, vvhich I haue lost thorough myne ovvne sinne? I demaund a great thing of thee, according to my faults but in deede verie little according to thy povver. All that I can request thee is nothing, in respect of that vvhich thou art able to giue me. O Queene of the Angels, amend my life, and dispose all my vvoorkes in such manner, that albeit I be but euill, yet I may deserue to be heard of thee vvith pitie. Shevv, o Lady, thy mercie in afording me remedie; that by this meanes those that be good, maye praise thee, and those that be euill, maye hope in thee. Let the sorovves, vvhich thou diddest endure in the passion of thy most louing sonne, and my Redeemer Iesus Christ, be alvvaies before myne eys, and let thy paines be the foode of my heart. Let not thy succour forsake me, let not thy pitie leaue me, let not thy memorie forget me. If thou, o Lady, abandon me, vvhoe shal vphold me? yf thou

forget

forget me, vvhoe fhal be myndful of me?
yf thou, that art the ftarre of the fea, and
the guide of thofe that erre out of the vvay,
doe not lighten me, vvhat fhal becom of
me? Suffer me not to be tempted by the
enimie; and yf he tempt me, fuffer me not
to fall; & yf I fall, help me to rife vp againe.
VVhoe, o Lady, hath called vppon thee, and
vvas not heard of thee? vvhoe hath euer ferued thee, that vvas not revvarded vvith
much magnificencie? Make, o moft glorious
virgin, that my hart may feele that pear-
fing griefe vvhich thou didft fuffer, vvhen,
after that thy moft pretious fonne vvas taken dovvne from the Croffe, thou diddeft
receaue him into thine armes, and vvaft not
able anie more to vveepe, beholding that
moft pretious image adored of the Angels,
but at that time defiled vvith the fpittle of
fo vile, and vnvvorthie perfons; and feeing
the crueltie fo ftraunge, vvith vvhich the
innocencie of the iuft, paied for the difobe-
dience of the finner. I doe contemplate
vvith my felf, o my vvoorthy Queene, in
vvhat fort thou diddeft remaine at that
time, vvith thyne armes open; thyne eyes
dimme; thy head hanging dovvne; vvithout colour in thy face: and feeling in the
fame more torment, then anie other could

Q   endure

endure in his ovvne bodye . Let those fo-
rovvful vvoords alvvaies found in myne
eares, vvhich thou diddest fpeake at that
time to thofe, that did behold thee, faying;
O you that paffe by the vvay . behold yf there be anie
forovv like to mine ; that by thofe vvoords I
maie deferue to be heard of thee. Fasten, o
Lady, in my fovvle , that fvvord of forovv,
vvhich paffed thorough thy fovvle, vvhen
thou diddest lay in the fepulchre that dif-
membred body of thy most pretious fonne,
that I may remember hovv I am of earth,
and hovv in the end, I must yeld to the
earth that , vvhich thence I receaued; that
fo the perifhing glory of this vvoorld doe
not deceaue me . Make me, o Lady, remember hovv often times thou didst turne
to behold the fepulchre, vvhere thou hadst
left fo great good inclofed, that I may therby deferue fo much favour at thy handes,
that thou vouchfafe to turne and regarde
my petition. Let my companie be that fo-
litarineffe, in vvhich thou diddest remaine
al that doleful night, vvhen thou hadst nothing more liuelie before thine eys, then
thy paines & forovvs; vvhen thou diddest
drinke the vvater of thy pitiful teares, and
eate the bread of thy heauie contempla-
tions: that I bevvailing the anguifh, and
dif-

diſtreſſe vvhich thou diddeſt ſuffer heere in earth, may, by thy meanes, atteine to ſee the glorie, vvhich thou haſt merited in heauen. Amen.

A PRAIER OF S. THOMAS OF
Aquine to demaund al vertues.

CHAP. XIII.

 Almightie, & moſt merciful Lord God, graunt me grace, that ſuch things as be acceptable to thee, I feruentlie deſire them, vviſelie ſeeke them, trulie knovve them, and perfectlie fulfill them, to the praiſe ad glory of thy holy name. Ordaine the ſtate of my life, & giue me light to knovv that, vvhich thou cõmaundeſt me to doe, and forces to put it in execution, as I ought, and as it is req. iſite for the ſaluation of my ſoule. Let the vvaie, o lord, vvhich leadeth to thee, be to me ſecure, right, and perfect, and ſuch, that I faile not betvvixt the p.operities and adue.ſities of this life, but that in proſperities I praiſe thee, and in adue.ſit es be not diſmaied; in proſperities I beçom not loftie and proude,

O 2   neither

neither vvaxe difconfident in aduerfities.

Let me take heauines or ioy of nothing, but onlie of that, vvhich may ioine me vvith thee, or feparate me from thee. Let me defire to content no bodie but thee, neither to difcontent anie bodye but thee. Let all tranfitorie things be vile vnto me for the loue of thee, and moft deare and pretious al things apperteining to thee, and thou, o mie God, aboue them all. Let al ioie be yrkfom to me vvithout thee, and let me not defire anie thing befides thee. Let al trauail be pleafant vnto me for thee, and noifom vvhatfoeuer repofe I take vvithout thee.

Graunt that I maie oftentimes lift vp my hart to thee, and yf at anie time I faile to doe this, that I recompence mie fault vvith thinking of the fame, and purpofing to amend it. Make me, o my lord God, obedient vvithout contradiction, poore vvithout lacke, chaft vvithout corruption, patient vvithout murmuring, humble vvithout fayning, merie vvithout diffolution, fadde vvithout deiection, graue vvithout heauines, quicke vvithout lightnes, fearful vvithout defperation, true vvithout doublenefle, dooing good vvithout prefumption, to amend my neighbour vvithout lafi-

loftinesse, and to edifie him in vvoords &
vvoorks vvithout difsimulation.

Giue me, o my moſt fvveete God, a verie
vvatchful hart, that no curious cogitation
maie vvithdravve it from thee. Giue me a
noble hart, that noe vnvvorthie affection
may dravv it dounevvards. Giue me a right
hart, that noe finiſtrous intention maie
turne it avvrye. Giue me an inuincible hart,
that noe tribulation maie breake it. Giue
me a free hart, that no peruerſe and violent
affection maie conſtraine it. Giue me, o
moſt fvveete and pleaſant lord, vnderſtanding to knovve thee, diligence to feeke
thee, vvifdom to find thee, conuerſation
that maie pleaſe thee, perſeuerance to faithfullie expect thee, and hope to finallie embrace thee. Graunt that I maye deſerue to
be nailed vppon the Croſſe vvith thee by
penance, to vfe thy beniſits in this vvoorld
by grace, and to enioie thy felicitie in
heauen by glorie : vvhoe, vvith the
father and the holy Ghoſt, liueſt
and raigneſt God, vvoorld
vvithout end,
Amen.

O 3   THE

THE THYRD

TREATISE, VVHICH
CONTEINETH AN
INSTRVCTION,

AND RVLE TO LIVE VVEL, GE-nerall to all fort of Chriftians.

HE greateft, and moft important affaire of all that be in ths vvorld (for vvhich onelie man vvas created, and for vvhich vvere created all things els that be in the vvoorld, and for vvhich the Creator, and lord of al things came him felf into he vvoorld, preached, and died in the fame) is the faluation & fanctification of man. He then that erneftlie, and vvith al his hart defireth to take in hand this fo greate an enterprife (in comparifon of vvhich, al that is vnder heauen, is to be efteemed as nothing) the fumme of al that he ought to doe, confifteth in one onlie thing, to vvit, that a man haue in his mind a moft ftedfaft, and determinate purpofe, neuer to commit anie mortal finne, for anie thing in the vvorld, be it goods, be it ho-

nour,

nour, be it life, or anie like thing vvhatſoeuer. In ſuch ſort, that euen as a faithful vvife, and a faithful captaine be reſolued to dye, rather then to commit anie treaſon, th'one againſt her huſband, and th'other againſt his king; ſo likevviſe a good Chriſtian man ought to haue this determination, to neuer commit this kind of treaſon againſt God, vvhich is donne by one mortall ſinne. And by mortal ſinne vve vnderſtand heere breeflie, vvhatſoeuer thing is donne againſt anie of the commaundements of God, or our holie mother the Catholique Church.

But albeit there be diuers ſorts of theſe ſinnes, yet the moſt ordinarie in vvhich men ar vvoont moſt to fall, be fiue; to vvit, Hatreds, Carnalities, Othes in vaine, Theftdoms, and Detraction or diffaming of our neighbours, and otherſuch like. He that ſhall vvithdrayve him ſelf from theſe, ſhall eaſilie auoide all the other ſorts of ſinnes. This is the abridgment of al that, vvhich a good Chriſtian ought to doe, comprehended in fevve vvoords, and this is ſufficient for his ſaluation. Yet becauſe to accompliſh this obligation, is a thing that hath greate difficultie, in reſpect of the great ſnares, and daungers of the vvoorld, and of the euil inclination of our fleaſh, and of the conti-

O 4 nual

mial combats of the enimie; therfore a man
must help him selfvvith al such things, as
may further him to this purpose, and in
this poinct consisteth the kaye of this
affaire.

The first Remedie.

NOVV amongst those things, the first
is to consider deepelie, hovv great an
euil one mortal sinne is, that so a man may
prouoke him selfto the abhorring, and de-
testing of it: and for this end he must consider tvvoe things, amongst manie others.
I The first is, vvhat is that, vvhich a man lo-
2 seth thorough mortall sinne. The second
is, hovv much almightie God detesteth and
abhorreth mortall sinne. As concerning the
first, a man thorough mortal sinne, commeth to lose the grace of God, and together
vvith it all the infused vertues, vvhich proceede from the same. And albeit faith, and
hope be not lost by mortall sinne, yet by
the same is lost at that verie instant, the right
& claime to euerlasting life, vvhich is not
giuen but to such vvoorks, as be donne in
grace. There is also lost the amitie of God,
the adoption and title of the children of
God,

God, the entertainment and cherifhing of
children, and the fatherlie prouidence,
vvhich almightie God hath of thofe,
vvhome he taketh to be his children. There
is loft alfo the fruite and merite of all thofe
good vvoorks, vvhich a man hath donne
from the time that he vvas borne, euen vntil that prefent hovvre. There is likevvife
loft the participation, and communication
of fuch good vvoorks, as a man doeth at
that prefent; and finallie by finne is loft God
himfelf (vvhoe is infinite goodnes) and is
gotten hell (vvhich is infinite euil) feeing
it depriueth vs of God, and dureth for euer.
Heerehence it enfueth, that the foule, vvhich
before vvas the liuing temple of God, and
the fpovvfe of the holie Ghoft, remaineth
the flaue of the diule, and the denne of Satan. And this in breefe is that, vvhich is loft
by finne.

But novv, hovv much almightie God
abhorreth finne, vve may vnderftand by
the terrible punifhments, that he hath vfed
againft it, euen from the beginning of the
vvorld : efpeciallie by the punifhment of
that greate Angel: and of that firft man; and
of al the vniuerfal vvorld vvith the vvaters
of the diluge; and of thofe fiue cities, vvhich
vvere burned vvith flames of fiar from heauen;

Ifai. 14.
Gen. 3.
Gen. 7.
Gen. 19.

uen; and of the deftruction of Ierufalem &
Babylon; and of manie other cities, king-
domes and empires; and aboue all, by the
puni hment vvhich is giuen in hell to
finne, and much more by that fo vvonderfull, and terrible punifhment and facrifice,
vvhich vvas donne vppon the fhoulders of
Chrift, vvhome God vvould haue to die,
by this meanes to deftroie, & banifh out of
the vvorld a thing, vvhich he fo greatlie abhorred, as is finne. He that fhall deepelie
and vvith attention confider thefe things,
can not but remaine aftonied. to fee the facilitie, vvith vvhich men at this time commit finne. This i then the firft thing, vvhich
helpeth exceeding much to efchevv and
abhorre finne.

The fecond Remedie.

THE fecond helpeth alfo heereunto.
vvhich is to auoide the occafions of
finnes vvith vvifdome, fuch as be gamings,
naughtie companies, conuerfations of men
vvith vvomen, and principallie the daungerous fight of our eyes, and other fuch like
things. For yf man be become foe fraile
through finne, that of him felf he falleth
from his ovvne proper ftate, and finneth.
vvhat

vvhat vvil he doe, vvhen occasion shall pluck him by the sleeue, alluring him vvith the presence of the thing set before his eys, and vvith the oportunitie and facilitie to sinne? much more sich that's true vvhich is commonlie saide, that the iust man sinneth by reason of the coffer set open before him.

The third Remedie.

THE thid thing that helpeth also for this purpose, is to resist in the beginning of temptation vvith greate speede and diligence, & to quenche the sparkle of euil thoughts, before it be kindled in the hart: for in this sort a man resisteth vvith greate facilitie and merite. But in case he make delaie, then is the labour in resistance much increased, and he committeth therby a nevv sinne vvhich at the least is veni-al, and somtimes deadlie. Novv the manner of resisting euil thoughts, is to se liuelie before the eys of oure sovvle, the image of our Sauiour Christ crucified, vvith al the angvvishes and painful passion, vvhich he suffred to destroie sinne, and by the same to demaund his assistance. Somtimes likevvise it is very good, to make vvith greate speede the signe of the Crosse vppon our hart, thereb thereby to driue avvay more easilie, the naughtie invvarde thought, vvith this externall signe.

The fourth Remedie.

IT helpeth also verie much for this, that a man examine his conscience euerie night, before he goe to sleepe, & see vvherin he hath sinned that daie, and accuse him self therof in the presence of almightie God, requesting pardon, & grace to amend the same. Let him also, in the morning vvhen he riseth, arme and fortifie him self vvith praier, & vvith a nevv determination against such a sinne, or such sinnes, to vvhich he seeeth him self most inclined; & let him there vse more diligence and circumspection, vvhere he feeleth more daunger.

The fift Remedie.

IT helpeth likevvise verie much to eschevv, so much as maie be, venial sinnes, because they doe dispose vs to mortal sinnes. For euen as those that doe greatlie feare death, doe prouide, as much as is possible, to escape those diseases, that doe dispose to that end;

end; fo alfo ought they, that defire to efcape mortal finnes (vvhich be the death of the foule) to efchevve likevvife, vvith all poffible diligence, venial finnes, vvhich ar the difeafes that doe difpofe vs to deadlie finnes.

Moreouer he that is careful and faithfull in a little, it is to be efteemed that he vvil be faithful likevvife in much; and that he, that vfeth diligence to efchevv the leffer euils, fhall be the more fecure from the greater. And by venial finnes vve vnderftand in this place, idle talke, inordinate lavvghing, eating, drinking, and fleeping more then is neceffarie, time euil fpent, light lies, and others the like, vvhich although they doe not depriue vs of Charitie; yet doe they quenche the feruour of the fame.

The fixt Remedie.

VV E ar alfo much holpen hereunto by the feuere, and fharp treating of our flefh, as vvel in eating and drinking, as alfo in fleeping and clothing, and in al the reft: vvhich flefh being a fountaine, and prouoker of finnes, the more feeble and vveake it is, the more feeble and vvveake

vveake fhal the paisions, and appetites alfo
be, vvhich fhal proceede of it. For like as
the drye & barren grond bringeth fourth
plantes vveake, and of fmale fubftance;
but contrari-vvife the batteful and fertile
grovvnd, efpeciallie that vvhich is vvel
vvatered and dounged, bringeth foorth
trees very greene, and verie mightie: fo likevvife it fareth vvith oure bodie, as much
as concerneth the pafsions, vvhich doe proceede from the fame, according as it is better, or vvoorfe dealt vvithall, or more, or
leffe fubdued. True it is, that al this muft be
donne vvith difcretion and moderation,
although this counfel, as the vvoorld goeth
novv a daies, be needeful to fevv. Yet to
obteine this, a man muft, as often as he
goeth to fable, not onlie bleffe the fame, but
alfo lift vp his hart to God, and demaund
this temperancie, and procure, vvhiles he
eateth, to obferue it.

The feuenth Remedie.

IT helpeth alfo much for this purpofe,
to take diligent and ftraite account of
our tovng, becaufe this is the part of our
bodie, vvith vvhich vvs offend God more
eafilie,

eaſilie, and often; for the toung is a verie
ſlippery membre, vvhich ſlippeth verie
quicklie into maine kindes of filthie, cole-
rick, boaſting, and vaine vvords, and ſomtimes alſo into lyeing, ſvvearing, curſing,
murmuring, ſlaundering, flattering, and the
like. For vvhich cauſe the vviſe-man ſaieth,
In much ſpeeche there ſhal not vvant offence. An 1 Prou. 1**.
againe, *Death and life are in the povver of the* 19.
tounge. And therfore it is verie good coun- Prou. 18.
ſel, that as manie times as thou ſhalt haue 21.
occaſion to talk of ſuch matters, and vvith
ſuch perſons, by vvhich thou maiſt doubte
of ſom perill, either of murmuring, brag-
ging, lyeing, or of vaine-glorie &c. thou
doe firſt lift vp thy eyes to God, and com-
mend thy ſelf vnto him, and ſaie vvith the
Prophet. *Pone Domine cuſtodiam ori meo, &* Pſal. 14**.
oſtium circumſtantiæ labijs meis, That is to ſaie. 3.
Apoint, O lord, a cuſtodie or garde to my mouth,
and a dore of circumſtance vnto my lippes. And
vvith this alſo, vvhileſt thou art in communication, be vvel aduiſed in thy vvords (as
he that paſſeth ouer a riuer vppon ſome
ſtones, that lie ouerthvvarte the ſame) that
thou ſlippe not into anie of theſe perils.

The

The eight Remedie.

IT helpeth also verie much to this ende, not to entangle thy hart vvith too excessiue loue of anie visible thing, vvhither it he honour, goods, children or anie other temporal thing; forsomuch as this loue is a great occasion, in a manner of al the sinnes, cares, fantasies, vexations, passions, and disquietnes that be in the vvorld. For vvhich cause the Apostle saieth, that *Couetousnes* (vvhich is the ouergreedie affection of temporall things) *is the roote of all euills.* And therfore a man must liue alvvaies vvith attention, and carefulnes, that he suffer not his hart to cleaue ouermuch to these temporall things; but rather pluck it back alvvaies, vvith the bridle, vvhen he perceiueth that it rangeth abrode fantasticallie, and not desire things more then they deserue to be desyred: that is to saie, as things of small account, as fraile, vncertaine, and such as passe avvaie in a moment, vvithdravving his hart from them, and fixing it vvhollie vppon that cheefest, onlie and true felicitie.

1. *Timoth.* 6.

He that shal loue temporall things after this manner, vvil neuer despaire for them, vvhen he vvanteth them, neither vvilhe be dismaied, difmaied, vvhen they ar taken from him, neither vvil he commit infinite forts of finnes, vvhich the louers of thefe things doe commit, either to obteine them, or to increafe them, or els to defend them. Herein confifteth the keye of al this bufines : for vndoutedlie he that hath fo moderated this loue, is novv becom lord of the vvorld and of finne.

The ninth Remedie.

TO this likevvife helpeth exceeding much, the vertue of almef-deedes and of me cie, by vvhich a man deferueth to obteine mercie at Gods hands; and this is one of the ftrongeft vveapons, that a man hath againft finne, for vyhich caufe the Ecclefiafticus faith. *VVater quencheth the burning fiar, and Almefdeedes doe refift finnes.* And againe in an other place. *The almes of a man is a pouche vvith him, and it fhal keepe the grace of a man, as the apple of the eye; and aftervvard it fhal rife againe, and yeeld them retribution, to euer e one vppon theire head: it fhall fight againft thine enemie, more then the fhield of a ftrong man, and more then the fpeare.* Let a man alfo emember, that al the foundation of Chriftian life, is Charitie, and that it is the marke, by

Ecclef. 3. 33. Ecclef. 29. 10.

P   vvhich

vvhich vve muſt be knovven to be the diſciples of Chriſt; and that the ſigne of this Charitie is Almes, and mercie tovvard ſuch as be ſicke, poore, afflicted, in priſon, and tovvards al other miſerable perſons, vvhome vve ought to helpe and ſuccour, according to oure poſſibilitie, vvith vvoorks of mercie, vvith comfortable ſpeeches, and vvith deuoute praiers, beſeeching God for them, and releeuing them vvith ſuch things as vve haue.

The tenth Remedie.

THE reading of good bookes, is alſo a greate helpe vnto this; as the reading of naughtie bookes, is a greate hinderance and impediment: for the vvoord of God is oure light, oure medicine, oure foode, oure maiſter, oure guide, oure vveapons, and all oure good; ſeeing it is it that filleth oure vnderſtanding vvith light, and cure ſovvle and vvil vvith good deſires, and the eby helpeth vs to recollect oure hart, vvhen it is moſt diſtracted, and to ſtirre vp our deuotion, vvhen it is moſt ſluggiſh and drovvſie. True it is, that this reading (yf vve mind to take profit thereof) muſt
not

not be a sleightie, or negligent careles running ouer of bocks, vvithout due vveigh-
ing of the same, and much lesse for onlie cu-
riositie sake, but contrarivvise, it must be
ioined vvith humilitie, and a desire to take
profit thereby.

The eleuenth Remedie.

IT is likevvise a great help for this purpose, to vvalke so, as though vve vvere
alvvaies in the presence of God, and to haue
him as present before our eyes, as much as
is possible, as a vvitnes of our dooings, a
iudge of our life, & a helper of our vveakenes, desyring him alvvaies, as such a one,
vvith deuout and humble praiers, to help
and succour vs vvith his grace. But this
continual attention ought to be had, not
onlie vnto God, but also to the ordering and
gouernment of oure life; in such sort, that
vve haue alvvaies one eye fixed vppon him,
for to reuerence him, and desire him of his
grace; and the other vppon that vvhich vve
haue to doe, to th'end that in nothing vve
passe the compasse of reason. And this sort
of attention and vvatchfulnes, is the principall sterne of our life; vvich manner of

P 2   attention,

attention, yf vve can not continue alvvaies
tovvards God, let vs yet at the least procure,
to lift vp our hart to him oftentimes, betvvixt daie and night , vvith som breefe
praiers , vvhich vve must alvvaies haue
readie for this purpose . And amongst
these is greatlie commended by Cassianus
that verse of king Dauid vvhich saieth.

Psalm. 69. 2. *Deus in adiutorium meum intende : Domine
ad adiuuandum me festina . That is, O God,
bend thy self to mie helpe: o lord , make hast to
succour me: or other such like as these be,*
vvhich ar easilie to be fo nd in the same
Prophet, almost in euerie place. VVhen vve
goe to bed, S. Iohn Climacus saith, that vve
must put our selus in such sort , as yf vve
vve e to lie in a sepulchre, that by this manner of lying , vve maie be moued to think
of the hovvre of death vvhich vve expect.
And it sha'l not be amisse , hat a man, to
this end, saie ouer him self a responsorie,
such as is vvoont to be saide ouer a dead bodie . VVhen in the night vve avvake out of
sleepe, let vs saie , *Gloria Patri, & Filio, & Spi-
ritui sancto* , or som such good and deuout
voords . And in the morning , vvhen vve

Psalm. 62. 2. open our eyes, let vs saie : *Deus, Deus meus ad
te deluce vigilo.* That is, *O God, my God, earlie doe
Psalm. 17. 2. I vvatch vnto me .* or els, *Diligam te Domine for-
titudo*

titudo mea ; dominus firmamentum meum , & re-
fugium meum, & liberator meus. I vvill loue thee o
lord my strength ; our lord is my fortreße, and my refuge, and my redeemer. Or som vvhat like this.
As often as the clock striketh , let vs saie.
Blessed be the time, in vvhich my lord Iesus
Christ vvas borne, & died for me : be mindful , o mie lord, of me in the hovvre of mie
death . And let vs then think, that vve haue
one houre leße of life, & that by little &
littel, this daie vvil be ended. VVhen vve
goe to table, let vs think hovv God is he
that giueth vs to eate, and that made al
things for our vse ; and let vs thank him for
the foode vvhich he giueth vs, and consider
hovv manie there be that vvant that, vvhich
to vs is superfluous , and hovv easilie vve
posseße that, vvhich others haue goten
vvith so great trauail and daungers. VVhen
vve be tempted of the enimie, the greatest
remedie is to runne vvith al speede to the
Croße, & there to behold Christ dismem-
bred and disfigured , out of vvhome issue
streames of bloud, and so to call to mind,
that the principall cause, vvherfore he put
him self there, vvas to destroy sinne, & to
praie him vvith al deuotion, that he suffer
not, that so abominable a thing reigne in
our harts, vvhich he vvith so great paines

P 3   ende-

endeuoured to deftroie. And fo vve muft
faie vvith all our hart. O mie lord, vvhoe
haft put thie felf vppon the Croffe, to the
end that I offend the not, maie it be that this
is not fufficient to make me vvithdravv mie
felf from finning! permit not this, o lord,
I befeeche thee, for thefe thy moft holy
vvoundes; forfake me not o my God, feeing I com to thee, or els fhevv me fom other
better harborough, vvhere I may haue mie
refuge. If thou, o lord, leaue me, vvhat
fhall becom of me? vvhoe fhall defend me?
Help me, o lord my God, and defend me
from this dragon, feeing I can not defend
my felf vvithout thee. It fhalbe alfo verie
good, to make fom times vvith fpeede the
figne of the Croffe vppon our hart, yfvve be
in place, vvhere vve may dee it, fo that vve
be not noted of others. And in this manner,
temptations, vvil be to vs an occafion of a
greater croune, as alfo to make vs lift vp
our hart to God more often : and in fuch
fort the diule vvhoe came, as they faie, for
vvool, vvil goe backe fhorne.

The tvvelfth Remedie.

ANother remedie is to frequent the Sa-
raments, vhich be certaine heauenlie
medi-

medicines that God hath ordeined againſt
ſinne, as remedies of our frailtie, prouokers
of our loue, ſtirrers vp of our deuotion, for-
vvarders of our hope, releeuers of our miſerie, treaſures of the grace of God, paunes of
his glorie, and teſtimonies of his loue. And
therfore the ſeruants of God ought alvvaies
to giue him thanks for this benifit, & to help
them ſelues vvith this ſo greate remedie, v-
ſing it in due times, ſom more, ſom leſſe, according as they feele deuotion, & according
to the fruite of theire auauncement, & the
counſell of theire ghoſtlie fathers.

The thirtenth Remedie.

A N other remedie is praier, vvhich hath
for office to aſk grace at Gods hands,
as the Sacraments haue for office to giue the
ſame grace, & ſo the revvard correſpondent
to praier, is to obtaine grace, vvhen it is
made as it ought to be . And therefore let
a man vvith praier, amongſt all other his
petitions, principallie demaunde this of
oure Lord, that he vvill deliuer him from
the ſnares of his enimie, and neuer permit that he fall into anie mortal ſinne.

P 4   Theſe

These be the principal remedies, that
vve haue againft all kind of vices; to vvhich
I vvil adde heere brieflie other three, no leſſe
profitable thē manie of the former. Amongſt
theſe the firſt is to flie idlenes, vvhich is as
it vvere the roote of al vices, for, as it is
vvritten, *Idlenes hath tougth much euill*. The
ground that is not laboured, becommeth
ful of thornes, and the vvater that ſtandeth
ſtill, is filled vvith toades, & other filthines:
ſo likevvife the ſovvle of one that is idle, is
filled vvith vices, and is made a framer and
inuentour of nevv euils.

The ſecond remedie is Solitarines, vvhich
is the mother and gard of innocencie, for
ſomuch as it cutteth of from vs at one
blovve, the occaſions of all ſinnes. This is a
kind of remedie, vvhich vvas ſent from heauen to the bleſſed father Arſenius·, vvhoe
heard from a-boue a voice, that ſaid vnto
him. *O Arſenius flie, keepe ſilence, and be quiet.*
Therfore the ſeruant of God muſt caſt of,
and forſake, as much as is poſſible, al viſi-
tations, conuerſations and compliments
of the vvorlde; for that ordinarile theſe
ar neuer vvithout murmuring, ſcoffing,
malice, fables, and ſuch like things. And yf
anie ſhould complaine of this, let him ſuffer theire ſayings for the loue of vertue: for
it is

Eccleſ. 33.
26.

it is lesse inconuenience, that men should complaine of him, then that God should be angrie vvith him.

The third remedie, vvich is verie profitable as vvel for this, as for manie other things, is to breake vvith the vvorld, not forcing vvhat shall be spoken of him, as long as he giueth no actiue scandall. For yf all these feares & respects be vvel examined, and vveighed in equall ballance, they vvil be in the end but blastes of vvind, and buggebeares to feare child en, vvhich ar afraid of euerie shadovve. To conclude, he that maketh anie g eate account of the vvorld, can not be the true seruant of God. Yf I should pleasse men, saith th'Apostle, I should not be the seruant of Christ.

Gal. 1. 10.

THE

THE FOVERTH

TREATISE, CONTEI-
NING AN INSTRVCTION
OR RVLE OF GOOD LIFE,

ESPECIALLIE FOR THOSE, THAT
begin to serue God in Religion.

TO THE READER.

A LBEIT the treatise that heere ensueth, serue principallie for such, as begin to serue God in Religion, yet neuerthelesal the contents thereof, serue as vvel alsoe for al those, that trulie and vvith al theire hart giue them selues to the seruice of our Lord, as in the beginning of this booke vvas mentioned. But that vvhich ought heere to be aduertised is, that *the end of Christian life*, to vvhich ar ordeined al Gods commaundments and counsels, and al statutes & voues of Religion, *is*, as th'Apostle saieth, *charitie*. VVhich although it be so, yet doe vve not, in the beginning of this treatise, straite vvaies speake of this end, but of that, vvhich apperteineth to him, vvhoe
takETH

taketh vppon him to inftruct a nouice,
newlie com out of the vvorld, vvith fuch
inclinations and vvicked cuftoms, as he
bringeth from the fame. For he that hath
this office, muft cheefelie attend to deftroye
and mortifie fuch euil habites, and inclinations; and to plant in theire place al thofe
vertues that be contrarie to them.

For euen as the Carpenter, vvhich preten-
deth to furnifh the timber, for building of
a palace of fom great lord, firft of al cutieth
avvaie the barks of fuch trees, as be brought
from the vvoode, & then doth favve, fquare,
and polifh them, vntill they be fit for his
purpofe; fo likevvife the good maifter of
nouices, and he that defireth to becom the
temple and dvvelling place of God, muft
vnderftand, that firft he muft caft out of his
foule, al the vvicked and peruerfe cuftoms
vvhich he bringeth from the vvorld, and
then muft adorne and beautifie the fame,
vvith the vvoorks of vertues. And this thing
vvhich is the end of him that bringeth vp a
nouice, is alfo a meanes to obteine the true
end of the lavve, vvhich is Charitie, as before hath ben faied. For vvhen the pafsions
be once mortified, and vertues planted in
theire place; Charitie remaineth as the ladie
and Queene of a man: for as our foyvle is a
                                              fpiri-

spi i ua. fubltance, fo is fhe a frind of fpiri-
tualthings . Neuertheles the affections of
this life d avve her dovvnevvards, and hinder her from flying vp to heauen, vvhere
fhe ha h her neaft.

Heerehence it is, that as a ftone, vvhich
by force of fom other thing is ho'den in a
higher place, then his nature requireth, as
foone as the impediments, that held it, be
taken avvay, ftraite vvais faileth dovvne to
the center, vvhich is his natural place:in like
manner, vvhen the difordred pafsions of
oure foule be once mortified and fubdued,
vvhich fhe hath to the things of this
vvorld, fhe fudainlie being holpen vvith
the grace of God, lifteth her felf vp to
heauen, vvhich is the proper place of her
abode.

This is then the reafon, vvherefore fo
greate account is made heere of the mortification of our pafsions, becaufe thefe be
the chaines, vvhich hold our foule bound &
hinder her from flying vpvvards. Vertues
al'o be necelfarie together vvith this mortification, becaufe they be the inftruments,
vvhich Charitie vfeth in al her vvoo ks;
no othervvife then our fovvle vfeth her
faculties, and naturall povvers in all her
functions.

AN

AN INSTRVCTION, OR RVLE OF
good life, for those that begin to serue God
especiallie in Religion.

BFORE vve begin to
treate of the exercises and
vertues, that he muſt haue,
vvhich beginneth to ſerue
God in Religion , it is
neceſſarie to declare the
end of this affaire ; becauſe the ignorance
of the ſame, is that vvhich maketh manie
erre out of the right vvaie.

The end then of this entrepriſe ſo important, is to correct , and mortifie al euil
inclinations, and diſordered appetites of nature, and to make a man ſpiritual, and vertuous , in ſuch ſort that he obteine the end,
for vvhich he vvas created , vvhich is God.
The end is to giue the fiſt being to a nevv
man, not of the earth , but of heauen ; not
of the fleſh , but of the ſpirite ; not conformable to the image of the earthlie Adam,
but like to that of the heauenlie ; not according to the affections and conditions of the
firſt generation, vvhich vvas by nature, but
according to the ſecond generation , vvhich
is by grace. Finallie the end is to dooe that,
vvhich

vvhich God commaunded the Prophet Ieremie, vvhen he faide. *I haue fet thee this daie*
ouer nations and kingdoms, that thou maiſt roote
out, and deſtroie, & diſperſe, & build vp, & plant.
VVhich is as much as to faie; that thou
pluck of from the foule all appetitee & inclinations, that men bring from theirs mothers vvombe, & the corruption of finne;
& that thou plant in theire places the plants
of vertues, vhich be agreable to the nevv re-
generation, & adoptio of the fonns of God.

 Heerehence it appeareth that like as he,
vvhoe deſireth to make a pleafant garden
in a hill ful of briars, fi st diggeth vp vvhatfoeuer hindereth him, and then planteth
in the fame al ſuch fruteful trees as he deſireth : fo one that purpoſeth to make his
fovvle a garden ſhut vp and incloſed, and
a paradiſe of pleafure for almightie God,
muſt firſt roote out all euil herbs, & al the
thornes of vices, and vvicked inclinations
of nature, and then forthvvith fet in theiſe
ſteede, al ſvveete plants & floyvers of vertues and graces. In like ſort dœ they that
mind to make a faire picture; for firſt they
prepare the matter, vvhereupon it is to be
painted, by plaining and poliſhing the
fame, and taking from it al roughnes :
vvhich being donne, they dravv in it vvhat-
     foeuer

Ierem. 1.
3 0.

foeuer they pleafe. Novv the verie like diligence is to be neceffarilie vfed in this ftate, in vvhich nature remained through finne (vvhich before vvas needles) to deftroye and abolifh the remaines of that firft generation, and to adorne the fovvle vvith the vertues of the fecond.

VVhe fore, as amongft diuers and fundrie kind of fruites, fom there be, that ar fit to be eaten, as foone as they be gathered of from the trees, and fom others that firft muft be boiled, or put in conferue manie daies, to affvvage and temper their natural fharpnes and bitternes, vvith vvhich they grevv; fo muft vve vnderftand, that mankind hath had tvvoe ftates or conditions of being, the one before he fel, the other after his finne committed: & that in the firft he vvas fo feafoned and ripe, that nothing vvas to be found in him vvorthie of blame or amendment; but in the fecond there is fo much to be amended, that fcarfe he hath anie thing, that needeth not to paffe firft through the fiar of the holie ghoft, that fo it maie lofe al the vvickednes it hath. And this is one of the chiefeft points and aduifes of this affaire; vvhence it appeareth, hovv great an error thofe bringers vp of nouices commit, vvhoe being intangled and intricated *Note this*

cated

cated in other things of lesse importance, imploie not al theire forces in this labour of mortification: vvhereof it ensueth, hat men remaine almoft as they vvere borne, that is in onlie natural goodnes or yll, vvhich is no lesse inconuenience, then to place a p ece of timber in a gorgeous pa'aice, no othervvise prepared, then euen as it vvas brought cut out of the vvoode; or to set vppon the table in a delicious banket greene olites, in such sort as they be gathered fiom the t ee.

Seeing then that the end of this entreprise, is to make a man good and vertuous, that thou be not deceaued vvith vvhatfoeuer fort of goodnes, thou muft vnderftand that there be tvvoe kinds of goodnes; th'one is naturall, and is proper to such, as be naturallie gentell and vvel condicioned; th'other is spiritual, proceeding of grace, and of the feare and loue of God, vvhich is propre to those that be iuft perfons. Betvvixt these tvvo kinds of goodnes there is fo great difference, that vvith the firft, vve nether merite grace nor glorie, but vvith the second vve obteine the one and the other. And for this p rpofe, the chiefeft care of a good maifter muft be, to attend that this spirite of the feare and loue of God, be poured into the fovvle of his nouice, procuring the same by
all

all meanes, that maie serue to this end, such as ar Praier, Meditation, and Vse of the Sacraments &c. For othervvise, vvhat soeuer he shal doe, vvil be a bodie vvithout sovvle, an Adam of earth vvithout spirite of life, vvhich is a thing of smal profit for Religion; because by experience vve see, that such, as in religion haue nothing els but this natural goodnes, ar no more to be esteemed then feelie soules, or folkes of good past, that ar led by euerie man yvhither he vvil, and can not saie naie to anie bodie, nor hold hand in anie thing that is commended to them. In so much, that a man othervvise yl bent by nature, vvhich striueth, alvvaies through the feare of God, against his vvicked inclinations, is much more vvorth, then is an other, verie vvel inclined by nature, yf he vvant this feare. For as the vvise man saieth, *Better is a liuing dogge, then a dead lion:* because vvithout spirite of life, not anie one thing, be it neuer so greate, can be grateful and acceptable to God.

Of that, vvhich hitherto hath ben said, it is manifest, hovv that this end, of vvhich vve haue spoken, comprehendeth tvvo things; th'one is to driue out of the soule al kind of vices; the other is to plant in the same al kind of vertues, seeing the one ne-

Ecclef. 9. 4.

Q   ceſſarilie

ceſſarilie goeth before the other. For like as in natural things, there can be no generation vvithout corruption; ſo vertues can not be engendred and brought forth in our ſoule, yf our vices be not fiſt dead: nether can the ſpirit freelie raigne and gouerne, yf the fleſh be not before vanquiſhed and ouercom.

Theſe tvvo ends the Apoſtle had then obteined, vvhen he ſaid, vvriting to the Galatians, *vvith Chriſt I am nailed to the Croſſe; and I liue, novv not I, but Chriſt liueth in me*. For by ſaying that he vvas *nailed to the Croſſe,* and that *he liued not,* he giueth to vnderſtand the death of the culd man, vvith al his vvicked inclinations and appetites; vvhich he had ouercom through the fauour of the Croſſe of Ieſus Chriſt: and by ſaying *Chriſt liueth in me,* he ſetteth before our eyes the reſurrection, and life of the nevv man, vvhich vvas not novv conformab'e to the affections of fleſh and bloud, but to the vertues and examples of Chriſt.

Theſe ſelfe ſame tvvo ends, did our Sauiour comprehend in thoſe vvoords of his, ſaying. *If anie man vvil com after me, let him denie him ſel; and take vp his Croſſe, and follovv me.* Fo— by ſaying, *let him denie him ſelf,* he laid before vs the firſt & immediate end, vvhich is that

Galat. 2.
19.

Matth. 16
24.

is, that a man denie his ovvne vvil, and natural inclination , vvith al the affections and
appetites thereof , and that he haue no lavv
vvith them , nor in anie vvise acknovvledge
them , thereby to folovv and obey them.
The fecond and laft end he declared, by faying *let him folovv me*, that is, let him folovv all
the pafes and examples of my life , and al
the vertues that he fhall find in me . And
in that vvhich he faied , *Let him take vp his
Croffe*, to vvit of trauail and aufteritie , he declared the chiefeft meane and inftrument,
neceffarie for the one and the other end : becaufe that neither rooting out of vices and
ouercomming of nature, nether planting of
vertues , can be donne vvithout trauail and
paine, for iomuch as there is great difficultie,
as vvel in the one, as in the other.

By that vvhich hath ben faied , vve maie
plainelie gather of vvhat condition this
nevv vvarfare is , to vvhich a man is called,
and vvhat fort of profeffion it is : for he is
not called to a delicate and quiet life (as fom
dœ imagin) but to the Croffe , to trauail,
to fight againft his paffions , to pouertie and
nakednes, to the facrifice of him felf, and of
his oune vvil, and finallie to that mortification , of vvhich our Sauiour faid ; *vnles the* Io m. 12,
graine of vvheate, falling into the ground , die, it 20.

Q 2   *felf*

selfe remaineth alone; but if it die, it bringeth much fruite. He that loueth his life shall lose it; and he that hateth his life in this vvorld, doth keepe it to life euerlasting. It is no matter of smal importance to vvin and subdue nature, and to make of flesh spirite, of earth heauen, and of a man an Angel. For if in deede to make of a greene hearbe, fine and delicate linnen cloth, there needeth so much mortifying & trauail about the same, by reason of the greate difference there is, betvvixt the one and the other; hovv much more is it necessarie, so the making of this so greate a change, of a man into an Agel? They report, that vvhen a snake vvil change his skinne, he entreth by a verie narovv and straite hole, that by this meanes he maie shift of his ould skinne: he then that mindeth to strippe him self of the ould man, & to put on the nevv, hovv can he bring this to passe, by leading a large & delicate life? There can be no generation vvithout corruption, nether can a man atteine to be that, vvhich he is not, yf first he leaue not to be that, vvhich he is: a thing that can not be donne vvithout great paine and labour.

The life of a Christian man is ordeined to a supernaturall end, and so presupposeth supernatural forces, and consequentlie this life

life it felf muſt be ſupernatural, to vvhich
thing fleſh and bloud can not arriue. VVoe
to that Religion, vvhoſe manner of life is
vvide and large, for in it a man ſhal goe alvvaies vv.th a vyeake and faint ſtomacke,
and one libertie vvil aſk an other, one delicacie vvil dravv an other. Religious life
ought to be ſuch, that like as the ſea caſteth
from it ſelf all dead bodies, and the pot, that
boileth, all the froth and ſcume, that is
vvithin it; ſo ſhee ſhould berid her ſelf of
all the ſcume that ſhe hath, & of al the dead
carcaſes vvhich ſhe findeth to be in her. Let
the ſeruant of God then force, and doe violence to him-ſelf; let him take a greate courage, and think that God ſaieth vnto him,
that vvhich the Angel ſaid to Elias: *Riſe vp,* ³·Reg. 19
eate, becauſe there reſteth yet a greate vvaie for the ⁷·
to goe.

Novv to turne back to our purpoſe, for
ſom uch as there be tvvoe things, vvhich vve
muſt alvvaies haue before our eyes in this
affaire, vvhich be to extirp vices, and plant
vertues: according to theſe tvvoe ends, ſhal
this preſent treatiſe haue alſo tvvoe parts.
The firſt ſhal be of the mortification of vices, and euil inclinations of nature: the ſecond ſhall be of vertues, & of al the renevv-
ing of the invvard man. Not that theſe

tvvoe parts be different betvvixt themselues in practife & vfe, feeing vertues can not
be planted, vnles vices be firft rooted out;
but onlie that the matter, of vvich vve treate,
maie be the better vnderftoode: efpeciallie
because vve knovve more euidentlie
the vices that vvar againft vs, then
vve doe the vertues, vvhich vve
haue neede of ; and fo that
vvhich vve get not by one
vvaie , vve fhal ob-
teine by an
other.

THE FIRSTE
PARTE OF THIS
TREATISE, SPEAKING
OF THE MORTIFICATION
OF OVRE VICES,

AND PASSIONS, AND OF THE meanes that serue for this purpose.

OLOvving then the order, vvhich vve haue heere set doune, the firft thing that vve muft pretend and feeke to bring to paffe is, to caft out of this kingdom al the Iebufites, and to purge this curfede earth from al thiftles and brambles; that is, vve muft labour to fubdue our nature, and to extirp all euil inclinations and appetites, vvhich partlie by the natural condition of eche one, partlie alfo by naughtie coftom, doe ftick and cleaue vnto h'm.

This being prefuppofed, the fift thing that he ought to doe, vvhoe defireth to be changed into an otherman, is to knovv the inclinations of the firft man; vvhich is nothing els but to knovv the enimies, againft vvhom vve muft alvvaies haue moft deadlie vvarre. Let him fearch vvel al the

coɾners

corners of his confcience; let him examen
all the vices, to vvhich he feeleth him felf
moft bent, as to hatred, to vvrath, to glot-
tonie, to flouth, to enuie, to too much talk,
to lying, to bofting, to vaine glorie, to lightnes and eafines of hart, to pleafure and pam-
pering of the bodie, to pride, to prefumption,
to difhoneftie, to pufillanimitie & vveakenes of mind , to couetoufnes and pinching, and to fuch other vices and defects:
and let him determine vvith him felf , to
take this fo glorious and vvorthie an enterprife in hand, as is to vanquifh and fubdue
him felf , and caft out of his fovvle al thefe
monfters , and not to giue ouer, nor take
repofe, vntil he fee an end of that, vvhich he
pretended . Novv thefe vvicked inclinations & vices he fhall neuer by anie meanes
vnderftand better, then by labouring to
obteine vertues, vvhich be contrarie vnto
them : becaufe vvhen it commeth to the
point, to embrace vertue earneftlie, & as it
behoueth vs to doe , then the contradiction
of that vice, vvhich repugneth to vertue,
declareth and fhevveth it felf; vvhich yet before laie hidden. And to faie the truth, a man
neuer commeth to knovv vvel his natural
imperfections and vices, vntil he haue a
vvil & defire to leaue them; no othervvife
then

then the bird, vvhich is taken in the snare, feeleth not that he is taken, vntil that he seeke to get out of the same.

And becauf there might be much said of this matter, yf a man vvould runne through euerie particular vice, and inclinati.n of ours, & the breefenes of this little treatise suffereth not that I be ouerlong; I shal be content for this present, to remit the vertuous and diligent reader, to the springs and fountaines of this matter, that is, to the holie fathers and doctors, that vvrite of the same.

To this helpeth verie much also, the ordinarie examining of a mans oyvne conscience, vvhich at the least ought to be donne euerie daie once, in vvhich he must enter into iudgment vvith him self; laying doune before him, al his euil inclinations and affections; and examen al his vvords, vvorks and thoughts; and the intention vvhich he hath in al his actions; and the feruor and deuotion vvith vvhich he vvoorketh; and to chasten him self, and doe penance for that vvhich is il donne, hauing alvvaies readie som sorts of penance for this purpose; and demaund instantlie, at almightie Gods hands, grace to remaine at the end victorious and triumphant. I knovv a certaine
                                            person,

perfon , vvhoe, in the examen at night, vvhen he found that he had exceeded in anie vvoord, vvas vvount to byte his toung in penance of that, vvhich he had mifpoken: and an other that for this vvas vvont to take a difcipline , as alfo for vvhatfoeuer other defects . And fo maie euerie one take to him felf, fom particular manner of penance, thereby to chaften the faults, vvhich he euerie daie committeth.

It auaileth alfo much , and is a thing of great profit , to procure earneftlie euerie vveeke the victorie of fom particular vices, and to haue about a man fom thing , to vvaken him, and put him in mind of this enterprife, as maie be to gird him felf vvith fom thing, that caufeth paine, or fom fuch like: to the end that this maie ferue alvvais to admonifh , and prick him forvvards to that, vvhich before he had purpofed , and make him ad ifed, that he fleepe not in this affaire.

It helpeth alfo , and that verie much, that a man doe oftentimes renounce , and giue ouer his ovvne vvil , euen in thofe things that be lavvfull; that by fo doeing , he maie be the more prompt and redie , to denie the fame in fuch things , as be vnlauful and forbidden ; and that he occupie him felf in fom
labours

labours leſſe neceſſarie, thereby not to faile
in ſuch as be of neceſsitie: in like manner,
as men report, that Socrates the philoſo-
pher did, & as they doe, vvhich vvil goe to
vvarre, vvhoe in time of peace doe exerciſe
thoſe things vvhich they muſt vſe in time of
vvarre. And let him not ceaſe in this affaire,
vntil ſuch time as his ovvne vvill be dead
& buried (yf poſsible it vve e) to the end
that there be no hinderance againſt Gods
vvil, nor againſt the vvil of thoſe that be in
his place.

Novv a general meane and inſtrument,
that ſeemeth neceſſarie and requiſite for all
theſe exerciſes, is that general ſtrength, of
vvhich vve ſpake before, to ouercom thervvith all the difficulties, vvhich offer them
ſelues vnto vs in this enterpriſe : For ſomuch as heere muſt be vanquiſhed tvvoe
of the moſt potent things in the vvorld,
vvhich be *nature* and *reaſon*; vvhich can not
be donne vvithout this general courage
and ſtrength, vvhich vve haue made men-
tion of. Heere-hence it is that our Sauiour
ſaid. *The kingdome of heauen ſuffereth violence,* Matth. 11.
and the violent beare it avvay. And therefore 12.
as he that laboureth yron-vvoorke, muſt
neuer let goe the hammer out of his hands,
for the hardnes and reſiſtance of the matter,

on

on vvhich he vvoorketh; so he that laboureth on the matter of vices & vertues, must net moue one pase vvithout this strength and constancie, by reason of the perpetual difficultie, vvhich is in this matter. And let him be assured, that manie occasions vvil be offred heere, to make him relent, and be dismaied in the beginning, and that he shall haue manie falls, and spend manie teares for them, & shall haue great discontentment and diffidence of him self. But yet let him vnderstand, that this is the roial and beaten vvaie of all Saincts, and the true profe and exercise of vertue, and the true penance and file, vvith vvhich al the rustines of vices is made cleane: & that there is no other vvaie more assured, as vvel to com to the knovvledge of God, as to the knovvledge and contempt of him self. Nether let him be discouraged, though he fall manie times, but rather, yf he fell a thovvsand times a daie, let him a thousand times rise vp againe, stil trusting in the superabundāt goodnes of God: nether let him be troubled, seeing that he cannot at euerie moment oue: com & subdue som of his passions, because eftsones it falleth cut, that that is ouercom after manie yeares, vvhich could not be ouercom in long time before; that

by

by this meanes a man maie see manifestlie of vvhome this victorie is . And som times it pleaseth our lord that som Iebusite remaine in our land, as vvel for the exercise of vertue, as also for the safegard of humilitie.

Aboue al this, the diligence of a good maister vvil help much to this mortification, for that to him it apperteineth principallie, to haue knovvledge of the naughtie inclinations of his disciple, and to seeke alvvais medecines and remedies for them . Amongst vvhich remedies one of the chiefest is, to rest the speare , and incountre him in those passions, and inclinations that he hath, setting him a vvoork in base and humble offices, yf he be loftie and proude ; in things that be austere and hard , yf he be tender and delicate; spoiling him of that vvhich he hath, yf he see him bent to proprietie ; and aboue al making him denie his ovvne vvil in diuerse things, euen in those that be lauful , to the end that he be more easie, vvhen neede shal so require, to denie the same in things that ar forbidden . In such sort, that as he vvhich breaketh young horses, to make them manureable and pliant to the bridle, is not content to make them runne the right race onlie , but giueth them a thousand gire-volts, or turnings to the one side and the other,

that

that by this meanes in time of necessitie he
maie vvith facilitie turne him at his pleasure; so likevvise the good maister, must so
often exercise his scholar in renouncing his
ovvne appetites, that novv his vvil being
habituated, and madeto plie it self, doe not
stand stubborne, stiffe, and vntractable, but
be gentle, easie, & obedient to that, vvhich
they shal dispose of her: for othervvise shee
vvil becom as hard as an oke-tree, vvhen
you vvould bend her anie vvaie, such as
vvas that people, of vvhome God saied by
the Prophet Isaie. *I knovv that thou art stub-*
borne, and that thie neck is an yron sinevve. And
againe. *From the vvombe I haue called the a trans-*
greßour, to vvit of mie commaundements
and vvil, to doe thine ovvne.

This is then the chiefest point of this instruction, vvithout vvhich al the rest is nothing vvorth, or of exceeding smal value.
For to goe to the quiar in time appointed,
and to doe such offices as all others doe, anie
vertue be it neuer so little, is sufficient; nether is there in this anie matter vvhereby to
exercise such vertues as be of importance,
to vvit Patience, Obedience, Charitie, Humilitie, Discretion, Subiection and the like;
vvhich all ar more perfectlie discouered in
labours, in reprehensions, in base offices, in
    punish-

Isai.48.4
Ibid. v.8.

punifhments, and particularlie in penances, vvich be giuen vvithout fufficient caufe; for in thefe things vve fhevv patience, vvhich is the touch-ftone of vertues perfection and finenes.

And therfore it is a fingular kind of probation, to giue the nouice oftentimes this manner of penance, for by this meanes is knovven the valour and vertue of eche one. In this fort thofe auncient holie fathers vvere vvoont to proue, and exercife theire difciples, vvhich they brought vp; and yf they vvere brought vp in like manner novv, Religious houfes vvould be peopled not vvith men, but vvith fo manie Angels: becaufe vvith this kind of flaile, they vvould eafilie feparate the ftravv and chaffe from the threffing floare, and the corne vvould remaine alone. But fince the time that this auncient difcipline hath ceafed, things goe as novv a daies vve fee.

Novv the felf fame force and feueritie vvhich the difciple ought to vfe vvith him felf, muft the maifter alfo vfe vvith him, chaftifing feuerelie and religiouflie his imperfections, to the end he feare him; and auifing and vvarning him fecretelie, to the end he loue him, taking alvvaies heede, as much as poffiblie he maie, that he nether haue, nor

fhevv

shevv auersion from anie one, nor vtter anie
angrie, or iniurious vvoords ; because as
soone as this shall be noted in him , the
vvhole enterprise vvil be dissolued and broken of, seeing that the chiefest meanes to
compasse the same , is kindnes and loue.
Nether, because som be frovvard & vveake,
ought the good maister therfore to haue
lesse care of them, but rather (as S. *Bernard*
saith) to others he must be as a companion,
to vveakelings onlie as a father and Superior : hauing for his enterprise to be neuer
vvearie, nor to take repose , vntil such time
as he shall gaine them to Christ. And vvhen
som times he is forced to chasten and punish, let him procure to obserue diligentlie
that vvhich S. *Gregorie* admonisheth , that
his speeche be svveete, and his hand seuere:
and in this sort he shall easilie amend
vvhat is amisse , and not scandalize
anie bodie. Manie other things might
be saied to this purpose , but that,
vvhich hath ben hithertooe set
doune , sufnseth for the present : and so let vs novv
gœ forvvard to speake
of that vvhich yet
remaineth.

THE

THE SECOND
PARTE OF THIS
TREATISE

VVHICH SPEAKETH OF vertues.

T HE ground of our hart being once cleanſed, and alſo purged from all the thornes, and naughtie vveedes of vices & paſſi-ons, vvhich vvere in the ſame, it remaineth that novv vve ſet in it diuers flouers & plantes of vertues; that ſo this garden incloſed, and this paradiſe of pleaſure, in vvhich God him ſelf mindeth ro dvvel, maie be brought to an end and perfection.

Of Charitie.

T HE firſt plant then, vvhich is as the tree of life, that muſt be ſet in the mid-deſt of this paradiſe, is *Charitie*, vvhoſe pro-pertie is to loue, and eſteeme God aboue all things. To this vertue it apperteineth to laie the firſt ſtone of this building, vvhich

R   is a

is a stedfast purpose and determination, not to doe anie thing through vvhich this treasure maie be lost, vvhich yet is lost by one mortal sinne. Let this therfore be the first foundation, and dermination of a Christian man, to esteeme, and make such account of God, and to procure so much to obserue this manner of loialtie and fidelitie, that he vvould rather endure al the torments and paines in the vvorld, euen as the holy martyres suffred them, then commit but onlie one mortall sinne. This must be alvvaies before his eyes, this he must feare in all his affaires, this he must demaund in al his praiers, yea this must be the greatest, and the most continual of al his petitions.

Vnto this same Charitie it apperteineth to purifie the eye of our intention in al our vvorkes, pretending in them not our ovvne commoditie and interest, but the onlie vvel pleasing and contentation of God. In such sort that vvhatsoeuer vve doe, either folovving cure ovvne vvil, o the vvil of anie other vve doe it not for com liment, nor for a bare cerem nie, nor for necessitie, nor by constrainte, nor to please the eyes of men, nor for anie vvorld ie gaine or profit, but purelie for the loue of God: like as an honest vvoman serueth her husband, not for anie

anie commoditie that fhe hopeth at his
hands, but for the loue vvhich fhe beareth
vnto him. And this intention ought a man
to haue, not onlie in the beginning & end
of his vvorkes, but alfo in the time that he
doeth them, he ought to doe them in fuch
manner for God, that in doing them he
actuallie exercife him felf in louing of God:
fo that vvhileft he is in vvorking, he maie
feeme rather to be louing, then to be vvorking. And after this fort, he fhal not be
diftracted in the vvcorks that he doeth. For
foe vvere the Sainds vvont to vvorke, and
therfore vvere not diftracted. VVe fee that
vvhen a mother, or good vvife doth anie
feruice to her child, or to her hufband,
vvhich com from abrode, fhe doth both
loue them, and ferue them together; deli-
ting her felf, and taking great pleafure and
contentation in that feruice vvhich fhe
doeth vnto them. In like manner ought our
hart to be affected, vvhen it mindeth to doe
anie feruice vnto his Creator.

To this felf fame Charitie it appertaineth
not onlie to loue God, but alfo al things
that be his, and efpeciallie reafonable creatures, made to his image & likenes, vvhich
be his children, and the membres of his mi-
ftical bodie; and fo vvith one onlie felf ha-

bite of Charitie, ought vve to loue both God and them; God for him felf, and them in God, and for him, for vvhofe fake it is reafon that vve refpect & loue them, although of them felues they deferued not to be beloued. This loue requireth of vs, that vve hurt no man, that vve fpeake euil of no man, that vve iudge no man, that vve keepe in greate fecrefie the good name & fame of our neighbour, yea and rather to clofe vp our mouthes vvith feuen knottes, then once to touch him in his good name.

Nether is it fufficient onlie to doe no hurt to others, but it is alfo requifite to doe good to al, ro help al, to giue countel to al, to forgiue vvho'oeuer hath offended thee, to afk pardon of him, vvhome thou haft offended, and aboue al to fuffer and beare the greeuances, iniuries, rudenes, fimplicitie, humors, and conditions of al men, according to the faying of the Apoftle. *Beare ye one an* Galat. 6. 2 *others burden, and fo fhal ye fulfil the lavve of Chrift.* This is that vvhich Charitie requireth, vvherein is conteined the lavve and the Prophets: vvithout vvhich, he that vvil goe about to found a Religion, fhal doe as litle as he, that vvould forme a liuelie bodie vvithout a foule; vvhich bodie maie vvel be ftravve or ftone, but not a liuing creature.

Of

Of Hope.

THE second vertue sister of *Charitie*, is *Hope*, vnto vvhich it apperteineth to behold almightie God as a father, bearing tovvards him the hart of a sonne: becaufe that in verie deede, as there is no good in this vvorld, that is vvorthie to be called good, yf it be compared vvith God; so is there no father in earth, that so tenderlie loueth those, vvhome he hath accepted for his sonnes, as almightie God doeth. And so, vvhatsoeuer shal happen vnto a man in this vvorld, be it prosperitie or aduersitie let him be vvel assured, that al is for his commoditie and good, and that al commeth from Gods hand, sith no one sparovv falleth into the snare vvithout his prouidence: and in al these things let him foorthvvith haue recourse vnto him, vvith entiere confidence opening vnto him al his troubles, trusting in the passing great bountie of his liberalitie, in the fidelitie of his promisses, in the pledges of the benifits alreadie receaued, and aboue al in the mer tes of his sonne, that although he be a sinner and verie miserable, yet vvil God be merciful vnto him, and direct al things for his commoditie.

R 3 And

And for this purpose let him alvvaies beare in mind that verse of Dauid, *I am a begger & in pouretie, but our lord is careful for me.* And yf he vvil regard vvith attention the scripture of the psalmes, of the Prophets, and of the Euangelistes, he shall find it al ful of this kind of prouidence, and hope, vvherevvith he shal dailie take greater encouragement to trust in God. And let him be assured, that he shal neuer haue true peace, and quietnes of mind, vntil such time as he hath this manner of securitie and confidence; for vvithout this confidence, euerie thing vvil molest, disquiet, and dismaie him. But vvith this confidence there is nothing that can trouble him, for so much as he hath God for his father, for his protector and defender (as he is of al those that hope in him) vvhose povver and strength no arme is able to resist.

Psal. 39.
18.

Of Humilitie.

THE third vertue is *Humilitie* as vvel invvard as outvvard, vvhich is the roote and foundation of all vertues, & to vvhich it apperteineth, that a man account him self for one of the most vile, and vngrateful creatures of the vvorld, most vnvvorthie of the bread that he eateth, of the earth vvhich he trea-

he treadeth vppon, and of the ayre vvherevvith he breatheth ; and that he esteemeth him
self no better , then a stinking & abominable carcasse , stuffed full vvith vvormes, the
stenche vvherof he him self can not abide;
and for this cause let him desire to be despised, and dishonoured of al creatures, sith he
hath so dishonoured and dispised his Creator. Let him loue thoſe offices that be most
base and vile, as to vvasshe & vvipe disshes,
to svveepe the house, to vvash and make
cleane the necessities of others, as vvel sick
as vvhole, and let him esteeme this for a most
high glorie, that he is becom as a drudge,
& a scullion of al men for the loue of God,
sith he became , and made him self much
lesse then anie of these things be, vvhen he
offended almightie God.

Of Patience.

THE fourth vertue is *Patience*, vvhich
as S. Iames saith, is a vvork of perfection; & as the Apostle nameth it, a token
of proofe, because this vertue is a greate
discouerer (as vve haue said before) of the
finenes of all vertues, but principallie &
notoriouslie of prudence and discretion.
This vertue hath three degrees. The first is
R 4   to suffer

Iacob. 1.4.
Rom. 5.4.

to suffer vvhatsoeuer tribulations or iniuries, vvithout murmuring and quarrelling.
2. The second is not onlie to beare them pa-
tientlie, but also to desire them for the loue
of God. The third is to reioice in them, as it
3 is recorded of the Apostles that they did,
vvhen *they vvent from the sight of the Councel*
reioicing, becau∫e they vvere accounted vvorthie to
∫uffer reproche for the name of IESVS *:* And
albeit this be a vvork of greate perfection,
yet the nouice, vvhoe in the beginning of
his conuersion (vvhen the feruors of charitie, and the consolations of the holie Ghost
doe most abound) arriueth not to this, let
him be vvel assured, that he is not yet a good
nouice, nether hath he begunne prospe-
rouslie to runne this race.

Actor. 5.
41.

Of Pouertie.

THE fift vertue is *Pouertie of ∫pirite*, to
vvhich it apperteineth, not onlie that
a man posse∫se nothing as proper, but also
that he despi∫e, and contemne vvhatsoeuer
riches for Christ, as things that be the matter and obiect of pride, of enuie, of coue-
tou∫nes, of vvrath, of contention, and of al
the cares and troubles of the vvorld. To
this vertue it belongeth not onlie to be
poore

poore in deede, but alſo to loue and affect
pouertie; nether onlie to loue pouertie it ſelf,
but alſo al the companions of pouretie, as
hunger, thirſt, vvearines, a poore hovvſe, a
poore bead, a poore table, poore apparel,
poore houſhold ſtuffe, and euerie one that
is poore, thereby to be in ſom part like to
our Lord, vvhoe vvas borne ſo poorelie, liued ſo poorelie, died ſo poorelie, and vvas ſo
poorelie buried . And that nouice or religious perſon, vvhoe is not yet arriued to
this terme, hath not atteined to the perfection of pouretie, nether to the feruor of
ſpirite, and conſequentlie he ſhall not find
nether in God, nor in him ſelf, that perfect
peace and repoſe vvhich he deſireth.

Of Chaſtitie.

THE ſixt vertue is *Chaſtitie*; the office
vvhereof is to haue a bodie and mind
euen of an Angel yf poſsible it vvere, & to
flie both heauen and earth, from all com-
munications, ſights, familiarities, conuer
ſations, frindſhips or acquaintance, that
maie be anie preiudice to the ſame ; yea
though it be ſomtimes euen of ſpiritual perſons. For as S. *Thomas* ſaith ſingularlie vvel,
oftentimes the ſpiritual loue commeth to be
chaunged

chaunged into a carnall loue, by reason of the likenes, vvhich is betvvixt the one loue, and the other. And therfore let a man endenour in this point, to be so chast and faithful to God, that he vvould rather pluck out his eys of his head, yf it vvere possible, then behold anie thing, that might offend the giuer of them. And vvhen anie occasion shall be ministred vnto him to see anie thing, that maie moue him vnto vnchast thoughts, let him saie mildlie in his hart. O mie lord, let me not haue eyes to behold anie thing, vvherevvith I maie offend thine eyes. Let it not please thy goodnes, that, vvith the eyes vvhich thou hast giuen me, and vvhich thou doest novv illumina e vvith thy light, I make vveapons to offend thee. He that shal haue this honest & careful regard in the gouernment of his eyes, maie be vvel assured that God vvil prese.ue him, and that thereby he shal escape manie battailes and perils, & shall liue in greate peace and quietnes.

Of Mortification.

THE seuenth vertue is *Mortification*, *of
qvvre appetites and selfvvil*, vvhich is noe
particular vertue, but vniuersal and general, that comprehendeth all vertues, vvhich
haue for theire office to moderate and subdue the passions of our hart. To this vertue
apperteineth to contradict, and mortifie
not onlie those appetites and desires, vvhich
extend them selues to vnlauful things, but
also to such as ar not forbidden; to the end
that by the exercise of the one, a man maie
be more readie to the vse of the other. And
therfore it is in deede a verie commendable
exercise, and vvorthie of greate praise, that
as often as a man hath vvil to eate, to drink,
to speake, to recreate him self, to vvalke a-
brode, to see this or that thing; he so often
contradict his vvil in these things, and
breake his ovvne appetite, that in so dooing
he maie becom more fit to suffer the bridle
of reason in other his appetites and desires,
vvhich be lesse vvel ordered, as ar those of
honoure, of interest, of delights, and such
like...

It is also verie expedient, that the ma-
sters exercise theire nouices oftentimes, and
almost

almost alvvaies in these things, as hath ben saied before, that thereby the natural stubburnnes, and hardnes of theire ovvne vvils maie be broken, and a man maie becom more obedient & tractable, and not breake in peeces aftervvards (as drie vvoode is vvont toe doe) vvhen he must be plied and bent. And as often as the seruant of God shal ouercom him self in anie of these things, let him esteeme that he hath vvonne a great croune, and that he hath donne **2. Regum.** God such seruice, as vvas that vvhich Da-**23.15.** uid did him, vvhen he vvold not drink the vvater of the cisterne of Beth-lehem, vvhich he had so greatlie desired, but resisting his greedie appetite, did sacrificie the same to almightie God.

Of Austeritie.

THE eight vertue sister of *mortification*, is *Austeritie* and *rigorousnes* of al things, in the table, bed, disciplines, and all those things, vvhich the Apostle signified vvhen **2. Corint.** he said, *In labour & miserie, in much vvatchings,* **11.27.** *in hunger and thirst, in fastings often, in could & nakednes, beside all those things vvhich ar out-vvardlie.* In all vvhich things this vertue is exceeding profitable for euerie exercise, be-

çause

cauſe ſhe puniſheth the fleſh, ſhe lifteth vp the ſpirite, ſhe ſubdueth the paſsions, ſhe maketh ſatisfaction for ſinnes, and, that vvhich is moſt to be vvondered at, ſhe cutteth of the roote of al euils, vvhich is couetouſnes; ſith the man that is content vvith litle, hath no occaſion to deſire much.

Neither doeth this vertue onlie deliuer a man from other euils, but alſo from al diſcourſes, cares, and vnquietnes, to vvhich thoſe ar bound that vvil liue deliciouſlie, and vſe them ſelues vvel: and by this meanes a man remaineth free and vnoccupied, to giue him ſelf vvholie to God, for vvhich cauſe thoſe holie fathers of Egypt vvere giuen ſo much to this vertue. Neither vvas S. Francis of anie other ſpirite, vvhoe ſo highlie commended the pouretie of bodie and mind; for in the end al commeth to one account, to vvit the auſteritie of the one, and the pouretie and nakednes of the other.

VVhen this vertue ſhall vvant in religious, then ſhal they fal to ruine and decaie; becauſe the vice contrarie to this vertue, vvhich is to eate, drink, and cheariſh the bodie, is not content to breake one onlie lavve of faſting, but alſo al other lavves and ordres; for ſo much as to ſeeke and procure the pleaſures, and delicacies vvhich the bellie

lie requireth, permitteth not that anie lavve of Religion remaine entire, and in his due force: especiallie becaufe one delicacie requireth another, and one vice dravveth another, euen as one vertue bringeth an other vertue.

Novv he that defireth to be free from fo greate euils, let him fettel vvel in his hart, thofe vvordes of the Apoftle that faieth. *Philip.* 3. *Manie vvalke, vvhome often I told you of, and novv* 18 *vveeping alfo I tell you, the ennimies of the croffe of Chrift, vvhofe end is deftruction, vvhofe God is the bellye.* By vvhich vvords thou maift vnderftand, that it muft be no fmall euil, vvhich the Apoftel fo much bevvaileth.

Of Silence.

THE ninth vertue is *Silence* vvhich is the keie of deuotion, of difcretion, of chaftitie, of fhamefaftnes, of innocencie, and of al vertues, fith the vvife-man faied. *Prouerb.* *Death and life lie in the hand of the toung.* VVhofe 18. 21. praifes and commendations yf anie man defire to fee, let him reade the booke of *Sapience*, and there fhal he finde maruailous things touching this vertue. And therfore let a Ch iftian man alvvaies praie to almightie God for this vertue, and faie vvith the Pro-

Prophet Da.id. *Pone Domine custodiam ori meo,* & *ostium circumstantiæ labijs meis* . *Set , o lord ,a garde to mie mouth , and a doore of circumstance to mie lippes.* And let him be assured, that it is no more possible to keepe other vertues vvithout this , then to preserue a great treasure vvithout keie and locke. Novv heere it seemeth conuenient to vvarne those that speake, of the Circumstances vvhich they ought to obserue in the time of speache, to vvit vvhoe speaketh, to vvhome , vvhen, vvhereof, to vvhat end, vvhere, and vvith vvhat inteñtion he speaketh ; that by this meanes he maie keepe him self from al the rocks vvhich be in this nauigation.

Of Solitarines.

THE tenth vertue sister and Companion of *Silence* , is *Solitarines* , vvhich is a rauelin of Silence ; vvhich Solitarines, he must greatlie loue , and procure vvith al diligence, vvhoe desireth to keepe innocencie, to conserue peace , to spend vvel his time, to enioie the pleasures and comforts of the holie Ghost, and to mount vp, and descend by the degees of that ladder, vvhich S. *Bernard* describeth vvriting it to Religious folkes, vvhich be *Reading, Meditation,*

Bernard.
de scala
Clauftra-
lium.

tion, *Praier* and *Contemplation*. For the obteining of this vértue it is neceſſarie that a man ſubdue nature, and force him ſelf, vntil he haue góten a cuſtom to flie companie, to loue recollection and ſolitarines, and to leade his life vvith her: but chiefelie it is neceſſarie to flie the cōpanie of diſtracted, and light perſons, becauſe this is one of the greateſt diſeaſes that the vvorld hath, ſeeing that neither a mad dogge, nor a venimous ſnake doeth ſo much harme, as doeth euil cōpanie: ſor it is moſt certaine (as the Apoſtle ſaieth) that *Euill ſpeaches corrupt good manners*. Moreouer let the ſeruant of God vvrite in his hart that ſaying of the vviſeman; *He that vvalketh vvith vviſemen, ſhal be vviſe; the frind of fooles ſhalbe like them*. And that alſo. *He that toucheth pitch, ſhaibe deſiled therevvith; & he that dealeth vvith proude men, ſhal put on pride*. Novv the maiſters of nouices muſt be verie zealous of this vertue, yf they deſire not to loſe that in fevv hovvers, vvhich hath ben goten vvith greate trauail, and diligent bringing vp in manie yeares.

1. Cor. 15.
33.
Prouerb.
13. 20.

Eccleſiaſt.
13. 1.

Of invvard compoſition.

THE eleuenth vertue is the *meaſure* and *Compoſition of the invvard man*, to vvhich vertue

vertue apperteineth that saying of S. Augustine; *In your going, standing, apparel, and in*
al other your motions , let nothing be donne, that
maie offend anie mans eyes, but that vvhich be-
commeth your holines; becausethe contrarie is
a token of a light hart,of small vertue,smal
substance and small deuotion . And therfore
one of the chiefest cares of a good maister
must be to teache his nouice hovv to goe,
hovv to speake , hovv to apparel him self,
hovv to conuerse vvith others , hovv to dis-
pute, hovv to laughe, hovv to vse his armes
in theire gestures , hovv to   recollect his
sight, vvith other such like things. Also
vvith vvhat temperance he must behaue him
self at the table , vvith vvhat comelines he
must lie in his bed , vvith vvhat measure
and deuotion he must be in the Church,
vvith vvhat invvard and outvvard reuerence before the altare , and so in al other the
like places.

Likevvise vvhen he dealeth vvith other
men , he ought to conuerse vvith them in
suche manner , that they remaine edified
vvith his good example,and that he be vvith
al men , and to all an image and patterne of
holines: in such sort, that as one vvhoe toucheth som things that be odoriferous and
svveete , beareth and reteineth vvith him

August. in
regula
clericorum

S   self

self the sent of that vvhich he did touche;
and as he vvhoe in the old lavve touched
anie holie thing, remained halovved ther-
bie, so it is great reason that he remaine in
like sort, vvhoe hath had communication
vvith anie seruant of God.

Of invvard loue to the ceremonies of a mans Religion.

THE tvvelfth vertue is an invvard and
hartie loue to al the ceremonies and
obseruations of a mans profession, not onlie
to those that be great and essential, but also
to all the others, hovv litle and small soeuer
they seeme: for in verie deede none of those
things ought to seeme small, vvhich be ordeined to so high an end, as is to loue God.
Let a man remember vvel hovv it is vvriten, that *he vvhich maketh no account of small*
things, shal fall toe greater: and that *he vvhich*
is faithful in litle, shal be also faithful in more.
My meaning is that he vvhich feareth to fal
in small things, shal be more secure from
falling in greater. And contrarievvise from
smal offences, men com by littel and littel
to fall into verie great euils. It is a thing
vvel knovven that goeth in the common
prouerbe, hovv for a naile vve loose a horse-
shue

Ecclesiast.
19. 1.
Lucæ 16.
10.

fhue, and for a horfefhue a horfe, and for
a horfe the horfeman alfo. In like manner
vve fee, that for a littel rippe, al a vvhole
garment commeth to be rent, and for a little peece that falleth out of a vvall, falleth
aftervvards a great ftone, and thence goeth
to decaye the vvhole building. None vvas
euer at the firft leape verie euil, but by littel
and little men clim as it vvere, and get vp
from fmall euils to greater. There is nothing in Religion that ought to be efteemed
littel, becaufe, be it neuer fo littel, by reafon of the vovve that a Religious perfon
maketh, it is novv becom an act of Religion, & of Obedience, vvhich be tvvoe moft
excellent and high vertues. For Religion
is the moft excellent of al moral vertues,
and this notvvithftanding, Obedience is
fuch a vertue that the Prophet faid of it,
Better is Obedience then Sacrifice. Aboue al this 1. *Regum*
let him be mindful, that a religious perfon 15.22.
is bound vnder paine of mortal finne, to
goe forvvards in that perfection vvhich he
hath profeffed, and that he vvhoe maketh
noe account of fmall things, is not far from
this peril and daunger.

But albeit all obferuations and cceremo-
nies, doe deferue this eftimation and reuerence of vvhich vve haue fpoken, yet more
S 2 noto-

notorioullie and vvorthilie thofe merite
the fame, vvhich be ioined vvith difficultie
& aufteritie: fuch ar fafting, filence, abftinence from flefh, vvatchings at midnight,
clofure, difciplines and the like; becaufe
thefe make Religion to be an imitation,
& Croffe of Chrift, and thefe principallie
doe fingle, and make vs different from
vvordlie men, thefe doe tame the pride of
the flefh, and prouoke vs to the exercifes of
the fpirite. VVhich being foe, there is no
thing that our nature refufeth more then
thefe aufterities; becaufe fhe is a frind of
pleafures, and an enimie of paines. And therfore it is neceffarie to make more refiftance
heere, and to put more ftrength, vvherethe
building is more heauie, as vvel for the importance of the affaire, as alfo for the greatnes of the danger.

Of Imitating the founders of Religion.

T H E thirtenth vertue is the *Imitation*
of the father of that Religion, vnder vvhofe
ftadard eche one is a fouldiat, as the Francifcans
doe imitate S. Francis; the Dominicans,
doe folovv S. Dominicke. And in thefe
theire children ought to imitate the greatenes of theire Charitie, theire zeale of the
falua-

faluation of fovvles, theire perfeuerance in
vvatchings, theire continuation in praiers,
theire rigour in abftinence, theire loue of
pouertie, theire going a foote, theire fleeping in theire clothes, therby to rife more
fpeedelie at midnight, and fuch other like
things ; vvhich thofe that be theire true
children ought to folovv, that fo they may
refemble the fpirite, & fafſhions of theire
father.

Of Difcretion.

THE fourtenth vertue is *Difcretion*,
vvhich is as a miſtres of al the others,
and as a torche that is caried before, to
ſhevve the vvaie of al other vertues : of
vvhich *Difcretion* the vviſeman ſaid. *Let thine* *Prouerb.*
eyes behold the thiags that be right, and let thie 4. 25.
eye-liddes goe before thy ſteppes . This *Difcretion*
hath for her helpers and companions Grauitie, Silence, Secrefie, Counfel, Praier, Repofe and compoſition both of the invvard
and outvvard man, and a profound Confideration of al that, vvhich a man doeth or
faieth, to the end that al be meafured and
compaffed vvith Reafon, al other paſſions
and affections fet a fide.

Of Obedience.

THE laft vertue is *Obedience*, vvhich I
place heere in the end, not as the laft of
al, but as the abridgment and fumme of al
vertues, taking the fame *Obedience* in as
much as it is a General vertue, to vvhich it
apperteineth, that a man haue his ovvne
vvil vvholie refigned, and as it vvere dead
(as much as may be pofsible) to the end that
there be nothing in him, that maie refift or
contradict the vvil of almightie God.

In this *Obedience* there be fiue degrees,
1 amongft vvhich the firft is to obey the com-
2 maundements of God. The fecond is to
3 obey his counfels. The third is to obey his
diuine infpirations and callings, vvhen vve
fhal once vnderftand that they com from
4 him. The fouerth is to conforme our felues
to his diuine vvil, in vvhatfoeuer he fhal
doe or difpofe of vs, or by vvhat meanes it
fhal beft pleafe him, be it profperous or ad-
uerfe, trufting that al commeth from his
hand, and for our good, as hath ben faied
5 before. The fift is to be obedient to thofe,
vvhome God hath put in his place, as to his
miniftres & vicars, in al that they fhal commaund vs, calling to mind that vvhich is
vvriten.

vvriten. *He that heareth you, heareth me ; and he* Lucæ 10.
that despiseth you, despiseth me. Novv in this fift 16.
degree of Obedience , there be yet three
other degrees. The first is to obey onlie by   **1**
dooing the outvvard vvoork that is commaunded , vvithout that the vvil giue her
consent thereunto , or the vnderstanding
approue and allovv of it . The second is to   **2**
obey both vvith vvorke and vvil , but not
vvith the vnderstanding. The third is to   **3**
obey vvith vvorke , vvith vvil , and vvith
the vnderstanding , iudging that to be expedient vvhich is commaunded, and so appro-
uing it : and this is the most substantial, and
most high degree of Obedience , vvhich can
not be found , but vvhere there is greate
Humilitie , greate Resignation & , greate
Discretion.

These be then , most gentle and louing
reader , the principal vertues , vvith vvhich
he must adorne and deck his sovvle , that desireth to make the same a liuing temple of
almightie God, and a vessel of election and
choise , of vvhich maie be said that vvhich
the vviseman vvriteth , *As a massie vessel of* Ecclesiast.
gold , beset vvith al kinde of pretious stones. Fi- 50. 10.
nallie al these things haue ben treated of
heere vvith much breefenes, that so the di-
lating and amplifying of them maie re-
S 4   maine

maine to him , that shall teache this doctrine vvhich he maie accompanie vvith
manie goodlie examples of Sainctes , vvith
manie goodlie testimonies as vvel of holie
scripture as of auncientfathers , and vvith
vvhat els soeuer that either reading, or experience , or the holie Ghost shall teache
him.

OF SVCH THINGS AS MAIE
help vs to put in practise al that, vvhich
hitherto hath ben saied.

T can not be denied, but
that there is great labour,
and difficultie in al those
things , vvhich hitherto
vve haue treated of, be-
cause as vvel the breaking
of nature and old customs, as also the obteining of vertues, is not vvithout difficultie, sith this is the common obiect, and matter of vertue. It therfore remaineth novv, for
the accumplisshing of that vvhich hath ben
saied , to prouide som remedies , vvhereby
to make this affaire more easie , because
vvithout these remedies, it vvil little auaile
vs to knovv vvhat is good, yf vve vvant
forces to put it in execution : no othervvise
then it

then it little profitteth a sick man to haue
meate before him, yf he haue no appetite
to eate the same.

Of Deuotion.

NOVV for this purpose, one of the
chiefest meanes that vve haue, is *Deuo-*
tion, sith it apparteineth principallie to this
vertue, to make a man prompt and fitte to
the vvoorks of almightie God: in such sort
that other vertues be as it vvere the burden
and yoke of our lord, but this vertue of deuotion, is as the shoulders and vvings that
help to lift and beare it vp. For the vnderstanding of vvhich thing *it is to be noted*, that Note this
the difficultie vvhich is in this affaire, grovveth not out of the condition of vice, nor
of vertue, (because vice is contrarie to nature, and vertue is conformable to the same,
and so by reason there should be difficultie
in vice, and facilitie in vertue) but it grovveth of the corrupted subiect, vvhich is
the hart of man, corrupted and vitiated
through sinne. VVherfore as to a sick mans
tast the meate seemeth vnsauourie and vn-
gratefull, vvhich to one that is in good
health, is svveete and pleasant; and as to
vveake and feeble eyes the light it self is
com-

combrefom , vvhich to fuch as haue good
eyes is moft grateful : fo vertue feemeth
fovver , and vice fvveete, not in comparifon of themfelues, but in refpect of the euil
difpofition of the fubiect , vvhich is our cor-
corrupted hart.

This then beeing foe, it is neceffarie to
prouide fom kind of plaifter and medicine;
to amend this vvickednes of our hart, and
to put it in fuch difpofition, that it maie loue
vvhat is good , and abhorre the contrarie;
feeing that vvithout this it is impoffible,
either toe fhake of vices, or to obteine vertues. Therfore this is that vvhich moft properlie apperteineth to deuotion , vvhich is
as it vvere a refrefhing & devv of heauen;
a breathing of the holie Choft; an exhala-
tion and yffue of his grace; a kendling of
Faith, Hope & Charitie; and a maruailous
brightnes and fvvetenes , vvhich rifeth of
the meditation and confideration of diuine
and godlie things; and fo transformeth a
mans hart , that it maketh him heauie to
al euil, and fvvift to all good things, and giueth him a taft in thofe thinges that belong to almightie God , and a difguft of
thofe things that be of the vvorld, as S. *Auguftine* declareth in the beginning of the
ninth booke of his Confefsions, vvhere he
recounteth

recounteth of him self saying, that al vvordlie things gaue him difcontentment, in comparifon of the fyveetenes vvhich he found in God, and of the beautie of his houfe, vvhich he fo greatlie loued. This is that vvhich fpiritual perfons feele euerie daie by experience, vvhoe, at the time that they haue anie greate deuotion, find them felues exceeding prompt and redie to al that, vvhich is good, and verie vnvvilling to anie thing that is euil, and fo in the one they find great contentment, and in the other great difpleafure.

So that for this, one of the chiefeft cares of him that defireth to goe forvvards, muft be, that he procure to keepe, and encreafe this noble affect of deuotion, by al fuch means as poffiblie he may: for fo much more eafie fhal the chaungement of his hart be vnto him, hovv much more he fhal haue it deuoute. And therfore, as thofe that mind toe vvorke or print anie thing in vvaxe, doe firft make it foft and fupple betvvixt their hands, and then ftraite giue it the figure that they lift: fo likevvife he that vvil labour his hart, and print in it the Image of verttue, muft endeuour to make it foft vvith the heate of deuotiõ, & fo fhal he doe vvith it, vvhatfoeuer he defireth. So vve

fee,

see, that al such as pretend to vvork anie thing, in a matter vvhich is difficult & hard of it self, doe vse this manner of proceeding. So those that purpose to breake anie hard stone, doe first soften it vvith fiar and vinager, and then doe set vppon it vvith theire yron tooles, and instruments to breake it. Those also that vvil make right a staffe that is crooked, doe first make it supple and pliable at the flame of the fiar, and then bend it as it pleaseth them. Moreouer, hovv can a smith vvork on so hard a mettal as yron is, vvithout the heate of his forge? vvith this heate he doth mollisie the hard yron, and so maketh it pliable and obedient, as yf it vvere vvaxe, to the strokes of the hammer. In so much that the one vvithout the other, vvould not suffice for his office, because the hammer vvithout the forge, vvere, as men saie, to strike vppon cold yron; and the forge vvithout the hammer, vvere to soften the yron, but not to change the forme and figure thereof. And therfore these tvvo things be, in theire manner, necessarie to our purpose, that is the hammer of mortification, to breake and make right the euil inclinations of nature, and the fiar of deuotion, to make the hart softe and obedient to the blovvs of the hammer.

I haue

I haue laide doune thefe things vvith fo
manie vvords and comparifons, becaufe it
feeme h to me, that heerein confifteth the
key of this affaire, and heere-hence is difcouered more cleerelie, hovv great necefstie
vve haue of this deuotion, for the chaung-
ment of our life : and confequentlie hovv
the bringing vp of nouices, and of fuch as
begin a nevv life, is far other then it ought
to be, vvhen vve take no care to traine
them vp in thofe exercifes.

OF DIVERS MEANES VVHEREBY
to get Deuotion ; and firſt of the vſe
of the holie Sacramentes.

IT then remaineh novv
that vve fpeake of thofe
meanes, by vvhich vve
may obteine this good
effect of deuotion ; a-
mongft vvhich meanes
the firit is, the vſe of the holie Sacraments, efpeciallie of the bleffed Communion, becaufe the
proper effect of this moft noble Sacrament,
is the fpirituall refection of the foyvle,
vvhich is a fingular and verie excellent deuotion : for fomuch as the fame doth cherifh

cherifh & ftrengthen vs, & giue vs breath
for this viage. And here a good maifter may
take occafion to faie much, as vvel ofthe in-
eftimable vertue ofthe holie Sacraments,as
alfo of the máner, hovv vve ought to prepare oure felues for the receauing of them;
becaufe he that approcheth to them as he
fhould, can not but receaue moft greate vi-
fitations & illuminations of almightie God.
But cheefelie before Cómunion, & after the
fame, it becommeth vs to haue more particular recollection and praier, becaufe
heere is fom times receaued fuch a fvveete
and maruailous refection, that it dureth aftervvards for manie daies. And he that hath
not yet tafted of this fvveetenes, let him
beleeue that he hath not arriued to feele the
moft noble effect of this Sacrament ; fith
that holding this honie combe and this
bred of Angels in his mouth, he hath felt
nothing that furpaffeth nature.

Of the meditation of heauenlie things.

THE fecond means that ferueth for
this, is *the Meditation and confideration of*
fpiritual things, as the holie doctor S. *Tho-*
mas expreffie determineth, efpeciallie of
almightie Gods benifits, & of the life of
our

our Sauiour Chrift, &c. Becaufe of this
confideration of our mind and vnderftanding, refulteth and rifeth in our vvil this
good affection and feeling, vvhich vve call
deuotion. This is then one of the firft things,
vvhich the maifter muft giue the nouice to
dooe, that by this means deuotion maie be
fo printed in his hart, that he neuer forget
the fame at anie time: & like as nature be-
ginnerh to fafsion the bodie of a liuing creature from the hart, becaufe life doth proceede from the fame to al the other membres; fo muft he begin this fpirituall life by
Praier and Confideration, feeing that from
hence he fhal dravve the fpirite of loue and
feare of God, vvith vvich he muft giue life
to all his vvorks. To this end he muft af-
figne him his times, and manner of exercifes, teaching him, and inftructing him in
particular, and vvith good leafure of that,
vvhich in this parte he ought to dooe, &
afking him euerie daie account of that,
of vvhich he hath praied & meditated vpon, that dooing foe, he maie by littel and
littel teache him this vvaie.

Of Reading spirituall and deuoute bookes.

THE third means is *the reading of spirituall bookes, and of such as be deuoute,* especiallie yf they be redde vvith Attention, &
vvith defire to take profit by them ; becaufe
this manner of reading is verie like to Meditation , except that Meditation doth ftaie
it felfe fomvvhat more in things, and doth
ruminate and digeft them more at leafure,
vvhich he alfo maie , and ought to doe that
readeth, for fo he fhal reape not much leffe
fruite by the one, then by the other. And
the reafon is , becaufe that the light vvhich
the vnderftanding receaueth heere, defcen-
deth and is communicated to the vvill, and
to all the povvers of the foule, no othervvife then the vertue and motion of the firft
heauen , is communicated to all the other
inferior celeftial globes and fpheres. And it
is an excercife vvorthie to be much commended, to reade euerie daie to the nouices, in cómon, fom fpiritual booke, conteining aduertifements & documents of good
life, fuch as is the Treatife made by S· Vin-
cent of fpiritual life,& others like: & vvhen
Reading is ended , to make fom fpiritual
fpeache vppon that vvhich hath ben reade.

Of

Of Attention in the time of the diuine seruice.

AN other thing that helpeth verie much tō the fame deuotion , is *the diuine seruice,* in vvhich manie times the foule is caried avvaie in ecftafie , and becommeth as it vvere dronk vvith an extraordinarie fvveetenes, yf fhee endeuour to afsift there, vvith fuch attention and deuotion , as is requifite . And for this purpofe , one of the maifters cares muft be, to explicate and declare, in vvhat manner the nouice ought to prepare him felf by time , to com to the quiar ; and in vvhat fort he muft affift there, not as one heauie , cold , and redie to fall dovvne, but as one that is quick, vvaking, attent, deuout, and as one that ftandeth amongft the Angels, docing the office and dutie that they doe . Becaufe of thefe tvvoe things dependeth principallie the fruite, vvhich is gotten by this vvoork ; to vvit of the manner of preparing our felues before the diuine feruice, and of the Attention that is to be vfed in the fame. And heere it is requifite to declare the Obligation , vvhich the nouice hath , to faie the diuine feruice vvith Attention , and hovv there be *three forts of Attention*, one, vvhich is good , to the

T vvoords;

vvoords; an other, vvhich is better, to the
sense and meaning of the vvoords; and the
third, vvhich is best of all, to God him self,
setling our hart in him, & reposing in him.
And heere the maister maie also teache his
nouice, to haue Attention to diuerse misteries of the Passion of IESVS Christ, re-
parting them for the seuen Canonical hovvers, vvhich is a verie good remedie for
such, as vnderstand not vvhat they sing
or saie.

Of hearing and seruing masse.

A N other exercise also is *to serue, and*
assist at masse, considering there the
misterie, vvhich in the same is represented
vnto vs, vvhich is the Sacrifice of the blessed
Passion of our Sauiour IESVS Christ: in
so much that a man seruing, or assisting at
masse, doth the Office of Angels, vvhoe minister and assist before the diuine maiestie of
almightie God. So likevvise as often as he
shal be present, or goe before the most blessed Sacrament, let him endeuour to stand
there vvith such feare and reuerence, as is
due to so greate a maiestie: vvhich is a thing
vvorthie to be much accounted of, and to
be amended also, because of the great negligence

gence and carelefnes, that men doe vſe in
this affaire of ſo great importance.

Of dailie exerciſe.

THE morning vvhen he riſeth out of
his bead, let him doe theſe three things
that folovv . The firſt is to giue moſt hartie
thanks to our lord , for that he hath giuen
him that night reſt and repoſe , and for al
other benifits . The ſecond is to offer him
ſelf, & al the things vvhich that daie he ſhal
doe or ſuffer, to the glorie of his holie name.
The third is to demaund his grace to emploie, and ſpend al that daie in his ſeruice,
and particularlie to reſiſt thoſe vices , to
vvhich he findeth him ſelfe moſt inclined.

Of fridaies exerciſe.

EVERIE fridaie in remembrance of
the paſsion of our Sauiour IESVS
Chriſt, he ought to doe ſom particular thing
as to faſt or to giue Almes, or to take ſom
diſcipline that maie greeue him, or to vveare
ſom auſtere thing vppon his bodie, for the
loue of his Sauiour, that endured ſo much
for him. It is alſo reaſon that he ſhould doe
the like, the euenings before he goe to Communion,

munion, thereby to prepare him felf the better to this miſterie; and vvhen he taketh a diſcipline, he muſt diuide the ſame into three parts, allotting the one for him felf; the other for the ſovvles that be in purgatorie; and the third for thoſe that liue in mortal ſinne, that God graunt them grace to amend them ſelues.

Theſe be the ſpiritual exerciſes, vvhich the good maiſter muſt teache his diſcipſe, becauſe theſe be the chiefe means and inſtruments, by vvhich the holie Ghoſt is vvont to make men becom ſpiritual, and to vnfleſh them of al fleſh, and to make them fit for all vertue. And it is alſo a verie good meane for this, to let the nouice be vnoccupied, the firſt daies of his conuerſion, from al external affairs, as much as maie be poſſible, and to teache him, being ſo retired in ſilence and ſolitarines, the manner that he muſt obſerue in thoſe exerciſes, eſpeciallie in Praier and Meditation. And euerie daie at a certein hovver, let the maiſter take a reckoning of his nouice, hovv he hath behaued and found him ſelf in eche of theſe exerciſes; hovv in his meditations, and vvhat he thought of in them; hovv in the quiar, & at maſſe time, & in the examining of his conſcience; hovv in reading of

ſpi-

spiritual bookes; novv he recollected him
felf before, and after the receauing of the
bleffed Communion, and vvhat hedid re-
hearce, or meditate at thofe times; hovv he
did beare him felf touching fuch thoughts,
as came there to his mind; and finallie
vvhat patience, and longanimitie he hath
in expecting the vifitation of our Lord, &
the devv of deuotion vvhen it is differred,
yea vvhen it is vvholie denied him. And fo
vvhen he giueth account of him felf in this
manner, the maifter fhal com to knovv, and
vnderftand by little and little, vvhat he
hath in him, and confequentlie hovv to deale
vvith him, as his office requireth.

A BREEFE SVMME OF AL THAT
vvhich hitherto hath ben faid.

VT novv to abbreuiate,
and laie doune in fevve
vvords all that vvhich hitherto vve haue treated
of, it remaineth that there
be three things neceffarie,
for the good order & redreffing of our life.
One is to mortifie, and caft out of our fovvle,
al our vvicked inclinations and vices. An
T 3   other

other is to adorne and beutifie the same
vvith vertues. The third is to procure, by
al the aforesaied meanes and exercises, the
grace of deuotion, that through it vve maie
performe the one and the other. Amongst
vvhich things, the tvvo first be as the ends,
the third is as a most principal meane to
obteine these ends. And yf vve doe this that
hath ben saied, vve shall not climme vp to
heauen vvithout a ladder, as those doe,
vvhich pretend to get vp to the toppe of
Perfection, vvithout deuotion.

Of diuerse Temptations of those that be nevv in Religion.

ALBEIT this little booke is nothing
els but a breefe memorial of that,
vvhich a good maister must teache his disciple (and therfore it doth but onlie point
those things, vvhich he must treate of) neuer
theles, it hath seemed to me expedient (besides that vvhich hath ben saied) to touche
heere in the end of this Rule, vvith like
breefenes, the most ordinarie temptations,
that ar vvont to assault such persons, as begin to serue God in Religion: that by this
meanes they may at lest knovv them to be
temptations, because this is a verie good
vvaie to ouercom and vanquish them.

VVhere-

VVherfore, vvho foeuer hee be, that doth put on his harneis, and arme him felf toe fight in this kind of battail, let him firft of all prefuppofe, that he muft abide great incounters, & manie temptations of the enimie. For not in vainethe vvife-man fore-vvarened vs faying. *O mie fanne, vvhen thou commeft to the feruice of God, ftand in iuftice and feare, and prepare thy fovvle to temptation.* *Ecclefiaft. 2. 1.*

Of Temptation in matters of faith.

AMONgft thefe Temptations the firft is *in Matters of faith*: for vvhere as a man, vntil the time of his conuerfion, remained as it vvere in a fleepe, touching the confideration of fuch matters as apperteine to Catholique faith, novv, vvhen he nevvlie beginneth to open hiseyes, and to fee the myfteries thereof, he beginneth forth-vvith, like a ftraunger in a foraine countrye, to vvauer in thofe things, that ar laide before him. And this is by reafon of the little light, and fmall vnderftanding, vvhich he hath of them; vntil that after-vvards perceiuing by vfe, to vvhat purpofe eche thing doth ferue, he quieteth his mind, and is perfvvaded that fuch things be verie conuenient, as feemed to him before verie ftraunge.　　　　T 4　　Of

Of Temptation of Blasphemie.

AN other temptation there is, vvhich is *of Blasphemie*: and this representeth vnto a man the shape of certaine filthie, and abominable things, vvhen he is set to meditate vppon heauenlie things: for as he bringeth his imagination from the vvorld, being yet ful of the shapes and figures of the same, he can not sodainlie cast out of his mind the figures of such things, as haue ben by long continuance imprinted therein: and therfore together vvith spiritual shapes and formes, ar also represented vnto him certaine carnal figures, vvhich doe torment him verie much, that is troubled vvith them. Albeit hovv much more trouble they giue him, so much they be lesse daungerous, because he is farther of from giuing anie consent to them: and so the best vvaie that maie be to ouercom these temptations, is to make no account of them, for so much as they be indeede rather a kind of frighting, and fearing of our enimie, then anie true daunger.

Of temptation of Scruples.

AN other temptation is of *Scruples*, vvhich doe proceede of the ignorance that young beginners haue of spiritual matters; and therfore they goe as a man that vvalketh in the night, vvho doubteth at euerie steppe to fal. This commeth to passe especiallie, for that they vnderstand not the difference betvvene a thought, & a consent, and therfore they imagin that they giue theire consent in euerie light motion. But this temptation, vvith time and vnderstanding of spiritual matters, is cured by little and little, especiallie in those that be humble, and subiect them selues to the iudgment and direction of others.

Of temptation of Scandales.

AN other temptation is *to be quicklie scandalized*, *and offended at euerie little trifle*, and this by reason of the smal experience, vvhich they haue of things. For as they conceiued in theire mindes, that Religion is a most exact and perfect schoole of perfection, and a life of Angels, and as yet knovv not the greatnes of mans frailtie, in

atteining

atteining thereunto; they be easilie scandalized, and vvonder at euerie thing that they
see. These haue not yet atteined vnto the
vnderstanding of that place of S. Gregorie
vvhere he saieth, that *True holines hath com-*
passion, but feined or imperfect holines is disdaine-
full.

To this temptation maie be reduced an
other, vvhich is, vvhen a Religious person
taketh scandale at the lavves, and rules of
his Religion, making him self a Iudge, and
interpreter in the exposition of such things
as his Rule commaundeth, and geuing rash
censure, vvhither his rule be good or euil.
VVhich generallie is a téptation of prouude
and presumptuous vvittes, and of such, as
haue more affiance in them selues, then in
the experience of theire forefathers, vvhich
ordeined these Rules. The remedie is, that
a man submit him self to other mens aduise
and gouernment, and vvholie renounce his
ovvne opinion.

Gregor.
hom. 34.
in euangel.

Of temptation of ouermuch desire of
spiritual Consolations.

AN other temptation is *to desire ouer-*
much spiritual Consolations, and to be
ouer heauie, and discomfited, vvhen he vvanteth

teth them, and to esteeme him self better
then others, vvhen he hath them, measuring perfection by consolation; vvhereas in
deede this is not the true measure, but the
profit in mortification and vertue, is the
touchstone of perfection. Som others there
be likevvise, vvhich, vvhen they vvant spiritual consolations, doe seeke for sensual
consolations, the vvhich is no lesse inconuenience then the former.

Of temptation of vttering Gods fauours.

AN other temptation is, not to keepe
secreate such visitations and fauours,
as they receaue of almightie God, but to
publish and disclose that to others, vvhich
they ought to keepe secrete; and to make
them selues preachers, and doctors before
the time, and begin to be maisters, before
they be good schollers. And al this they doe
vnder a pretence of goodnes, & vvith the
shadovve of vertue, not considering that
the fruitefull tree must yeeld his frute in
time, and that the proper office of a beginner, is to laie his finger on his mouthe, and
to keepe silence.

Of

Of temptation to flitte from place to place.

AN other temptation , and that verie common, is, *to be disquieted vvith the de-fires of chaunging from place to place,* feeming to them, that they maie be in fom otherplace much more quiet and deuout , or els vvith greater profitand more clofe recolleċtion of their minde. Nether doe they confider, that by chaunging the place , the ayer is chaunged , but not the hart, and that to vvhat place foeuer a man goeth, he carieth him felf alvvaies vvith him; that is to faie a mind rent and torne vvith finne (vvhich is a continual ſtore-houfe of miferie and trovvbles) and that this is not remedied vvith chaunging ofplaces , but vvith the fiar of mortification , and vvith the oint-ment of deuotion . VVhich deuotion (as hath ben faied before) doth alter the mind ofa man in fuch fort , that for the time that it dureth, the ftincking filth, vvhich iffueth from the finke of our flefh , is not perceiued. VVherfore the beſt remedie , that a man can take to flie from him felf, is to approche neere vnto almightie God , & to comuni-cate vvith him: for by dvvelling in him by aċtual loue, he remaineth forthvvith fepa-rated,

rated, and abfent from himfelf.

Of temptation of vndifcretion, and of too much difcretion.

AN other temptation is, vvhen men ar in this nevv taft and feruour of fpirite, to giue them felues to vndifcreete vvatchings, praiers, & abftinences, vvhere-by they com to deftroie their fight, their heads, and ftomakes, and to remaine in a manner al theire life afrervvards, vnable for fpiritual exercifes, as I my felf haue feene in manie Religious perfons; and others fall thereby into grieuous difeafes, and fo vvhat vvith the cheriffhing in time of theire fick-nes, vvhat vvith vvant of fpiritual exerci-fes, vvhich they omit, enforced by theire difeafe, theire temptations begin to in-creafe in fuch fort, as that they maie eafilie caft dovvne vertue, being fo abandoned of the aide and ftrength of deuotion.

Others againe being accuftomed to deli-cate cheriffhing in theire infirmitie, doe continue in fuch euil cuftoms, as they vfed in the fame; and others (as *S. Bonauenture* faieth) doe fall by this occafion to loue them felues aboue al meafure, and to hue not onlie more delicatelie then before, but alfo more diffo-

diſſolutelie, making theire ſicknes a pretended colour, to giue licence to al theire appetites, and delicate cheriſſhings.

Som others contrarievviſe doe offend
through ouermuch diſcretion and ſlacknes,
refuſing to doe euerie honeſt vvoork for
feare of peril, ſaying that it is ſufficient for
theire ſaluation, to keepe themſelues from
deadlie ſinnes, albeit other auſterities, and
ſmal things be not obſerued. Of theſe men
S. Bernard ſaith thus. *The man vvhoe is nevvlie*
entred into Religion, and being as yet ſenſual, is be-
com diſcreete, and being but a nouice, is becoin vviſe,
and being but a beginner, is alreadie prudent, can
not poſſiblie perſeuer anie long time in Religion.

Bernard.
de vita
ſolit. ad
frat. de
moute Dei.

Of temptation of forſaking a mans
firſt vocation.

BVT the moſt common temptation of
young nouices is, to forſake the vvaie,
that they haue begonne, and to turne backe
againe to the vvorld; to vvhich purpoſe the
diule vſeth a thovvſand deuiſes. For ſom
times vvith temptations of puſillanimitie
and vveakenes, he putteth into theire head,
that they ſhal neuer be able to endure, and
goe through vvith this kind of auſtere life.
Other times vvith ſtrong temptations of
the

the flefh, he reprefenteth vnto them the
ftate of mariage, as a fure hauen, and quiet
life, vvhich is neuertheles (to faie the truthe)
a goolf of continual troubles and torments;
alleaging for this purpofe the examples of
manie Patriarches, vvhoe being maried
vvere Sainćts; and bearing them in hand,
that they fhal finde for that ftate of life a
meete companion, that fhal be of the fame
intention and mind that they be of, and that
they fhal bring vp theire children in the
feare of God. And here he alfo reprefenteth
vnto them vvhat almes they maie beftovve
in this ftate, vvhich they can not doe remaining in Religion, telling them moreouer,
that this giuing of almes is a greate meane,
to be affured of the kingdom of heauen, at
the daie of iudgment.

Other times contrarie to this, he goeth
about to deceaue them vvith higher imaginations, fetting before them other ordres
of Religion vvhich be more ftraite, and efpeciallie that of the Carthufians; the vvhich
thing he doeth, to once allure and dravv
them out of theire Religion vvith this hal-
ter, that foe hauing gotten them out of the
barres, in the middeft of the tilt he maie fet
vppon them, and carrie them avvaie vppon
his hornes.

Som

Som other times he bringeth them to be in loue exceedinglie vvith folitarie life, vfing therevnto the examples and liues of the holie fathers in the defert, that by this meanes hauing feparated them from all companie, and ledde them through this folitarie vvalke, vvhen they be alone vvithout the fhadovve and counfel of their fpiritual fathers, he maie the more eafilie preuaile againft them.

Of temptation vvhich is couered vvith the cloke of vertue.

BVT amongft al thefe kinds of temptations, the moft dangerous ar thofe, that com vnder pretenfe of goodnes, and doe beare a fhevv of vertue. For fuch things as be openlie naught, carrie vvith them theire ovvne filthines & fuperfcription, by vvhich they be both eafilie knovven, and abhorred: but things, that haue fom ovvtvvard apparence & fhevv of goodnes, ar more perilous, becaufe vvith this colour and cloke of vertue, they maie the more eafilie begui'e vs. And by this vvaie our aduerfarie preuaileth more, then by anie other, in tempting the feruants of God. For vvheras he knovveth right vvel, that they be alredie determined

ned

ned to abhorre the euil, and to embrace the good, he procureth to giue them to drinke the poifon of finne, mingled vvith this deceitful honie of the fhevv of vertue. VVherfore vve ought to fufpect euerie exceffiue and vehement affection, for fo much as the exceffe in euerie thing, is alvvaies to be feared.

Thefe be the moft common temptations of fuch as begin to ferue God, for vvhich the good maifter muft haue his medecines, aforehand, vvel ftudied and prouided for, and a greate part of thefe medecines confifteth in this, to knovve that the things before mentioned, be in deede temptations : becaufe the chiefeft deceite of the enimie is, to make thefe young beginners beliue, that temptations be not temptations but reafons, and thofe alfo vvel grounded, in theire opinion and conceite.

V   HO VV

HOVV A MAN OVGHT TO BEHAVE
him self tovvards God, tovvards him self, and
tovvards his neighbours.

LBEIT I haue suffici-
entlie spoken of vertues in
general , yet that euerie
mā that beginneth to serue
God, maie more easilie put
them in practise, I shal ap-
plie al that hath ben said vnto three principal bounden deuties, vvhich be our devvtie
tovvards God, tovvards oure selues, and
tovvards our neighbours , vvhich deuties
vvere signified by the Prophet Micheas
Mich. 6.8. vvhen he saied, I vvil teache thee, o man, vvherein
goodnes consisteth: and vvhat our lord requireth of
thee, to vvit, to doe iudgment, tovvards thy self;
to loue mercie, tovvards thy neighbour; and
to vvalk caresullie vvith thy God, vvhich
apperteineth vnto the seruice, honour, and
reuerence of God.

Of our devvtie tovvards God.

TO beginne vvith the chiefest of these
deuties, it is to be noted, that amongst
vertues som doe of theire ovvne nature in-
com-

comparablie exceede al others;such be thofe
vertues, that haue theire eye to God, and
be therfore called *Theological*, as *Faith, Hope,*
and *Charitie*, vnto vvhich vve maie adioine
the feare of God, and vvithal *Religion*, vvhich
confifteth in the honour & feruice of God.
Thefe be the moft principal vertues, and
the ftirrers vp of al others; and therefore he
that defireth to atteine to the perfection of
Chriftian life, muft labour to increafe and
profit efpeciallie in the forfaid vertues: for
the more he fhal profit in them, the greater
fhal his perfection be. And for this caufe
it is to be thought, that manie of thofe auncient Patriarches vvere fo notable in vertue,
and fo holie men, becaufe they had thefe
moft excellent vertues; as it appeared in the
Faith and Obedience of Abraham, and in
the loue and confidence vvhich Dauid had
in almightie God, in that he had fuch re-
courfe to him in al necefsities, and did put
fuch truft in him, as a child doth in his father, yea and much more faying. *My father* *Pfalm.26.*
and my mother haue forfaken me; but oure Lord is 10.
careful for me.

Novv to obteine thefe fo noble vertues,
there is no meane more conuenient, then to
pefvvade our felues vvith all the hope that
is pofsible, that almightie God is our true

father: for fomuch as neither in the hart, nor in the prouidence, neither yet in the loue of a father, there is anie comparable vnto him; fith none hath created vs, but he; none defireth more our profit, then he. Let vs therfore fettle this moft ftedfaftlie in our harts, and endeuour alvvaies to behold God vvith fuch eyes &hart, as a child doth his father: that is vvith a hart louing, tender, humble, reuerent, obedient to his vvil, ful of confidence in al aduerfities, and covvched vnder the vvinges of his fatherlie prouidence. And becaufe this hart and affection cannot be obteined vvith oure forces onlie, therefore a man ought continuallie to defire the fame of God.

And to fpeake fomvvhat more particularlie of this, the holie father S. *Vincentius* faieth, that a man ought to haue feuen forts of affections, and vertues tovvards God in his hart: to vvit a moft feruent loue; a verie greate feare; an humble reuerence; a moft conftant zeale; a grateful giuing of thankes; a fvveete mouthe ful of praifes; a readie Obedience; and a pleafant taft of diuine fvvetenes.

Note this

Oj

Of our devvtie tovvards our selues.

A MAN ought also to haue tovvards him self (saith the same holie father) seuen other affections and vertues; amongst vvhich the first must be, to be confounded and ashamed for his sinnes committed. The second, to bevvaile his sinnes, and be hartilie sorovv that he hath offended God, and hurt his ovvne sovvle. The third, that for this he desire to be despised of all men, as vnvvorthie of all honour and fauour. The fourth to make leane, and chastice his bodie vvith al seueritie and rigour, as one that hath ben the prouoker and mouer of al these sinnes. The fift, to conceiue an irreconciliable anger and hatred against al vices, and against al inclinations and rootes of the same. The sixt, to be verie vigilant and attent to gouerne and direct al his vvorkes, and vvordes, and al his senses, and passions, that nothing doe vvithdravv him from the iustice and lavve of God. The seuenth that he haue a most perfect modestie, and discretion in keeping Temperance, and measure in all things; but especiallie to discerne betvveene little & much, betvveene lesse and more, to the end that there be nothing ei-

1

2

3

4

5

6

7

V 3   ther

ther superfluous , or to litle ; nor that he exceede , or vvant vvhat is necessarie.

Of our devvtie tovvards our neighbours.

IN like manner (as the same Saincte teacheth vs) a man ought to haue seuen other special vertues & affections tovvards his neighbour. First he ought to haue an invvard hartie compassion of other mens miseries, and to be grieued at them, as yf they vvere his ovvne. Secondlie he ought to haue a charitable gladnes at the prosperitie, and felicitie of others as he vvould haue, in case it vvere his ovvne. Thirdlie he ought to haue a quiet and seeled patience, vvillinglie contenting him self to suffer all that shalbe donne vnto him, and readie to forgiue al men, vvith al his hart. Fourthlie he ought to haue a gentel benigne behauiour and affabilitie tovvards al men, vsing him self in conuersation, amongst them, vvith al courtisie, mildnes, and gentlenes, and vvisshing them al vvel. Fiftlie he ought to haue an humble reuerence tovvards al men, accounting them for his betters, and submitting him self to all, as yf they vvere his Superiours. Sixtlie he must haue a perfect concord vvith al men, to the end, that

(so

(fo much as in him lieth, and God fhall giue
him grace) he maie faie one felf-fame thing,
and agree vvith al men in opinion, & be
perfvvaded that al men ar euen him felf.
Seuenthlie he ought to haue a mind to offer
him felf for al men, that is, to be readie, to
beftovve his life for the faluation of all men,
and toe praie alvvaies, and to endeuour,
that they al may be one in Chrift, and
Chrift in them. Yet muft he not for this
frequent the companie of naughtie perfons,
but rather flie from them as from ferpents.
Albeit, fetting this occafion afide, the feruant of God ought to be fimple in his con-
uerfation vvith his neighbours, and either to vvinke at theire defectes, or
els, yf he muft needes fee them, to
beare them vvith patience, or to
admonifh them charitablie,
vvhen there is hope of re-
dreffe by fo dooing.

7

V 4   THE

THE FYFT

TREATISE OF THE
SACRAMENT OF
PENANCE.

THE PREFACE.

 MONGST diuers euils that raigne in the vvorld, one most to be lamented, is the manner that manie Christians doe vse in making the Confession of their sinnes. For som fevv excepted, the most part doe com to this Sacrament vvithout anie repentance, and vvithout anie examination of theire consciences. Hence it ensueth, that soone after their Confession, they returne to their vvicked life, and to the same filth in vvhich they vvallovved before. This is a great contempt of God, of his ministers, & of his Sacraments; and it seemeth that these men com to confession onlie to dallie and mock vvith almightie God, for in confession they desire him pardon of theire sinnes, they protest an amendment of life, & yet out of hand beginne a fresh

to

to offend him more then before.

The punifhment that fuch perfons deferue, is fuch as God for the moft part permitteth : that is to leaue them in this euil
ftate, al the daies of theire life, euen til the
houre of death, vvhen theire end vvil be
fuch as vvas theire life, that is vvithout anie
fruite. Yf therfore anie one haue defire to
conuert him felf earneftlie vnto almightie
God, and to doe true penance, I fhal heere
declare vvhat he ought to obferue concerning this matter. And becaufe the *Sacrament
of Penance* conteineth three principal parts,
vvhich be *Contrition*, *Confeßion and Satisfaction*, I vvil breefelie declare
vvhat is to be donne in eche
of thefe parts.

OF CONTRITION, AND OF THE
tvvo partes vvhich it conteineth.

CHAP. I.

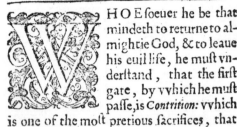

HO E foeuer he be that mindeth to returne to almightie God, & to leaue his euil life, he must vnderstand, that the first gate, by vvhich he must passe, is *Contrition:* vvhich is one of the most pretious sacrifices, that vve are able to offer vnto almightie God, according as the Prophet Dauid saith.

Psalm. 50.
19.

A sorovvful minde is a sacrifice to God, a contrite and humble harte, thou o Lord vvilt not despise.

This *Contrition* hath tvvoe parts. The one is a repentance for the sinnes past; and the other is a stedfast purpose of amendment in time to com. The reason of this is, because *Contrition* is a detestation of sinne, aboue al things that maie be hated, in regard that it offendeth the maiestie of almightie God. And because God is offended as vvel vvith those sinnes that ar to com, as vvith those that ar past; therfore *Contrition* doth include the detestation of the one and the
other;

other; vvhich is as much to faie, as that a
man muft be fory for his finnes paft, and
muft determine to efchevve fuch as maie
com heere after. And heerehence it is, that
the firft thing in a true penitent, muft be to
haue forovve for his finnes, not p inc pallie
for that by them he hath deferued hel, and
loft heauen (although to be fory for this
caufe be good alfo) but for that he hath loft
God, and moft grievoufíie offended his diuine maieftie. And as God deferueth to be
loued aboue al things, fo fhould vve be
more grieued for offending him, then for al
other things vvhatfoeuer; albeit the mercie
of our lord is fuch, that though the forovv
be not fullie anfyverable to the finne committed, yet the vertue of the Sacrament
ioyned therevvith (yf there be no impediment in him that receaueth the fame) fhal
fuffice to reftore him againe to faluation.

Novv heere it is to be noted for the fcru-
pulous and vveake perfons, that this forovv
vvhich is required is not fo of necefsitie, that
it be alvvaies as other fenfible griefes ar, but
that our vvii doe deteft and abhorre finne,
aboue al things that maie be detefted, vvhich
maie be vvithout vveeping or ovytvvard
forovve.

The fecond thing requifite to Contrition,

tion, vvhich is a moſt ſtedfaſt purpoſe neuer
to offend almightie God, muſt likevviſe
not principallie be intended for heauen,
hel, or anie other particular intereſt of our
ovvne, but for the loue of God : albeit to
feare hel, or to deſire heauen, ar not to be re-
proued, but ar verie laudable & profitable,
yea and a gift of God alſo. And as a man
muſt haue a reſolute purpoſe to eſchevv
ſinnes that ar to com, ſoe muſt he leaue &
forſake his preſent ſinnes, othervviſe his
confeſſion ſhould be no confeſſion, but a
ſacrilege. And therfore he that beareth anie
hatred againſt his neighbour, muſt put it
out of his mind, yea and ſpeake to him alſo,
yf anie ſcandale ſhould be feared of the
cõtrarie. He that vvithholdeth anie mans
goods, againſt the vvill of the ovvner, muſt
reſtore them vnto him forvvith, in caſe he
be able to doe it preſentlie, although by this
reſtitution he ſhould caſt him ſelf far behind
hand, eſpeciallie vvhen the devv ovvner
ſtandeth in ſuch, or like neceſſitie of it him
ſelfe. In like manner ought vve to make
Reſtitution of fame, and of honour, yf vve
haue publiſhed abroade anie grieuous, & ſe-
crete crime of our neighbour, or donne him
anie iniurie by vvoord or deede. And this
is that vvhich apperteineth to the tvvoe
prin-

OF THE MEANES BY VVHICH
Contrition is obteined.

CHAP. II.

E novv that defireth to obteine this moſt pretious ievvel of *Contrition*, muſt knovv that the firſt meane for the getting of it , is to demaund the ſame of almightie God, vvith al humilitie and inſtancie that is poſsible ; becauſe the ſame is a ſpecial grace and gift of almightie God, and a vvork exceeding al the povver and force of mans nature . The reaſon of this is , for that God created the nature of man vpright, and lifted vp vnto him ſelf by loue , but ſinne hath crooked it, and inclined it doune to her ſelf , that is to the loue of viſible things : & therfore as a man borne vvith a crooked backe from his mothers vvombe, can not find anie natural remedie to reſtore him to his ſtreightnes ; ſo vve being borne vvith this kind of ſpiritual crookednes throrgh originall ſinne , there is no thing that can ſtreighten vs, but onlie the ſame

lord

lord that made vs. And becaufe this ftreightnes confifteth in the loue of God aboue al things, vvhich no man can haue but by God him felf; fo no man can haue forovve for finne aboue al things for the loue of him, but by the fpecial loue of God him felfe, for fomuch as the one folovveth of the other. If this then be a vvorke of God, and fo greate a vvorke, it folovveth that vve ought to demaund the fame of him vvith al humilitie and inftancie pofsible.

The fecond meane to obteine Contrition , is for a man to keepe a parliament vvithin him felf, & to confider fuch things, as maie prouoke and incline him to get forovv for his finnes. For the more he fhal confider the caufes that maie moue him thereunto, the more clearelie fhal he perceaue , hovy much it importeth him to bevvaile his miferable ftate. For he that knovveth hovy to confider his finnes , as they ought to be confidered, knovveth alfo hovy to bevvaile them, as they ought to be bevvailed. Let a finner therfore open his eyes, and fixe them firft vppon the multitude of his finnes, and aftervvards vppon almightie God againft vvhome he hath finned; for eche of thefe confiderations vvil teach him , hovy good caufe he hath to bevvaile
                                                                    his

his finnes.

Novv to ftirre vp thy fovvle to this forovve, thou muft firft of all fet before thine
eyes all the finnes of thie life paft, & vvithal hovv thou haft abufed the benefites receaued of almightie God. And becaufe finne
is a fvvaruing from the end, for vvhich man
vvas created, let him firft confider this end,
vvhich vvas to knovve and loue God, and
to keepe his commaundements, and therby
to atteine to the chiefeft felicitie : for by this
he fhal fee more clearelie, hovv far he hath
ftraied from this end . In confideration
vvhereof God gaue him *a Lavve* to vvit his
Commmaundements, vvherein he fhould
liue ; and *Grace* vvhereby he might obferue
his lavve ; and *Sacramentes* by vvhich grace
be miniftred vnto him ; and *Teachers* that
might inftruct him therein ; and *Infpirations*
that might prouoke him thereunto ; and finallie *him felf*, to be the price and remedie
of al his finnes . Likevvife for this end he
gaue him *the gifts of nature*, vvhich be Life,
Health, Strength, The povvers of the
fovvle, The fenfes, and membres of the bodie, to the end that he fhould applie all
thefe in his feruice, vvhoe had beftovved
them vppon him. And for this fame end he
gaue him alfo the goods, called the goods

of

I

of fortune that vvith them he might fufteine his ovvne life, and relieue the necefsitie of others, and ſo merite the kingdome of heauen . Theſe and manie others be the benifits and helpes , vvich God hath giuen vs to emploie them in his ſeruice. Let a man therfore conſider hovv he hath vſed theſe benifits, and he ſhall find, that he hath made vveapons of them to fight againſt God ; and vvith vvhat things he vvas bound to doe him greater ſeruice , vvith the ſame he hath committed greater ſinnes . He then that ſhall conſider this, hath he not good cauſe to bevvaile and lament his offences ?

2   The ſecond meane is to conſider vvhat is loſt by ſinne , vvhereof becauſe vve haue ſpoken ſufficientlie in the third treatiſe pag. *236.* it ſhalbe neceſſarie onlie to aduertiſe euerie man , that he conſider vvith him ſelf, vvhether he hath not good cauſe to be hartilie ſorie, that hath loſt ſo manie benifits as ar there mentioned.

3   The third meane is to conſider the greatnes of the maieſtie , and goodnes of God, againſt vv home thou haſt ſinned . For it is certaine , that the greater the perſonage is that is offended , the greater is the offence committed againſt him ; and ſo the more that a man ſhal vnderſtand the exceeding
greatnes

greatnes of the maieftie of almightie God, the more fhall he penetrate the malice of his finne. Confider then the nobilitie, the riches, the dignitie, the vvifdome, the beutie, the glorie, the goodnes, the maieftie, the benignitie & povver of this Lord, & hovv al creatures ar bound vnto him; and fo calling to mind hovv thou haft offended him, thou fhalt not onlie vnderftand the heynoufnes of thy finnes, committed againft him, but alfo haue good caufe to be fory and to lament.

The fourth meane is to confider the iniurie donne to almightie God by finne. For as often as vve finne this iudgment paffeth fecretelie, in practife vvithin our harts, though me perceaue it not; to vvit, of the one fide is fet before vs the profit of finne, vvhich is the delite or commoditie that enfueth of finne, and of the other the offence that vve comit againft God, & man being placed in the middeft, refolueth vvith him felfe rather to leefe the friendfhip & fauour of God, then the comoditie vvhich is to com by finne. Novv vvhat can be more horrible, or more vnfeemelie then this; to preferre fo bafe a thing before God? or vvhat can more refemble that vvicked fact of the Ievves, vvhoe vvhen choife vvas offered

X   fered

fered vnto them, vvhether they vvould haue
Chrift or Barrabbas, anfvvered, that they
vvould rather haue Barrabbas then Chrift.
VVhich things yf a man confider vvel, he
vvil vndoubtedlie be afhamed of him felf,
and moued to forovve.

5 The fift meane is to confider the great
hatred, that God beareth againft finne,
vvhich is fo great, as no vnderftanding is
able to comprehend it. The reafon is, for
that the better a man is, the more he loueth
that vvhich is good, and abhorreth that
vvhich is vvicked; and therefore God being
infinitelie good, he muft needes beare infinite loue tovvards goodnes, and infinite
hatred tovvards finne, and fo he revvardeth
the one vvith euerlafting glorie, and the o-
ther he punifheth vvith euerlafting paines.
But becaufe of this hatred againft finne,
cnough hath ben faid in the third treatife
pag. 257. procure by the confideration
thereof, to abhorre finne fo much as is poffible for thee to doe, and praie God to encreafe in thee this hatred of finne, and forovv
for the fame, for therein confifteth a greate
part of true penance.

6 The fixt meane is to call to remembrance
the paines of hell, and the vniuerfall laft
iudgment, as alfo the particular iudgment
at eche

at eche mans death, vvhich things vvil
moue vs to conceaue hartie forovv and feare
for our sinnes, sith that eche one of them
doth threaten such great terrible calamities
to him, that shall be found guiltie of anie
one deadlie sinne. And therfore better it is
novv for euerie one, to enter presentlie into
iudgment vvith himself for his sinnes, that
he be not then iudged for them of almightie
God; especiallie considering that the holie
scripture assureth vs, that in case vve shall
iudge our selues, vve shall not be iudged.

1. Cor. 11.
31.

The last meane is to consider the multitude of the benifits of almightie God, and
especiallie of thy Creation, Conseruation,
Redemption, Baptisme, Vocation, Diuine
inspirations, Preseruation of thee from dangers and miseries, vvith other innumerable benifits. Novv vvhat thing is more to
be lamented, then that thou hast liued so
long time, in such a greate forgetfulnes
and ignorance of such a louing Lord, in
vvhome thou diddest moue, liue, & hadest
thy being? vvhat greater iniquitie could
be deuised, then to offend him vvhoe hath
trauailled for thy sake so manie vvaies,
fasted so manie and so long fastes, shedde
so manie teares, made so manie prayiers,
suffered so manie iniuries, taken so greate

7

X 2   paines,

paines, fufteined fo manie difhonours, fo manie infamies, fo manie, yea and fo greate torments? For it is moft certaine that al thefe he fuffered for thy finnes, as vvel to fatisfie for them, as to make thee vnderftand the hatred he beareth againft them, fith he tooke fuch paines to deftroye them. Confider therfore, vvhether thou haft not good caufe to be forie, and to refolue thy felfe vvholie into teares.

OF CONFESSION, AND VVHAT
vve ought to obferue in the fame.

CHAP. III.

AVING treated of the firfte parte of Penance, vvhich is *Contrition* for our finnes, let vs novv fpeake of the fecond, vvhich is *Confefsion*, vvherein a man ought to obferue thefe things that folovve. The firft is that he take fom time before to examin his confcience, and to cal to mind al his deadlie finnes paft, efpeciallie yf he haue difcontinued anie long time from *Confefsion*; in vvhich examination he ought to attend vvith greate diligence and care, as in a
matter

matter of moſt great importance. This exa-
minatiõ is ſo neceſſarie, that vvhen it vvanteth (in caſe the Ghoſtlie father ſupplie not
this vvant) the Confeſſion is of no effecte;
euen as that Confeſsion ſhould be, vvherein
the ſinner doth vvillinglie leaue out of his
Confeſsion ſom deadlie ſinne vnconfeſſed,
and ſo is bounde toe make his Confeſsion
againe. Therfore to auoide this inconuenience a man ought to prepare him ſelf, and
to examin his conſcience diligentlie, by per-
vſing the ten Commaundements, and the
deadlie ſinnes, vvhich he ought to conſider
euerie one, hovv often he hath ſinned in eche
of them by thought, vvoord, or deede, vvith
al the circumſtances that happened in the
ſinne; vvhen the circumſtances be ſuch, as
of neceſsitie ought to be confeſſed.

The ſecond aduiſe is to declare in Confeſsion the number of the deadlie ſinnes. **2.**
And in caſe he doe not remember hovv often he hath committed ſuch or ſuch a deadlie ſinne diſtinctlie, yet let him giue a gheſſe
thereof, as neere as he can poſsiblie, more or
leſſe, or els declare vnto his Ghoſtlie father
hovv long time he hath continued in the
ſame deadlie ſinne; or at the leaſt let him declare vvhether he hath accuſtomed to offend
in that kind of deadlie ſinne as often as

opportunitie vvas offered, or did some times vppon remorse of conscience refraine him selfe.

3   The third is to confesse and specifie the Circumstances, vvhen they doe greatlie aggrauate the sinne, although the kind thereof be not thereby chaunged. For although the acte of deadlie sinne is but one thing, yet it maie be accompanied vvith som vvickednes of such qualitie, that of necessitie it ought to be confessed. As for example; yf one had stollen armour, vvith intent to kill an other man, and take avvaie his vvife from him : it is heere manifest, that albeit this be but one onlie act, vvhich is to robbe, and consequentlie but one sinne, yet this act hath tvvoe other offences annexed vnto it, vvhich be, a vvil to commit murther, & to commit adulterie. But this is a thing that apperteineth more to the ghostlie father, then to the penitent, except he be such a one, as is able to knovve these circumstances.

4   The fourth is to confesse the kind of the deadlie sinne, as thefte, fornication, adulterie or such like, vvithout rehearsall of the vvhole historie as it passed, by onlie saying, I haue often times robbed, killed, committed fornication, adulterie, periurie, &c.
                                                    Like-

Likevvife it is not neceſſarie to ſpecifie in vvhat manner the ſinne vvas committed, eſpeciallie being a ſinne of the fleſh, but to declare the kind onlie. And albeit this matter be verie lothſome and filthie, yet it is to be noted, that a diſhoneſt ſinne maie be committed by thought, by vvords, or by touching, or by doing the verie deede. It the act be donne in deede, it is ſufficient to tell the name of the act, as Adulterie, Inceſt, ſimple fornication, &c. If it vvere by touching, it is ſufficient to ſaie, I haue touched ſuch a kind of perſon, vnles there folovved ſom thing that might change the kind of the ſinne. If it vvere by vvordes, it ſhal ſuffice to ſaie, I haue ſpoken filthie vvords, and ſuch as prouoked to ſinne, or to delite mie ſelf therein; and not to name the vvordes.

The fift is, to confeſſe the ſinnes of the thought, and heere I vvil declare hovv this ought to be donne. It is then to be vnder-ſtoode, that in an euil thought a man may behaue him ſelfe after one of theſe foure vvaies that folovv. The firſt is, vvhen he endeuoureth ſpeedilie to repell avvaie the euil thought, in vvhich caſe it is cleare, that, albeit this reſiſting & ſtriuing ſhould continue all a vvhole daie, yet therein is no

5

Note this vvel

1

X 4   ſinne,

sinne, but a merite and revvard, and so it requireth no Confession. The second is, 2 vvhen he staieth him self in the euil thought for a short time ; and then it is a veniall sinne, vvhich is more or lesse grieuous, according as the staying in it vvas more or lesse. The manner to confesse it is to saie. I accuse mie self to haue had a dishonest thought, or of anger, &c. and haue staied in it longer then I should haue donne. The 3 third is, vvhen he giueth consent to the euil thought, and determineth to put it in practise, though aftervvards he doe it not in deede, and it is manifest that this is a deadlie sinne, and of the same kind, as if it 4 had ben executed in acte. The last is, vvhen one continueth vvillinglie, or suffereth him selfe to continue in thinking, & taking delite in an euil thought, albeit he intend not to put it in execution ; & this is also a deadlie sinne, called by the learned diuines *a lingring delite* ; vvhich is, as they ar vvonte to saie. *Though I drinke not in the tauerne, yet I take delite therein.*

Novv that vve haue vnderstoode these foure differences of thoughts, it shalbe easie to knovv hovv to confesse them, yf the penitent declare vvhether he staide him self in the euil thought, or consented thereunto,

or

or vvhether he had anie lingring delite therein, by continuing vvillinglie in taking delite in the same euil thought.

The sixte is, that the penitent be careful **6** to preserue the good name and fame of his neighbour, confesing his ovvne sinnes in such order, that he discouer not the sinnes of others, nor speake of anie person by name, but let him onlie saie, I haue sinned vvith a maried vvife, or vvith a single vvoman, &c. And in case the circumstance be such, as the ghostlie father maie therby knovv vvhome he meaneth, then ought he to seeke for that time, som other ghostlie father, that knovveth not the person. And yf he can not possiblie so doe (vvhich yet he must endeuour as much as he maie) then (the ghostlie father being such a person) he maie vvel confesse ynto him this circumstance.

The seuenth is, that in his confession he **7** excuse not his ovvne sinnes, nor yet charge him selfe vvith more then is true; neither yet vtter that vvhich is doubtful for certaine, nor such things as ar certaine for doubtful; but let him declare eche thing in his place as it vvas in deede, vvithout adding or diminishing.

The last is, that he be careful to seeke **8**

out a good phisition for his sovvle, as he vvould if he vvere sick for his bodie, for this is a matter of more importance: and to seeke out an ignorant ghoftlie father, is as much to saie, as to seeke for a certaine guide to bring one to hell: for so much as if the blind leade the blind (as Chrift saith) both fall into the diche.

Matth.15. 14.

IN VVHAT CASES THE CONFES-
sion is of no value, but ought to be
made againe.

CHAP. IV.

O the end that euerie one may knovv of vvhat importance the things before declared be, I fhall heere brieflie expreffe, in vvhat cafes the Confeffion is of no effecte, but muft be made againe. The firft is, vvhen the penitent maketh a lie in confeffion, in a matter of deadlie finne. The fecond is, if in confeffion he did vvillinglie conceale from his ghoftlie father anie deadlie finne, vvhen he vnderftoode it to be a deadlie finne. The third is, if being long time from confeffion, he hath not examined his confcience, before

1

2

3

he

he commeth therunto : for in this cafe forgetfulnes excufeth not the penitent, but
doth rather accufe him the more. The
fourth is, vvhen the penitent mindeth not   **4**
to leaue the deadlie finne, vvherein he hath
offended; or intendeth not to make reftitution of fuch goods as he ought to reftore.
The fift is, vvhen the penitent is excom-   **5**
municated, and procureth not to be firft ab-
abfolued from the excommunication. The
fixthe cafe is, vvhen the Ghoftlie father   **6**
being ignorant, and the penitent him felfe
is not learned, there ar notvvithftanding
greate matters to be difcuffed in his Confefsion: for in this cafe it can not be, but
that fom errors vvil happen, that haue neede
of a further cure.

But heere it is to be noted, that in euerie
one of thefe cafes, vvherein it is neceffarie
to iterate the confefsion, if it be donne vvith
the felfe fame ghoftlie father, it is not
needeful to repeate al thofe finnes a frefhe,
vvhich he confeffed before, in cafe the
ghoftlie father be mindful of them ; but it
fhal fuffice to faie, I accufe mie felf of fuch
finnes, as at fuch a time I confeffed to you
mie ghoftlie father, and befides I accufe mie
felfe of fuch, and fuch a deadlie finne, for
vvhich I am novv bound to iterate mie
con-

confeſsion.

Novv for help of memorie it ſhall doe
vvel, that vve laie doune heere a briefe memorial of deadlie ſinnes, to the end that the
penitent maie therebie more eaſilie examin
his conſcience, and prepare him ſelf for this
ſacrament of penance , vvhich is the firſt
of the aduiſes that vve haue before ſpecified.
Hovvbeit this vve vvil doe, not by diſco-
uering infinite kinds of exquiſite ſinnes, but by laying doune the moſt
common ſinnes that ar vvont
to happen, and leauing the
reſt to the penitent,
and the Ghoſt-
lie father.

A ME-

A MEMORIAL

OF SINNES AS VVEL
TOVCHING THE TEN
COMMAVNDEMENTS,
as other matters vvherein a
man maie finne mor-
tallie.

Of the firſt commaundement . *Thou
ſhalt honour God aboue all
thinges.*

ONSIDERING that
God is honoured vvith the
three Theological vertues,
Faith , *Hope*, and *Charitie* , let
the penitent examine him
felf in theſe.

As concerning *Faith* , if he hath beleeued
vvhatſoeuer the holie Catholique Romane
Church beleeueth, or hath doubted, or vvith
vvords , and outvvarde ſignes hath made
anie ſhevv of infidelitie or hereſie . If he
hath ben ouer curious in ſearching the matters of faith . If he hath kept bookes of He-
retiques , or ſuch as ar forbidden by the
Church . If knovving anie man to be in-
fected vvith hereſie , and incorrigible by
other

other meanes, he hath not detected him to whome he ought. If he hath learned thofe neceſſarie things, vvhich euerie Chriſtian is bound to knovve, as ar the commaundements of God, and the principal miſteries of oure faith. If he hath beleened in dreames, enchauntments, deuinings, or anie ſorts of ſuperſtition, or counſeled others to credit them. If he hath caried about him ſuperſtitious vvritings for hauing his health, or for anie other end, or induced others to doe the like. If he hath blaſphemed God or anie of his Sainćts. If he hath ben angrie vvith almightie God, or murmured of him, for ſuch aduerſities and troubles, as he hath ſent vnto him, as though he vvere vniuſt or vnmerciful. If in his rage he hath deſired his ovvne death, or els vviſhed that God vvould take him out of this life

As concerning *Hope*. If in his troubles he hath had ſuch confidence in God, as he ought. If he hath put more confidence in creatures, and in theire helpes, then in God. If he hath miſtruſted to obteine pardon for his ſinnes, or amendment of life. If hoping to haue pardon of his ſinnes, he did perſeuer in his euil life, or minded to differ his repentance vntil he vvaxed old, or vntil the houre of his death.

As

As concerning *Charitie*. If he hath not loued God aboue al things as he is bound to doe. If he hath persecuted, or iniuried vvith vvords such deuout persons, as doe frequent Confession, Masse, &c. Or if he hath mocked and scoffed at them; and in particular, if he hath dissuaded or hindered anie from going into Religion. If he hath exposed him self to anie daunger of mortal sinne, or taken delight of anie sinne donne before.

Of the second commaundement. *Thou shalt not take the name of the Lord God in vaine.*

IF he hath svvorne falslie, knovving it vvas false, or doubting it to be soe, or being careles vvhat he svvare. If svvearing he did promise anie layvful thing, and not fulfil it, nor hath intention to performe it. If he hath ben cause that anie did svveare false, or not keepe theire lauful oth once made. If he hath svvorne in manner of cursing, to vvit; if I doe not such a thing, let such euil happen vnto me. If he hath svvorne to doe anie sinne, or euil, or not to doe that vvhich is good. If he hath made anie vovve vvith a mind of not fulfilling it. If he

If he haue differred the fulfilling of his laufull vovve anie long time . If he hath vovved to doe anie vvicked acte , or not to doe anie good deede , or to doe a good thing for an euil end , for such vovves bind not.

Of the third commaundement . *Thou shalt keepe holy the Sabboth-daie.*

IF he hath not kept the holiedaies, but either hath donne , or commaunded to be donne anie seruile vvorke vppon the same daies, vnles it vvere som litle thing. If he hath omitted to heare masse throughout euerie Sondaie and holidaie , vvithout lauful cause . If being present at masse vppon anie holidaie , he hath ben for anie notable time voluntarilie distracted , by talking, laughing, or busying him self in impertinent things. If he hath not procured that such as be vnder his charge, should heare masse vppon the holidaies. If he hath not gone to Confession at the lest once a yeere, or hath gone vvithout due examination of his conscience . If euerie yeere at Easter he hath receiued vvith due disposition , or rather vvith a conscience or doubt of mortall sinne. If he hath fasted the lent, vigils and

and Ember daies being bound thereunto, or hath eaten forbidden meates. If he hath spent all the Holidaies in paftimes, gamemings and vanities. If being excommunicated he hath ben prefent at Catholique diuine feruice, or receiued anie Sacrament during that time, or hath conuerfed vvith excommunicate perfons, or fuch as vvere fufpeded of herefie. If being bound to faie his office, he hath omitted or all, or anie part thereof, or in the faying of it hath ben voluntarilie diftracted.

Of the fourth commaundement. *Thou fhalt honour thy father and thy mother.*

IF he hath defpifed or not honoured his father and mother, or hath offended them in deedes or vvords, or not obeied them in matters that vvere iuft, and fuch as might refult to notable detriment of theire familie, or of theire ovvne fovvle. If he hath not fuccoured his parents in theire necefsitie vvhen it vvas in his povver. If he hath ben afhamed of them, by reafon of the bafenes of their familie, or poore eftate. If he hath defired theire death, to enioie their lands or goods. If he hath perfor-

Y   med

med theire teftaments and laft vvills. If he
hath fo loued them, that for theire loue,
he cared not to offend God. If he hath not
obferued the iuft lavves, and decrees of his
Superiours. If he hath detracted, or fpoken
euill of Superiours, Ecclefiafticall, or Se-
cular, of Religious perfons, or Prieftes, or
Teachers, &c. If he hath not fuccoured
the poore, if he could, efpeciallie in extreme
or grieuous necefsitie, or if he hath ben
cruell vnto them in vvoords or deedes. If
thofe vvhich be fathers and mothers haue
curfed : or vvifhed euill vnto theire children. Alfo if they haue brought them vp as
they fhould, teaching them theire praiers.
and Chriftian doctrine, and reprehending
and correcting them, efpeciallie in matter of finne, and occupying them in fom
honeft exercife, to the end they be not idle,
and take fom euil courfe. And that vvhich
is faid of Children, is to be vnderftoode alfo
of feruants, and others of the familie, of
vvhome care is to be had, that they knovv
things vvhich be neceffarie, and obferue the
commaundements of God, and of the
Church.

Of

Of the fift Commaundement. *Thou shalt not kill.*

IF he haue spirituallie slaine his neighbour, by pesvvading him to Scisme or Heresie, or by prouoking him, or giuing him counsaile, or occasion to sinne deadlie. If he hath caried hatred tovvards anie person, desiring to be reuenged, and hovv long he hath staied therein. If he hath killed, or procured, or desired the death of his neighbour, or anie other greate euil or domage, as vvel in his bodie, as in his good name, honour, temporal and spirituall goods, or geuen counsaile, aide, and fauour thereunto. If hauing offended others by vvoord, or deede, he hath refused to aske pardon or reconciliation, either by him self, or som other; or hath not sufficientlie satisfied for the offence; or hath not forgiuen such, as haue humblie desired pardon of him. If he hath ben occasion of factions, or fauoured them, or threatned anie vvith euil speeches, not being vnder his gouernment. If he hath refused to speake to anie, or to salute them, and hath thereby giuen scandall, or offence to his neighbour. If in aduersities and misfortunes he hath desired

death,

death, or vvith furie ftrooken & curfed him
felf, or mentioned the diule . If he hath curfed others either aliue, or dead, and vvith
vvhat intention . If he hath fovved difcord,
or caufed enmitie betvvene others, and
vvhat harme hath com thereof. If for hatred
or enuie, he hath ben immoderatlie forie
for the good, and profperitie of others, as
vvel Temporal as Spiritual, or hath reioi-
ced at anie harme, or notable domage of his
neigbour, manifefting anie fecrete fault of
his to difcredit him , or caufe him other
harme . If he haue ftrooken iniuriouflie anie
ecclefiaftical perfon, vvherein alfo there is
Excommunication.

Of the fixt and ninth commaundement.
*Thou fhalt not commit fornication. Thou
fhalt not defire they neighbours vvife.*

IF he hath had anie difhoneft and vn-
cleane thoughts, and voluntarilie hath
ftaied and taken delite in them, or not refifted them fo fpeedilie as he ought. If vvith
deliberate mind he hath defired to finne
vvith anie man or vvoman, vvhich finne is
of the fame kind, of vvhich the vvoork it
felf vvoold be. If vvith libidinous intent he
hath

hath beheld vvomen, or other perfons . If
he hath fpoken lafciuious and difhoneft
yvoords, vvith intention to finne, and to
prouoke others ; or hath vvillinglie and
vvith delite heard fuch fpeeches. If he hath
actuallie finned vvith anie vvoman, and of
vvhat qualitie fhe vvas; or vvith anie perfon
againft nature . If he hath vncleanlie touched him felf or others, or permitted the
fame; & vvhether at that time he thought
of anie perfon vvith vnlauful defire: for in
this cafe there be tvvoe mortal finnes . If
vvith defire of finne, he hath fent letters,
meffagers, or prefents, or hath kiffed others;
or hath ben a meane to induce others vnto
finne, or giuen counfel or ayde thereunto.
If he hath gone to anie place vvith euil intention, or paffed by the fame, or decked
him felf to fom euil end ; vvhere he muft tel
of dangers of finne, to vvhich he hath ex-
pofed him felf, and of the occafions vvhich
he hath not auoided. If he hath had pollu-
tion in fleepe, or avvake, or hath giuen anie
caufe, or voluntarilie taken delite therein:
or reade anie bookes that might prouoke
to flefhlie finne . If he hath borne carnal
loue to anie perfon, vvith defire of finne,
and hovv long he hath perfeuered in the
fame, and yf by his occafion, fuch perfons

hath

hath ben noted vvith anie infamie. Thofe that be maried muft examine them felues in particular, if in theire mind thinking of other perfons, or vvith intention not to beget children, but onlie for carnal delite, or vvith extraordinarie touchings and meanes, they haue finned againft the end, and honeftie of mariage.

Of the feuenth & tenth commaundement.
Thou fhalt not fteale. Thou fhalt not defire they neighbours goods.

IF he hath taken anie thing belonging to others by deceite or violence, expref-fing the quantitie of the theft, and if he hath taken anie facred thing, or out of anie facred place. If he hath holden ought vvith-out the ovvners confent, and hath not refto-red it being able. If for not paying of his debts, his creditours haue fuftained anie do-mage. If he hath not made reftitution of fuch things as he hath found, or came to his hands, knovving them to belong to others. If buying, or felling he hath vfed anie de-ceite in the vvare, in the price, meafure, or yveight. If he hath bought of thofe that could not fel, as ar flaues, or children ynder
age.

age . If onlie in refpect of felling vppon credit , he hath fold aboue the iuft price, or bought for leffe then the iuft price, in refpect of paiment made before hand. If he hath had a determinate vvill to take, or retaine anie thing of others , and this by right, or by vvrong. If he hath committed anie vfurye , or made anie vfurarious contract , or entred into anie vniuft trafficke of marchandife or partnerfhippe. If he hath reteined the vvages due vnto others. If he hath plaied at prohibited games, or in playing vfed anie deceite , or plaied vvith perfons vvhich can not alienate , as ar children vnder age and the like. If he hath defrauded anie iuft impoft or tolles. If he hath committed fymenie in anie fort. If he hath not trulie paied his tythes vnto the Church . If by vnlavvfull meanes he haue goten anie thing that vvas not due vnto him; or hath vniuftlie hindred others, from the obteining anie benifit or commoditie . If he hath giuen anie help or counfel, or by anie other meanes abetted to fuch as haue taken other mens goods, or (being able and bound thereunto) hath not difcouered or hindered anie theft.

Y 4   Of

Of the eight commaundement.
Thou shalt not beare false vvitnes.

IF he hath borne anie false vvitnes in iudgement, or out of iudgement, or induced others to doe the like. If he haue spoken anie vntruthe, vvith notable preiudice or hurt of his neighboure. If he hath detracted from the good name of others, imposing falslie vppon them anie sinne, or exaggeratinge theire defects. If he haue murmured againſt anie other mans life and conuersation, especiallie in naughtie matters, and of qualified persons, as Prelates, Religious, and vvomen of good name. If he hath disclosed anie greeuous and secrete sinne of others, vvhere-vppon hath insued Infamie : vvhich although it vvere true, & not spoken vvith euill intention, yet is the speaker bound to reſtore the good name. If he hath vttered anie secrete vvhich vvas committed vnto him, or vvhich secretlie he came to see or heare, in vvhich case he is bound to reſtore all domages, that afterwards happen by such reuelations. If he hath opened other mens letters vnlavvfullie, or vvith anie euil intention. If he
hath

hath rafhlie iudged the deedes or fpeeches
of his neighbour , taking in euil part that,
vvhich might haue ben vvel interpreted,
and condemning him in his heart of mortal
finne . If he hath promifed anie thing
vvith intention to bind him felf; and aftervvards, vvithout lavvful caufe , hath omitted to obferue the fame; for it is a mortall
finne , vvhen the thing vvhich is promifed
is notable , or vvhen, for vvant of perfor-
mance of the promife , our neighbour hath
had anie loffe , or domage temporall , or
fpirituall.

Of Pride.

IF that good vvhich he hath (be it of
the Sovvle , of the Body , or of fortune)
he hath not acknovvledged as of Cod, but
prefumed to haue it of him felf , or by his
ovvne induftrie, or if of God, yet by reafon
of his ovvne merites . If he hath reputed
vainelie to haue anie vertue , vvhich he hath
not; or to be that , vvhich he is not; or glo-
ried in anie thing, vvhich is mortall finne.
If to be efteemed for a perfon of value he
hath vaunted of anie good , or euil , vvhich
he hath donne, vvith the iniurie of God , or
his

his neighbour, & vvhether trulie or falflie.

Of other mortal finnes heere is nothing faied; becaufe enough hath bonfpoken alredie in the Commaundements. Onlie fuch as haue anie fpecial Office, degree or charge, muft examin them felues of the defects and finnes, vvhich in like Eftates and Exercifes maie particularlie happen, according vnto the obligation, vvhich euerie one hath.

A GENERALL ADVERTISMENT
to difcerne, vvhich is a deadlie finne, and vvhich a veniall.

CHAP. V

ECAVSE vve ar bound of neceffitie to confeffe al deadlie finnes, but not venial finnes vnles vve vvil; and for fo much as this thing, to vvit, vvhich is a deadlie, and vvhich a venial finne, can not be vvel declared in fevv vvoords, it fhal fuffice to giue fom general aduertifment concerning this point, for vvhich there ar vvont to be giuen tvvo Rules.

The firft and moft generall Rule is, that vvhatfoeuer is contrarie to *Charitie*, that is to the loue of God, and of our neighbour, is a deadlie finne. And fo by this Rule, vvhat-

vvhatfoeuer is againft the honour of God,
or the profit of our neighbour, in anie matter of importance, be it thought, vvoord,
or deede, is a deadlie finne; for this quencheth *Charitie*, vvherein confifteth the fpirituall life of the fovvle. But vvhatfoeuer
is not againft *Charitie*, but befides the fame,
is a veniall finne; as idle vvoords that hurt
no man; or fom kind of little vaine glorie, of
anger, of negligence, &c.

The fecond Rule is more fpeciall; to
vvit, that vvhatfoeuer is contrarie to anie
one of the Commaundements of almightie
God, or of the Catholique Church, is a
deadlie finne. But heere it is diligentlie to
be noted, that that vvhich is of his ovvne
nature a deadlie finne, maie be a veniall
finne, by one of thefe tvvo vvaies; either becaufe the matter is of fmall importance (as
yf one fhould fteale a pinne, or a point) or
becaufe the vvork is imperfect, by reafon
that it vvanted a ful confent, as it maie happen in euil thoughts, vvithout anie confent
giuen vnto them, but yet euil refifted.

Likevvife it is to be confidered, that the
Commaundements be of three kinds. Som
ar *negatiue* as *Thou fhalt not kill* &c. VVhich
doe bind vs for euer and euer, that is in
euerie time, and at all times. Others be *af-*
firmatiue

2

firmatiue, as *to giue almes*, *to haue contrition for our finnes*, &c, and thefe doe bind vs euer, but not in euerie time, but in time of necefsitie, and then vve ar bound of dutie to doe them. There be other *compounded of both*, to vvit of negatiues, and affirmatiues, *as to restore other mens goods*. For this commaundeth to reftore, and alfo not to vvithhold our neighbours goods. And thefe commaundements doe bind vs to obferue them, in both manner of vvaies, to vvit euer, and at all times.

A BRIEFE MANNER OF CONFESsion, for fuch as be vvont to confeffe often.

CHAP. VI.

ANIE deuoute perfons be fore vexed & troubled vvith fcruples, becaufe in examining theire confciences, they find not, fom times, vvhereof to make theire Confefsion. For as on the one fide they knovv, and beleeue certeinlie that they ar not vvithout finnes, and on the other fide, at the time of confefsion, they find them not, they ar in great perplexitie, and

and doe fullie perfuade them felues, that
they ar neuer rightlie confeffed.

Of this vvee may gather tvvo thinges.
The one is, that it is in deede a verie hard
matter for a man to knovv him felfe, and
to vnderftande throughlie all the fecrete
corners of his confcience, in fo much that
the Prophet faid not in vaine, *vvhoe is he* Pfalm. 18.
that knovveth his finnes? deliuer me, o Lord, from 13.
my fecrete offences. A n other is, that the finnes
of iuft perfons (of vvhome the vvife man
faieth, vhat they fall feuen times in the daie) Prouerb.
ar rather finnes of *omitting* then of *committing*; 24. 17.
vvhich kinde of finnes ar hard to be knovv-
en. For vnderftanding vvhereof, it is to be
noted, that all finnes ar committed by one
of thefe tvvo vvaies , to vvit, either by
vvaie of *Committing* (that is by doing fome
vvicked thing, as by robbing, killing &c.
or by vvaie of *Omitting* (that is by leauing
fome good thing vndonne, as for not louing God, not fafting, not praying &c.)
Novv of thefe tvvo kind of finnes, the firft
(becaufe they confift in doing) ar verie fenfible and eafie to be knovven; but the fecond (vvhich confift not in doing , but in
leauing vndonne) ar much harder to be
knovven ; becaufe that thing , vvhich is
not, hath no meane to fhevv it felf. VVherfore

fore it is not to be maruailed at , that fpirituall perfons (efpeciallie if they be fimple)
doe not find, fom times, anie finnes, vvherof to accufe them felues . For as thefe perfons fall not fo often into thofe finnes of
Committing, of vvhich vve haue fpoken, and
the others , vvhich be of *Omitting* , ar not
fo eafie to be vnderftoode: hence it cometh
that they knovv not vvherof to confeffe
them felues , and therfore ar fo much vexed.

VVherfoie, for remedie of this , I haue
thought good to ordeine this *Memorial* , for
fuch perfons , vvherein is chieflie treated of
this kind of finnes, vvhich cocerne *Omitting*.
And becaufe thefe finnes maie be feither
againft God, or againft our felues, or againft
our neighbours ; therfore is this *Memorial*
diuided into three parts , vvhich doe treate
of thefe three kinds of negligences. And for
this end vve muft vnderftand, that there is a
difference betvvixt *imperfections* , and *venial*
finnes , vvherof it enfueth , that fom things
maie be imperfections , vvhich be not
finnes, as it chauceth vvhen vve leaue to doe
fom good vvorks , vvhich vve might haue
donne, to vvhich vve ar not alvvaies bound.
For it maie be, that one might beftovv more
almes , then he doeth , and praie more then
he praieth , and faft more then he fafteth,
and

and fo in other things; and to leaue thefe things is not finne, but it is a fault and imperfection, becaufe by doing them, a man might auance him felf, and profit much, vvhich he doth not in leauing them vndonne. Yet let no deuout perfon leaue to accufe him felf for this of fuch things, as vvel becaufe fom times they maie be venial finnes, as alfo to acknovvledge his imperfections, and fo to humble him felf before the Vicar of God, and to endeuour to get out of them. Hovvbeit this is not conuenient to be donne at al times, but at certeine times, (and efpeciallie vppon principall feaftes) to the end they vvearie not theire ghoftlie fathers vvith theire fuperfluous length: but at anie other ordinarie times, euerie one maie heere take his choice of that, vvhich he fhal thinke beft for the difcharge of his confcience.

Of that vvich goeth before Confeßion.

AT the beginning of his Confefsion, let a man accufe him felfe of that vvhich folovveth. Firft, for that he cometh not to this Sacrament vvith fuch forovv & repentance for his finnes, and vvith fo ftedfaft a purpofe to forfake them, as he ought;

ought ; and that he hath not so vvel examined his conscience, as reason vvould he
should haue donne. Let him accuse him self,
that the daie of his last Communion, he
vvas not so deuout nor recollected, as vvas
necessarie for so soueraigne a ghest ; and that
novv he commeth not prepared as he ought
to communicate, nether vvith such feare
and reuerence, as to so excellent a Sacrament is required. Also of the small amendment of his life, and that he doth no profit
in the seruice of God more one daie then
an other.

Tovvards God.

L ET him accuse him self for not louing God vvith all his hart, vvith all
his soule, and vvith al his forces as he vvas
bound. For that he hath not giuen him
thankes for the benifits receaued, and those
vvhich he doth dailie receaue, especiallie
for hauing redeemed him, and giuen him
knovvledge of him self, as he vvas bound.
For not doing that vvhich apperteined to
his seruice, vvith that puritie of intention,
nor vvith that feruor and deuotion, vvhich
he ought, but rather sluggishlie & coldlie.
For

For not anſvvering of his parte to the good inſpirations of God, and to the holie reſolutions vvhich he doth ſend him, and to the preparations & opportunities, vvhich he gaue him to liue vvel; by al vvhich he might haue profited him ſelf much more, yf it had not ſtoode by his ovvne greate negligence. For not hauing aſsiſted at maſſe, and at the diuine ſeruice, and in halovved places in the preſence of the moſt bleſſed Sacrament, vvith ſuch Deuotion, Attention, Feare and Reuerence, as the preſence of ſo greate a maieſtie demaunded.

Tovvards him ſelf.

A MAN conſiſteth of manie parts; for he hath a bodie vvith al his ſenſes; and a ſovvle vvith al her appetites, and a ſpirite vvith al his povvers, vvhich ar Vnderſtanding, Memorie and VVil; and ſo he maie offend againſt the order, vvhich he ought to keepe in euerie one of them. Let him then firſt accuſe him ſelf, for that he hath not gouerned his bodie vvith ſuch rigour, and ſeueritie as he ſhould haue donne, as vvel in eating, drinking, clothing, and ſleeping, as in al other things. For that he hath not his imagination, and other exterior ſenſes ſo

Z   recol-

recollected, as he ought, but hath suffred them to range, and vvander abrode, in hearing, feeing, talking and imagining manie things vvhich vvere idle, and not to the purpose. For that he hath not mortified his appetites, and resisted his ovvne vvil, as he ought to haue donne. For that he is not so humble in his hart, and vvoorkes, as he should be: nor esteemed him self for so vile, and miserable as he is, nor handled him self as such a one hath deserued. For that he hath not procured anie litle deuotion, nor geuen him self so much to praier, nor hath ben in the same vvith such closenes of mind, and diligent attention, as vvas requisite, but rather hath ben slovv, to rise at devv time to praier.

Tovvards his neighbour.

LET him accuse him self, for that he hath not loued his neighbours vvith such loue, as he vvould that others should loue him, as God hath commaunded. For that he hath not succoured them in theire necessities, vvith the help and reliefe that he might, or vvith the counsel that he ought. For that he hath not had such compassion vppon theire miseries, and praied God for them.

them, as he vvas bound to doe. Of the publique Calamities of the Catholique Church,
such as be Heresies, Captiuities and the like;
for that he hath not had such invvard feeling of them, as reason required, nor so re-
commended them vnto almightie God,
as they deserued to be commended. Such
as haue Superiours, let them accuse them
selfes, for not hauing obeied them, nor
borne them such reuerence, nor succoured
them as in deede they ought. And those
that haue subiects, children and seruants,
for not hauing taught, and chastised them,
& prouided for them such things as vvere
necessarie, and ben so careful of them as
reason vvould they should.

Of sinnes of Committing.

AFTER that the penitent hath so
accused him selfe of the sinnes of O-
mitting, then let him accuse him self of
those of Committing, running ouer the
ten commaundements, and seuen deadlie
sinnes, accusing him self of that in eche
one, vvherein his conscience shall find remorse. And yf he vvil goe more briefelie
to vvorke, he maie examin his thoughts,
vvords, and deedes, vvherein he shal think

Z 2   he

he hath offended, and so accuse him self
of the same. After all this he must accuse
him selfe, of all such sinnes as apperteine
to the state and office that he is of, decla-
ring vvherein he hath sinned against the
lavves and devvties of his state. As if he
be a Religious person, of his three vovves,
or anie other thing belonging to his Rule.
If he be a Iudge, Phisition, or marchaunt,
of such things as apperteine to his office.
If a Prince, of that vvhich concerneth his
gouernement . VVhen he hath ended all
these accusations, let him then conclude
as folovveth, saying . *Of al these sinnes, and
of all others vvherein I haue offended in thought,
vvoord , or deede I , grieuouslie accuse mie
self , and doe acknovvledge mie fault before God , mie fault , yea mie most
grieuous fault, and desire you mie
ghostlie father to giue me
penance and ab-
solution.*

OF SATISFACTION THE THIRD
part of Penance.

CHAP. VII.

ATISFACTION is
a ful & intiere paiment, of
that vvhich a man ovveth
for his sinnes commit-
ted. Novv sinne bringeth
vvith it tvvoe euils. The
one is the *spot* or *fault*; the other is the *paine*
and *punishment* due to the fault. In Confession by the vertue of the bloud of Christ,
vvhich vvorketh in this Sacrament, vve ar
clensed from the spot or filth of sinne, and
the fault is forgiuen vs, and so vve ar deliuered from euerlasting paine, due vnto
mortal sinne. But because all Temporall
paine is not alvvaies released, vvhen the
fault is pardoned, therfore Satisfaction is
necessarie, vvhich must be made or heere, or
in the life to com, in the paines of Purgatorie, vvhich (as *S. Augustine* affirmeth) ar
so greate, that they exceede all the torments, vvhich the holie martyrs suffered in
this life. Novv al sortes of Satisfactions ar
reduced vnto these three onlie: *Fasting or*

Z 3   *other*

other corporal austerities, *Almes*, and *Praier*, vvhich be correspondent to the goods of the Sovvle, of the Bodie, and of Fortune; and by *Almes* a man offereth to God his external goods; by *Fasting* he maketh a Sacrifice of his proper flesh, and by *Praier* he offereth to God his mind, & so consequentlie doth sacrifice to God him self, and al that vvhich he hath.

And although this Satisfaction maie be made in tvvoe manner of vvaies ; as first vvhen a sinner voluntarilie, and of his ovvne deuotion doth anie of these vvorks ; or secondlie vvhen he doeth the same being enioined him by his ghostlie father in Confession ; yet the Satisfaction vvhich is made for Obedience of the Confessor, in respect of the Sacrament, is much more fruiteful. Finallie al manner of scourges, and chastisements, vvhich almightie God sendeth vs, as Sicknes, Pouertie, and the like ; yf they be borne vvith Humilitie and Patience, ar of greate force, not onlie to satisfie for the temporal paines, devv for our sinnes, but also for increase of Grace and mercie.

THE SIXTH

TREATISE, HOVV VVE OVGHT TO PRE-PARE OVR SELVES

FOR THE RECEIVING OF THE
most blessed Sacrament of the Altare.

S amongst al the other Sacraments, the blessed Sa-
crament of the Altare is
the greatest, so is there requisite greater puritie and
preparation, for receauing
of the same : because in the other Sacraments, the vertue of God vvorketh, but in
this Sacrament is the real, and true presence
of God him self, and therfore, besides the
cleannes of the sovvle, vvhich must goe before, by meanes of the Sacrament of Penance, it requireth also especial deuotion,
to vvhich deuotion three things doe serue
verie notablie.

The first of these things is, the feare and
Reuerence of that diuine maiestie, vvhich is
in this Sacrament, for somuch as vve doe
trulie beliue, that in that little host is al-

Z 4   mighte

mightie God, the Creatour of heauen and earth, the lord of the vvorld, the glorie of the Angels, the repose of all those that be blessed, the iudge of the vvorld, vvhome the Angels, Archangels, Cherubines, and Seraphines doe praise, before vvhose sight the povvers of heauen doe tremble, not for that they haue offended him, but for that considering the highnes, and greatenes of that soueraine maiestie, they acknovvledge them selues to be but so manie vvormes before the same. True it is, that this feare causeth not in them anie paine, but a most high Reuerence; because they knovv, that as there is devv all loue to that infinite goodnes and bountie, so to his greatenes there is due all feare. This affection is also much increased in a man, by consideration of the greate number of his sinnes, and dailie negligences. For yf the Angels and Principalities of heauen doe feare him, vvithout hauing donne anie thing vvherefore, since theye vvere created, hovv much more ought a vile and vvretched vvorme to feare, vvhich so oftentimes, and in so manie manners offendeth his creator?

This is then the first thing vvhich a man ought to consider, vvhen he commeth

meth to this table, saying vvithin him selfe
vvith greate Reuerence. I goe novv to receaue almightie God , not onlie into mie
fovvle, but alfo into mie bodie.

Bnt novv this feare muft be tempered
vvith Hope, vvhich the fame lord of ours
giueth vs , by confidering that he vvith the
bovvels of pitie, and compafsion vppon our
vveakenes and miferie, inuiteth vs to his
table, & calleth vs vvith thofe moft fvveete
vvords, vvhich are. *Com ye to me, al that labour,* Matth. 1 :.
and ar burdened, to vvit vvith the heauines of 28.
your mortalitie, and of your pafsions , becaufe I vvil reftore and refrefh your foules.
And in an other place , vvhen the Pharifees
murmured of this lord , becaufe he did eate
and drinke vvith finners , he anfvvered
them, that *They that ar vvhole, neede not the Phi-* Luc. 5. 3 1.
fition, but they that ar yll at eafe; and that he *came*
not to cal the iuft, but finners to penance . So that
vvith thefe vvords, the finners , that repent
them felues of theire finnes, maie take hart
and confidence , to be bould to approche
neere to this heauenlie bankette.

But touching the hunger & defire vvhich
this heauenlie bread requireth, a greate motiue maie be to confider the effects thereof,
and the greate benifits , vvhich by the fame
ar communicated to thofe, that deuoutlie
doe

doe receaue it; vvhich be so greate, that no
man is able to recount them . For by the
same the Grace of God is giuen vs ; by it vve
becom vnited , and incorporated to our
head; vvhich is Chrift . By it vve ar made
partakers of the merites, and trauails of his
most sacred passion , and by it is renued
the memorie therof . By it Charitie is inflamed, our vveakenes is ftrengthned, and spiritual sweetenes is tasted euen in his ovvne
proper spring vvhich is Chrift ; and by it
ar stirred vp in our sovvles nevv purposes
and desires tovvards all goodnes. By it is
giuen vs a most pretious pavvne of euerlasting life. By it ar forgiuen the sinnes, and
negligences vvhich vve dailie commit , and
by it also a man becommeth of Attrite,
Contrite , vvhich is as much as to rise from
death to life . By it likevvise is diminished
the flame of our passions and concupiscen-
ces , and (that vvhich is more) by it Chrift
entreth into our sovvles to dvvel in them,
and dvvelling there (as he him self signified
vvhen he saied, that as his father vvas in
him, and therfore his life vvas like to the
life of his father) to make like him self in
pürenes of life , all those that vvorthilie receaue him into them selues , by meanes of
this Sacrament, that novv they maye saie
                                      eche

Effects of
Communio

Ioh. 6. 57.

eche one in particular, *I liue, novv not I, but* *Gal. 2.*
Chrift liueth in me.   20.

If therfore this celeftiall bread, vvoorke
all thefe effects in the fovvles of thofe, that
vvith a pure confcience doe eate it, vvhat
man is there fo infenfible, or fo great an
enimie of him felf, that vvil not haue hunger of bread, that vvorketh fo great effects
in him, that doth vvorthilie receaue it. A
man ought therefore to occupie him felf in
the confideration of thefe things, the daie
and the night before the bleffed Communion, to ftirre vp by meanes of the fame
thefe three affects aforefaid, in vvhich doth
confift actual deuotion, that is fo greatlie
requifite for this meate. To vvhich purpofe
the tvvoe praiers folovving vvil help verie
much, yf they be read vvith as much attention and deuotion as is pofsible ; becaufe in them the deuoute fovvle fhal
find vvoords, and confiderations to
ftirre vp in it felfe thofe three affections and feelings afore
mentioned.

A DE-

A DEVOVT PRAIER TO BE SAID
before the receiuing of the blessed
Sacrament.

I Giue vnto thee, o my Sauiour and Lord, most hartie thankes and praise, for all the benifits vvhich it hath pleased thee, to bestovve vppon this so vile and miserable creature. I giue the thankes for all the mercies, vvhich thou hast vsed tovvards mankind, for the misterie of thy holy Incarnation, and chiefelie for thie most holie Natiuitie, for thy Circumcision, for thy Presentation in the Temple, for thy Flight into Egypt, for the trauails of thy voiages, for thy going vp and dovvne in preaching, for the persecutions of the vvorld, for the tormentes and sorovves of thie passion, and for all that vvhich thou diddest suffer in this vvorld for me, and much more for the loue, vvith vvhich thou diddest suffer, vvhich vvithout comparison vvas farre greater.

Aboue all this I giue the thankes, that thou hast vouchsafed to set me at thy table, and to make me partaker of thy selfe, and of the inestimable treasures and merites of thy passion. O my God, O my Sauiour! vvher-

vvherevvith shall I repaie this thy nevv
mercie? vvhoe vvas thou, o Lord, & vvhoe
vvere vve, that thou, being the king of
maiestie, vvouldest com doune to these
our houses of claie? Heauen is thy seate, and
the earth thy footestoole, and the glorie
of thy maiestie doth fill all this. Hovv then
vvilt thou repose thy self in so vile cotages?
maie a man think (saith Salomon) *that God vvil* 3. Regn. 8.
dvvell in earth vvith men? If the heauen, and
heauens of heauens be not sufficient to giue
the place, hovv much les shall this so straite
roome suffice for thee? O hovv maruailous
a thing is it, that he vvhich sitteth aboue
the Cherubines, and from thence beholdeth the depths, doth novv com doune to
these depths, and place in them the seate
of his maiestie?

Seemed it little to thy infinite goodnes, to haue appointed vnto vs the Angels
for ovvre safegard, if thou thy self, being
the lord of Angels, hadst not com vnto vs
and entred into our sovvles, and handled
there, vvith thine ovvne hands, the affairs
of our saluation? There thou doest visit
the sicke; thou doest raise vp those that ar
fallen; thou doest instruct the ignorant;
thou doest teach those that haue erred,
the right vvaie; and finallie thou thy self
art

art he, that doft heale vs of all our difeafes, and this vvith no other hands, then
vvith thine ovvne, nor vvith anie other
medicine, then vvith thine ovvne moft
pretious bodie and bloud. O good pa-
ftour! hovv faithfullie haft thou fulfilled
thy vvord, vvhich thou diddeft fpeake
Ezech. 34 vnto vs by thy Prophet faying, I vvill
feede my fheepe, and giue them a fvveete
repofe; I vvill feeke that vvich vvas loft,
and vvill bring back againe that vvhich
vvas caft out.

But vvhoe maie be vvorthie of fuch
revvards? VVhoe maie be vvorthie to receaue fo greate benifits? Thie onlie mercie,
o Lord, maketh vs vvorthie of fo greate
goodnes. And forafmuch as vvithout it no
man can be vvorthie, let thie mercie, o mie
good God, be fauorable to me, and let the
fame make me partaker of this mifterie, and
thankful for this fo greate a benifit. Let thie
grace likevvife fupplie mie defects; let thie
mercie pardon mie finnes; let thy holie fpirite prepare mie foule; let thie merites enriche mie pouerties; and let thie moft pretious bloud vvafh al the fpots of mie life,
that fo I maie vvorthilie receaue this venerable Sacrament.

I doe exceedinglie reioice, o mie God,
vvhen

vvhen I remember that miracle, vvhich
Heliseus did after his death, vvhen he raised 4. Reg. 13
one that vvas dead, by touching him. For if 21.
the bodie of the dead Prophet vvas of such
force, of hovv much more force is the liue
bodie of the lord of Prophets? Thou, o lord,
vndoubtedlie art not of lesse povver, then
vvas thy Prophet; neither is my sovvle lesse
dead, then vvas that bodie; neither is this
touching of thine, of les vertue, then vvas
that of his; vvherfore then should I not
hope herehence an other like benifit? vvherfore should a bodie conceaued in sinne,
vvoork greater vvonders, then that bodie
vvhich vvas conceaued by the holie Ghost?
vvherfore should the bodie of the seruant,
be more honoured then the bodie of the
lord? vvherfore should not thie most sacred
bodie, raise againe the soules that approche
vnto thee, seeing that the bodie of thie seruant, raised the bodies that approched vnto
it? And for somuch as that dead bodie,
vvithout seeking for life, did receaue that
vvhich it sought not for, through the vertue of that holie bodie; let it please thie infinite mercie, o mie lord, that sith I seeke
the same by meanes of this most blessed Sacrament, through it I be so raised vp and
quickned, that hereafter I liue no more
vnto

vnto mie self, but vvholie vnto thee. O good IESVS, by that ineſtimable charitie vvhich made thee to take our fleſh vppon thee, and to ſuffer death for me, I moſt humblie beſeeche thee, that thou vvilt vouchſafe to make me cleane from al mie ſinnes; and to adorne and decke me vvith thie vertues and merites; and to giue me grace, that I maie receaue this moſt venerable Sacrament, vvith that humilitie and Reuerence, vvith that feare and trembling, vvith that ſorovv and repentance for mie ſinnes, and vvith that purpoſe and reſolution to leaue them, and vvith that loue and charitie, vvhich is requiſite for ſo highe a miſterie.

Giue me alſo, o lord, that puritie of intention, vvith vvhich I maie receaue this miſterie to the glorie of thie holy name, to the remedie of al mie vveakenes., and neceſsities, to defend me from the enimie vvith this armour, to ſuſteine mie ſelf in ſpiritual life vvith this foode, and to make mie ſelf one thing vvith thee, by the meanes of this Sacrament of loue, and to offer vp to thee this ſacrifice for the ſaluation of all faithfull Chriſtians, as vvel liuing, as dead, that all maie find help through the ineſtimable vertue of this Sacrament, vvhich vvas inſtituted and ordeined for the ſaluation

tion of all. Thou vvhoe liueſt and raigneſt
vvorld vvithout end, Amen.

O LORD God almightie, mie Creator, and mie Sauiour , hovv haue I
ben ſo bould as to approche vnto thee,
being ſo vile , ſo filthie, and ſo miſerable a
creature, as I am? Thou, o Lord, art the
God of Gods, the King of Kings, and the
Lord of Lords . Thou art the hight of al
goodnes, of al vertue, beutie and pleaſure.
Thou art the fountaine of light, the ſpring
of loue, and the embracing of moſt hartie
Charitie . And being as thou art, thou doſt
praie me, and I doe flie from thee; thou haſt
care of me , and I haue no care of thee;
thou doſt alvvaies regard me , and I doe
alvvaies forget thee ; thou doſt beſtovv
manie fauours vppon me, and I doe not
eſteeme them; and finallie thou doſt loue
me, that am vanitie and nothing, and I doe
make no account of thee , vvhich art an
infinite and vnchangeable good . I preferre
the baſenes of this vvorld, before thee moſt
gentel ſpovvſe; and the creatures moue me

A a   more,

more, then doth the Creator ; more detestable miserie, then the highest felicitie ; and more boundage, then libertie. And albeit it

Prouerb. 27.

be true, that the vvoundes of a frind ar to be more esteemed, then the deceitful kisses of an enimie; yet I am of such a condition, that I rather desire the deceitfull vvounds of him, vvhich abhorreth me, then the svveete embracings of him, vvhich loueth me. But remember not, o lord, mie sinnes, nether those of mie forefathers, but be mindful of thie merciful entrailes, and of the griefe of thie pretious vvounds. Consider not that vvhich I haue donne against thee, but that vvhich thou hastdonne for me : for if I haue donne manie things for vvhich thou maist condemne me, thou hast donne manie moe for vvhich thou maist saue me. Seeing then, o lord, that thou dost so loue me, as thou shevvest, vvherfore dost thou vvithdravve thy self from me? O most louing lord hold me vvith thy feare, constraine me vvith thy loue, and quiet me vvith thy svveetenes.

Luc. 15.

I confesse o Lord that I am that prodigall sonne, vvhoe liuing ouer rankly, and louing mie self and thy creatures disorderedlie, haue vvasted all the substance vvhich thou diddest giue me. But novv that I doe
knovv

knovv mie miferie and pouertie, and doe
returne pined vvith hunger to the fatherlie
bovvels of thy mercie, and doe approche to
this celeftial table of thy moft pretious body, vouchfafe to looke vppon one vvith
eyes of pittie, and to com forth to receaue
me vvith the fecrete beames of thy grace,
and to make me partaker of the maruailous
fruites and effects of this moft vvorthie Sacrament ; for fomuch as by it is giuen the
grace of the holie Ghoft; by it ar forgiuen
finnes ; by it ar pardoned the debts devv
vnto finnes ; by it deuotion is increafed; by
it is tafted fpiritual fvveetenes, euen in the
verie fpring of the fame; by it ar renued all
good purpofes and defires; and by it finallie
the fovvle is ioined vvith her heauenlie
fpoufe, and receaueth him into her felf, that
by him fhe maie be ruled, defended, and
guided in the vvaie of this life, vntil he
bring her to the defired harbour of his
glorie. Receaue then, o pitiful father, this
thy prodigal fonne, vvhoe trufting in thy
mercie, returneth to thy houfe. I acknovvledge, o my father, that I haue finned a-
gainft thee, & that I am not vvorthie to be
called thy fonne no nether a hired feruant;
yet for al this, haue mercie vppon me, and
forgiue me my finnes. I befeeche thee, o

Lord, commaund that the garment of Chāritie, the ring of liuelie faith, and the shooes of ioiful Hope be giuen me, vvith vvhich I maie goe securelie through the rough and cragged vvaie of this life. Let the multitude of vaine thoughts and desires depart out of me; for one is mie beloued, one mie desired, & one mie God and Lord. Let nothing heereafter be svveete to me, nor delite me but onlie he. Let him be al mine, and I al his, in such sort that mie hart doe becom one thing vvith him. Let me not knovv anie other thing, nor loue anie other thing, nor desire anie other thing, but onlie mie svveete Sauiour IESVS Chrisſt, and him crucified. VVhoe vvith the father and the holie Ghost liueth and raigneth vvorld vvithout end. Amen.

HEERE

HEERE FOLOVVETH A
PROFESSION OF THE CA-
THOLIQVE FAITH, SET
out according to the decree of
the holie Councell
of Trent.

. N . doe vvith a ftedfaft
faith beleeue, and profeffe
al and euerie point, con-
teined in the Simbole of
the Faith, that the holie
Romane Church doth vfe;
to vvit. I beleeue in *God the Father almightie*,
maker of heauen and earth, of al things vi-
fible, and inuifible; and *in one Lord IESVS*
Chrift the Onlie begotten Sonne of God, and
borne of the father before al vvorlds; God
of God, light of light, true God of true
God; begoten not made, of the fame fubftance vvith the father, by vvhome al things
vvere made; vvhoe for vs men, and for oure
faluation came dovvne from heauen, and
vvas incarnate by the holie Ghoft of the
Virgin Marie, and vvas made man; vvas crucified alfo for vs vnder *Pontius Pilate*, fuffered, and vvas buried; and rofe againe the
Aa 3   third

third daie according to the Scriptures; & ascended vp into heauen; sitteth at the right hand of the father; and he shal come againe vvith glorie, to iudge the liue and the dead, of vvhose kingdom there shal be no end; and *in the holie Ghost* our lord and giuer of life, vvhoe proceedeth from the father and the sonne, vvhoe vvith the father and the sonne is together adored, and conglorified, vvhoe spake by the Prophets; and one holie Catholique, and Apostolique Church. I confesse one Baptisme for the remission of sinnes, and I expect the Resurrection of the dead, and the life of the vvorld to come. Amen.

I doe most stedfastlie admit and embrace the *Traditions of the Apostles and of the Church*, and all other obseruances, and Constitutions of the same Church. I doe likevvise admit the holie Scripture, according to that sense, vvhich our holie mother the Catholique Church hath holden, and doth holde; vnto vvhome it doth appetteine to iudge of the true sense, and interpretation of the holie Scriptures: nether vvil I euer vnderstand, nor interprete the same, othervvise then according to the vniforme consent of the fathers.

I doe also professe that there be trulie, and

and properlie *Seuen Sacraments* of the nevv lavve, inftituted by IESVS Chrift our Lord, and neceffarie for the faluation of mankind, (although they be not all neceffarie for all men,) to vvit, *Baptifme, Confirmation*, *Euchariſt*, *Penance*, *Extreme Vnction, Order, and Matrimonie*; and that thefe Sacraments doe giue grace; and that of them, Baptifme, Confirmation and Order can not be reiterated, vvithout facrilege. I doe alfo receaue, and admit all the *receaued, and approued Ceremonies* of the Catholique Church, in the folemne adminiftration of al the aforefaid Sacraments. I doe embrace and receaue al, and euerie of thofe things, vvhich in the holie Councel of Trent haue ben defined, and declared touching *Original Sinne, and Iuſtification*. I doe profeſſe alfo that in the *Maſſe* is offered vp vnto God a true, proper, and propitiatorie facrifice, for the liue and the dead; and that in the moft holie Sacrament of the Altare, there is trulie, reallie, and fubſtantiallie the bodie and bloud, together vvith the fovvle and diuinitie of our lord IESVS Chrift; and that there is made a Conuerfion of the vvhole fubſtance of bread into the bodie, and of the vvhole fubſtance of vvine into the bloud; vvhich Conuerfion the Catholi-

Aa 4   que

que Church doth cal *Tranſubſtantiation*. I doe alſo confeſſe, that vnder ether kind onlie, is receaued Chriſt vvhole and intire, and the true Sacrament.

I doe conſtantlie hold that *there is Purgatorie*, and that the ſovvles, vvhich be there deteined, ar holpen by the praiers of the faithful. Alſo that the *Sainčts*, vvhoe reigne together vvith Chriſt, *ar to be vvorſhipped*, and called vppon, and that they offer vp praiers to God for vs, and that theire Reliques ar to be vvorſhipped.

I doe moſt ſtedfaſtlie affirme, that *the Images of Chriſt*, *of the mother of God alvvaies Virgin*, *and of other Sainčts*, ar to be had and reteined, and that due honour and reuerence is to be giuen to them. I doe affirme that *the authoritie of Indulgences*, vvas left by Chriſt in the Church, and that the vſe of them is verie behofeful for Chriſtian people.

I doe acknovvledge the holie Catholique, and Apoſtolique Romane Church, to be the mother and miſtreſſe of al Churches; and doe promiſe and ſvveare true Obedience to the Biſſhop of Rome, vvhoe is the Succeſſor of S. Peter Prince of the Apoſtles, and the Vicar of IESVS Chriſt. All other things alſo defined, and declared by the holie Canons, & Oecumenical Councels, and chie-

chiefelie by the holie Councel of Trent,
I doe vndoubtedlie receaue and professe;
and also al contrarie things, and vvhatsoeuer herefies condemned, reiected, and
accurfed by the Church, I likevvise doe
condemne, reiecte and accurse.

This true Catholique faith, vvithout
vvhich no man can be faued, vvhich novv
I doe vvillinglie professe and hold, I the
fame N. doe promife, vovv, and svveare to
hold and confeffe moft conftantlie, by Gods
helpe, intiere and vncorrupted euen to the
laft end of mie life; and to procure, as much
as fhal lie in me, that mie subiects, or thofe
of vvhome I fhal haue care in mie office,
fhal hold, teache, and preache the fame. So
God help me, and thefe holie Ghofpels
of God.

Laus Deo & Beatiſsima Virgini
Maria Dei Matri.

A TABLE OF THE THINGS CONteined in the sixe Treatises of this booke.

In the First Treatise, and first part of the same.

Satur-

In the second part of the first Treatise.

The 6.

THE TABLE.

The

THE TABLE.

Of

THE TABLE.

In the fift Treatise.

In the sixth Treatise.

of the

FINIS